The Future South

THE
Future South

*A Historical Perspective for the
Twenty-first Century*

EDITED BY

Joe P. Dunn

AND

Howard L. Preston

UNIVERSITY OF ILLINOIS PRESS
Urbana and Chicago

© 1991 by the Board of Trustees of the University of Illinois
Manufactured in the United States of America
1 2 3 4 5 C P 5 4 3 2 1

This book is printed on acid-free paper.

Library of Congress Cataloging-in-Publication Data

The Future south : a historical perspective for the twenty-first
century / edited by Joe P. Dunn, Howard L. Preston.
    p. cm.
    ISBN 0–252–01776–5 (cloth : alk. paper).—ISBN 0–252–06167–5 (paper :
alk. paper)
    1. Southern States—Civilization—Forecasting. 2. Southern
States—Civilization. I. Dunn, Joe P., 1945- . II. Preston,
Howard L.
F216.2.F88 1991
975—dc20   90-45170
                                                              CIP

For the students of Converse College—
past, present, and future

Contents

Preface ix

The Quest for the South's Future:
An Overview 1
JOE P. DUNN

1. The City as Southern History:
The Past and the Promise of Tomorrow 11
DAVID R. GOLDFIELD

2. The Future of Southern Politics:
New Directions for Dixie 49
ALEXANDER P. LAMIS

3. Variations on a Theme by Henry Grady:
Technology, Modernization, and Social Change 81
ROBERT C. McMATH, JR.

4. The Weight of the Past versus the Promise of the Future:
Southern Race Relations in Historical Perspective 100
HOWARD N. RABINOWITZ

5. The View from Atlanta:
Southern Women and the Future 123
MARGARET RIPLEY WOLFE

6. Many Souths and Broadening Scale:
A Changing Southern Literature 158
DORIS BETTS

7. Will Dixie Disappear?
Cultural Contours of a Region in Transition 188
HOWARD L. PRESTON

8. Tomorrow Seems Like Yesterday:
The South's Future in the Nation and the World 217
JAMES C. COBB

Notes on Contributors 239

Index 241

Preface

Although southerners revere the past, from earliest colonial days they have been future-oriented. Through the centuries, southerners, convinced that the superiority of their region would prevail in the future, held to a sense of place and a way of life and culture. Although the region's history of poverty, racial discrimination, and political backwardness fell far short of the dream, the faith in the future, the product of destiny, distinctiveness, and character, seldom wavered. The South has overcome the worst elements of its past to stake out national leadership and the bright future has never appeared more imminent, however southern distinctiveness is more threatened than ever before. The question, Will there be a distinctive South in the future? has never been as relevant. This is why Converse College chose to celebrate its history by hosting a symposium that addressed visions of the region's future.

"The Future South: An Historical Perspective for the Twenty-First Century," held October 20, 1988, the centerpiece of the college's centennial celebration, brought together six noted historians and a prominent political scientist, all experts in southern history. Each participant's presentation was followed by audience questions. In the evening, a panel discussion pursued the themes treated earlier in the day. Visiting academics, alumnae, and local citizens joined the Converse faculty and students for the conference.

The presenters were David R. Goldfield on urbanization; Alexander P. Lamis on politics; Robert C. McMath on technology, modernization, and social change; Howard N. Rabinowitz on black-white relations; Margaret Ripley Wolfe on women; Darlene R. Roth on cultural persistence; and James C. Cobb as keynote speaker and panel moderator. Six of the seven participants submitted their papers for this volume, and Howard L. Preston agreed to undertake the chapter on cultural persistence. Doris Betts was invited to submit a chapter on southern literature.

Joe Ann Lever, associate dean of arts and sciences and chair of the centennial committee, was the driving force behind the conference.

More than any other person, she is responsible for this volume. Jenny Dunn and Katharine Preston took time from busy professional and family lives to comment, critique, proofread, and assist in every other way, as both have done so many times before. Jarrett Dunn and Jay and Elizabeth Preston saw lots of each other's fathers as we shuttled back and forth between houses.

The Future South

The Quest for the South's Future:
An Overview

JOE P. DUNN

At an "Assembly on the Future of South Carolina," participants devoted four days to the socioeconomic, educational, environmental, and governmental problems which vex the state; yet the final report began with the proclamation that "South Carolina is a state where everyone has a great future." It was an archetypical southern response from a region which long has invoked the glories of the future as response to the inadequacies of the present. Nearly every decade since the late-nineteenth century has heralded a nascent New South. While the effusive optimism of the 1970s and 1980s on one hand merely reflects tradition, the fact is that lifting the dead weight of racial discrimination which retarded the region for so long, the migration of new industry from other areas of the nation, the attraction of foreign investment, and the expansion of southern cities provide the greatest promise in the region's economic history. Several southern states at the bottom of socioeconomic-indicator rankings for decades have leaped ahead of some southwestern, Great Plains, and Rocky Mountain states in per capita income and other measures of development.

Despite the undeniable progress, more than one study has warned about the "Shadows in the Sunbelt." Economic prosperity is not evenly distributed throughout the region or within individual states. While some communities blossom, others sink further and further behind creating "a tale of two Souths." The basic dichotomy is between metropolitan areas, especially along interstate highways, and rural areas distant from the cities. Today, few people are sanguine about the proposed panacea for the post-agricultural South—industry dotted through rural areas. In the era "After the Factory" (to quote the title of another study), growth has stagnated in many rural areas, especially in those with high concentrations of blacks and a minimal educational and cultural infrastructure. As employment opportunities change toward high-tech industry and the service sector, both increasingly concentrated in metropolitan areas, the old textile mills close and their village towns

1

wither. The young move to cities, and the older, unskilled workers find themselves locked in high unemployment ghettos. Where traditional manufacturing still prevails, per capita income has not kept pace with inflation. The gap between prosperous and poor communities ever widens, ratified by few employment opportunities, a poor educational environment, and a low standard of living. To depressed economies, the old approach, the continuous scramble to attract non-union-wage industry, is no longer practical.

Where growth is evident in the expanding areas around the cities, another set of problems exists. The rapid transformation of rural areas into metropolitan zones outstrips the ability of local governments to provide necessary amenities such as water, sewage treatment, highways, and land management plans. Often, local administrative structures are inchoate, annexation practices haphazard, former rural inhabitants forced off the land, the natural environment assaulted, and overcrowding prevails. Thus the latest of an inordinate number of New Souths faces the twenty-first century, replete with challenges but confident as ever that the distinctive region offers a model for the nation and the future. The southern obsession to explain itself and herald its future is one of the region's enduring passions as Fred Hobson's *Tell About the South: The Southern Rage to Explain* (Baton Rouge, 1983) demonstrates.

Although many have sought to define the distinctive nature of the region, any discussion must begin with four classics: Howard W. Odum, *Southern Regions of the United States* (Chapel Hill, 1936); W. J. Cash, *The Mind of the South* (New York, 1941); V. O. Key, Jr., *Southern Politics in State and Nation* (New York, 1949); and C. Vann Woodward, *The Burden of Southern History* (Baton Rouge, 1960). Earl Black and Merle Black, *Politics and Society in the South* (Cambridge, 1987), winner of the V. O. Key Award, is the most definitive contemporary source.

Other studies, such as Harry Ashmore's *Epitaph for Dixie* (New York, 1957), John Egerton's *The Americanization of Dixie: The Southernization of America* (New York, 1974), and Alexander P. Lamis's *The Two-Party South*, expanded ed. (New York, 1988), forecast the demise of a distinctive South. Among the hundreds of books that disagree are Thomas D. Clark, *The Emerging South* (New York, 1961); Pat Watters, *The South and the Nation* (New York, 1969); George B. Tindall, *The Ethnic Southerners* (Baton Rouge, 1976); Carl N. Degler, *Place over Time: The Continuity of Southern Distinctiveness* (Baton Rouge, 1977); Dewey W. Grantham, *The Regional Imagination: The South and Recent American History* (Nashville, 1979); Stephen A. Smith, *Myth, Media, and the Southern Mind* (Fayetteville, 1985); and Michael O'Brien, *Rethinking the South: Essays in Intellectual History* (Baltimore, 1988). But no scholar has addressed the subject more thoroughly than the sociologist John Shelton Reed, who explains a continuing southern culture in *The Enduring South: Subcultural Persistence in Mass Society* (Lexington, Mass., 1972); *One South: An Ethnic Approach to Regional Culture* (Baton Rouge, 1982); *Southerners: The Social Psychology of Sectionalism* (Chapel Hill, 1983), and his "Introduction," in *The Disappearing South? Studies in Regional Change and Continuity,* edited by Robert P. Steed, Laurence W. Moreland, and Tod A. Baker (Tuscaloosa, 1990).

A number of conferences and collections of essays have addressed the question of the changing South. Notable among these volumes are *The American South in the 1960s,* edited by Avery Leiserson (New York, 1964); *The South in Continuity and Change,* edited by John C. McKinney and Edgar T. Thompson (Durham, 1965); *You Can't Eat Magnolias,* edited by H. Brant Ayers and Thomas H. Naylor (New York, 1972); *Two Decades of Change: The South since the Supreme Court Desegregation Decision,* edited by Ernest M. Lander and Richard J. Calhoun (Columbia, 1975); Fifteen Southerners, *Why the South Will Survive* (Athens, 1981); *A Band of Prophets: The Vanderbilt Agrarians after Fifty Years,* edited by William C. Havard and Walter Sullivan (Baton Rouge, 1982); *The Evolution of Southern Culture,* edited by Numan V. Bartley (Athens, 1988); *The Prevailing South: Life and Politics in a Changing Culture,* edited by Dudley Clendinen (Atlanta, 1988); *Contemporary Southern Politics,* edited by James F. Lea (Baton Rouge, 1988); *The South's New Politics: Realignment and Dealignment,* edited by Robert H. Swansbrough and David Brodsky (Columbia, 1988); *The Disappearing South?,* edited by Steed, Moreland, and Baker; and *Searching for the Sunbelt: Historical Perspectives on a Region,* edited by Raymond A. Mohl (Knoxville, 1990). More specialized works address the question in a specific area such as civil rights or economic development.

While this volume addresses the same questions as those above, its scope is broader than most. It surveys the South in a systematic way from urbanization and race relations to literature and cultural persistence. The authors appreciate that any perspective on the future not grounded in the South's past, its change and continuity, as well as its dreams, lacks validity. As they envision the future, each addresses directly or indirectly the distinctiveness of the region. While their approaches are common, their conclusions vary considerably.

David Goldfield chronicles the growth of southern cities from the mid-nineteenth century to the present and assesses the impact of urbanization on the region. The South's vigorous pursuit of an urban future has had both positive and negative aspects. On one hand, boosterism and promotion sacrificed elegant buildings, open green space, and local charm; yet some cities worked hard to retain their historical past. In its rapid expansion, southern cities followed the negative patterns of the North—decaying central city, unplanned growth, sprawling suburbanization, and crass commercialism. Many cities managed to incorporate the worst aspects of both the Old and the emerging New Souths.

As he contemplates the problems which southern cities will continue to face in the future, Goldfield aptly quotes George Tindall's quip that if history is guide, "the South will blow it." But Goldfield is hopeful. He believes that a more favorable prediction for the urban South can be based upon several distinctive regional factors: smaller-scale, lower-population-density cities; ties to the rural heritage; a tradition of volunteerism; the moral reserve of religious institutions; and a respect for the past. As he concludes, "Both city and South are connected more intimately than ever before," and "the future of the South cannot be separated from the future of southern cities."

Alexander Lamis too is positive about the South's future, but unlike Goldfield, he forecasts the demise of regional distinctiveness. Lamis sees Dixie "fast on the way to rejoining completely the national political mainstream." He continues that demographic, social, economic, and historical differences, as well as varying traditions of individual states or groups of states, portend several "Souths." As the Republican party, already well established at the statewide level, competes more and more favorably on "down-ticket" elections, a true two-party system will function throughout Dixie by the turn of the century. Lamis also predicts a redefinition of the Democrat party in the next century as the vehicle of "those who have less" regardless of race. While he concedes that the short-run effect likely will be a sharp decline in Democrat strength in the South, he hopes that the new "purified and unified party" will emerge as a potential political force which could restore Democrats to the presidential dominance not enjoyed in the last two decades. Lamis calls this southern-led national political realignment "long-overdue," "just," "promising," and "exciting"—all words which parallel his view of the South's future.

The New South's greatest evangelist was Henry Grady, the prophet of industrialism and Sunbelt boosterism. Proclaiming the traditional agrarian society over northern-sponsored industrialism, populist Tom Watson offered a different New South vision. Robert McMath juxtaposes the Grady and Watson models in a brief historical survey of the economic-technological New South and commentary on the region's present stage of development. As he contemplates potential new technologies and organizational structures to save textiles and other tra-

4

ditional industries or speculates about new economic possibilities through biotechnology and microelectronics, he cautions that just as in the past these new "panaceas" will have social costs. Moreover, he warns that if the benefits accrued do not extend beyond the prosperous new urban citadels—the Atlantas, Charlottes, Austins, or Raleighs—to that South slowly sinking back into hopeless poverty, then Grady's dream of a New South will remain unfulfilled.

Thus like Goldfield and to a lesser degree Lamis, McMath issues caveats. George Tindall's pessimistic prophecy once again comes to mind. However, McMath ends on an upbeat note. He reminds us that by the choices they make, people determine their destiny and write their own history. By courageously addressing the future agenda with the understanding that all choices have ramifications, none are politically neutral, the South can choose technological paths compatible with human needs and its own survival "rather than assuming that the South is to be bulldozed out of existence."

Howard Rabinowitz confronts the central issue of southern distinctiveness—race. V. O. Key said it best in 1949, "the politics of the South revolves around the position of the Negro. . . . Whatever phase of the southern political process one seeks to understand, sooner or later the trail of inquiry leads to the Negro." Rabinowitz breaks black-white relations into six historical periods and comments on the degree to which the South's practices compared or contrasted with national patterns. When he comes to the present, Rabinowitz contends that the South today provides a distinctive positive environment for blacks. The majority of blacks now live in the South, and the migration to the northern cities which characterized most of this century has reversed. In conjunction with the migration from rural areas to southern cities, this has concentrated black economic and political power; and this power is being exercised throughout the region.

Rabinowitz warns, however, that heightened black expectations may outpace economic opportunities and fuel unrest; but for the most part, he is optimistic. He agrees with Lamis that class distinctions ultimately will supplant race in southern politics, but he explains that this will not necessarily mean total integration. He asserts that since the primary goal of the civil rights movement was freedom of choice and equal opportunity rather than integration per se, continuing aspects of voluntary segregation in the future will not necessarily "represent a failure of American democracy, but rather confirmation that America is a pluralistic society." Rabinowitz, like Goldfield, Lamis, and McMath, implies that the South has important choices to make, and wise decisions by prudent leaders can open untold possibilities.

5

While all recognize the centrality of race, Margaret Wolfe asserts that gender has not received adequate attention, and "it remains to be seen what impact the serious study of women's history may have on the future of the South." Her chapter sweeps widely over historical and contemporary examples of the diversity of women below the Mason-Dixon line, and she explains that the South is indeed the product of the multifarious experiences of southern women—white, black, Indian, poor, working class, and rich. The traditional image of the genteel "southern lady" addresses only a small percentage of "the daughters of Dixie."

Despite their diversity, southern women are distinctive, Wolfe avers. As products of a unique regional history and social context, they bear the stigma of southern history, mythology, and legends; the constraining images of belle and lady; the division of race and class; and, she emphasizes, a strong commitment to femininity and more tolerant relationship between the sexes. She remarks that "radical feminists are hard to find in the South; the great majority of females have no truck with lesbianism . . . they do not subscribe to the notion of an all-encompassing cross-cultural and historical patriarchal plot to subjugate women." Because southern women tend to eschew these "radical feminist rites-of-passage," Wolfe points out that scholars who study "the women of Dixie" should not be blinded by the New England model of feminism. From southern feminism, Wolfe perceives the opportunities for a changing, better, more equitable, distinctive South.

Like Wolfe, Doris Betts's analysis of southern literature surveys the ambiguities and diversity of the many Souths, a region simultaneously exhibiting ever-increasing sub-Souths and the powerful forces of national homogenization. She discovers that the tired, over-worked themes of traditional southern literature, the cliches, and the "outdated obsessions" are fading toward an attention to the agenda of the nation and the current South—technology, the environment, ecology, urban issues, feminism, mass culture, the global village, upward mobility, and those left out of the new order. Isolation, loneliness, and alienation no longer can be portrayed simply as product of region. Place and stock characters are changing. Gail Godwin's Asheville is not Thomas Wolfe's; Tim McLaurin's Fayetteville/Ft. Bragg is not Carson McCullers's; Truman Capote and Harper Lee's Monroeville, Alabama are not the same; and Bobbie Ann Mason's portrait of western Kentucky is not exclusive to region. No longer the "sons of the landed gentry educated in private schools," the new writers are "defiantly plebeian" in origins and subject matter. The voices of women, black, and hispanic authors add new dimensions; indeed, much of the energy of contemporary southern writing comes from feminists, especially black women.

Despite its changing nature, a definable southern literature still exists, which Betts believes can thrive, if through creativity it is "what it has always aspired to be—a local means to universal ends, not a de facto minor league of letters recognizable by outdated obsessions." If a southern literature continues, then a distinctive South may well remain.

None of the authors addressees southern distinctiveness as directly and broadly as does Howard Preston. Preston is less hopeful about the changing nature of racial accommodation than either Lamis or Rabinowitz, less optimistic about technological innovation than McMath, less enamored by the promise of the city than Goldfield. His chapter isolates aspects of southern life which have made the region different, and he speculates on their survival against the relentless forces of assimilation and national homogeneity.

Place is still essential to the South. In a region of small towns and rural areas, the bonds of community and the special qualities of the land undergird southern identity. Nowhere, Preston notes, is hunting and fishing, a communion with the land, more obsessive than in Dixie. Soil and blood, birthplace and lineage, continue to define the contemporary southerner. If Goldfield believes that the South's salvation is in its cities, Preston implies that its soul is in its small towns. While some focus on the glitter of the Sunbelt, he reminds us of the "shadows"— South Carolina's Jonesville's and Mississippi's Tchula's.

Southernness, Preston reminds us, is also a state of mind exemplified in southerners' values, social and family relationships, myths, food, and self-image. Religion is important in the South. Church affiliation and attendance are greater than in other parts of the country. Evangelicalism and fundamentalism have deep roots. One's church membership is a prime aspect of personal identity. Violence is also more prevalent in Dixie than in the rest of the nation. Preston speculates about a connection between this cultural characteristic and the southern mania for football. Preston concedes that inevitably southern distinctiveness will fade, but not as quickly, he contends, as many would predict, and never totally. It is a response as much from heart as from mind.

In the final chapter, James Cobb confronts Preston, and indeed all the other contributors, with the charge that they are misguided; he finds their conclusions irrelevant because they miss the point. On the issue of whether the South will remain distinctive, Cobb proclaims that the evidence is already in: "Americans . . . could care less whether the South has retained its uniqueness." And if "perhaps the whole notion of southernness itself, may have become too irrelevant to capture the attention of those outside the South" is there not "reason to question whether southernness has much of a future even inside the South." John Shelton

Reed's argument that southernness is an ethnicity clinging to its identity is dismissed by questioning "whether any such subgroup identity could survive through simple self-assertion so long as the larger society neither challenged it nor recognized it as especially significant."

Cobb traces the South's conception of itself as distinct from the larger nation and yet model for it, and the rest of the nation's perception of the South as separate and in dire need of reformation before being accepted into the mainstream. Thus, for decades the South awaited the hour of its ascendancy as the national model, and the nation devoted itself to making the region respectable enough to claim. By the mid-1970s, each believed that its mission had been accomplished. Suddenly, Dixie was transformed from wayward to chic, but the metamorphosis came too late. In the throes of Watergate, Vietnam, recession, runaway inflation, and foreign economic penetration, the nation, Cobb claims, awakened to the realization that the whole country had inherited the South's long-anguished status. Distinction between region and nation was irrelevant.

Cobb argues that the demise of southernness actually enhances the importance of southern history. As nation and region share a common future within a rapidly changing world, much can be learned from the South's experience as a benighted region struggling with limited resources and confronted by powerful forces bent on transforming its very soul. The mistakes of the South's past can serve as a lesson for an America thrashing in uncertain waters. For Cobb, "efforts to anticipate the region's future will consider that future less a challenge to the South's ability to measure up to national fantasies than a test of the capacity of the entire nation to cope with global realities."

If Cobb's thesis is correct, then the prognostications of the other authors are passé. Alexander Lamis already forecasts a future unitary nation. Possibly, Goldfield, McMath, and Rabinowitz, all optimistic about the region's future, might be persuaded that Dixie has triumphed—the nation has adopted the modern, upscale, urban South as model, and a unitary, uniform country collectively can address itself to eradicating the less savory aspects of the region and nation. If so, the further decline of regional idiosyncrasies is small price to pay. Margaret Wolfe, who advises the national women's movement to look to its southern sisters, and Doris Betts might be convinced to join the new consensus. Howard Preston probably would not.

Maybe Dixie has become the norm and is dying of homogenization, but copious reasons exist to question this. Cobb may have proclaimed the death of southernologists, but—to adapt Mark Twain's famous

8

quip—assuredly the news of their demise is greatly exaggerated. Until the evidence is more conclusive, the debate over southern distinctiveness and the region's future will continue well into the twenty-first century.

1

The City as Southern History:
The Past and the Promise of Tomorrow

DAVID R. GOLDFIELD

Not long ago I took a walk down Monument Avenue in Richmond. The avenue is a broad, tree-lined memorial to a pantheon of Confederate heroes. Foremost among the sculpted poses is the equestrian statue of General Robert E. Lee. The imposing statue rises seven stories above the street. As I maneuvered myself to get the best angle for a photograph, I recalled the stories of how the citizens of Richmond nearly a century earlier had carried sections of the statue from the railroad depot all the way out to what was then a corn field beyond the city limits. They were like medieval burgers carrying the stones that would become part of a new cathedral. They were pilgrims of the faith espousing a creed long dead but not buried, erecting an icon to the only dream that had mattered so they could keep on dreaming.

While I snapped some photographs, a well-dressed elderly gentleman approached me and commented matter-of-factly, "quite a man isn't he?" The question startled me a bit because I had never thought of the general in the present tense. Thinking about it later, I understood that the question was not surprising because time in the South seems to run together. As William Faulkner summarized the phenomenon, "yesterday, today, and tomorrow are Is: Indivisible: One. . . ."[1]

Looking Backward in a Forward Time

Although the Civil War provided the greatest impetus for timelessness, southerners maintained a loose definition of the present before then. Frederick Law Olmsted, farmer, landscape architect, and journalist, visited Richmond during the 1860s and came away convinced that the city was moving forward and backward at the same time: "[Richmond] is plainly the metropolis . . . of a people who have been dragged along in the grand march of the rest of the world, but who have had, for a long time and yet have, a disposition within themselves only to step backward."[2] And here was a city which, at that time, was among the nation's foremost industrial centers, a thriving port, and the terminus of two major rail lines.

There is no record that Olmsted stopped at Richmond's Hollywood Cemetery during his brief visit to the city. Had he done so, he might have happened on a ceremony that would have only confirmed his initial impression. The city was staging an elaborate celebration for the reinterment of ex-President James Monroe's remains. Monroe had died in New York City in 1830 and was buried there. New Yorkers graciously offered the bones to Richmond and assisted in their transfer to Hollywood. In the meantime, another group of Richmonders, led by women, was developing plans to purchase the decaying Mount Vernon estate of George Washington. Today, both of these events would likely make good cover stories for *Southern Living*. But, at the time, there was something queer about such nostalgic indulgence. It was a time of manifest destiny, of the steam engine, of improvement societies of every stripe. Holding onto the past reflected an ambivalence about the future, and the mid-nineteenth century was not a time of ambivalence.

Richmonders held legitimate concerns about the future, however. The age of Jackson had given free rein to greed, and although some southerners may have publicly disavowed the profit motive, most eagerly participated in the developing national economy. Southern cities became focal points for the scramble after commerce and industry. And most did quite well, especially during the prosperous 1850s. But it was a losing proposition for several reasons. First, railroads, credit facilities, distribution networks, information flows, and marketing connections favored northeastern cities, particularly New York. Second, a sectional political party emerged—the Republican party—that promoted, among other things, a vigorous program of economic nationalism. The new party favored a northern route for a transcontinental railroad, a high tariff to protect primarily northern industry, a homestead act designed to limit southern access to the West, and the use of the federal treasury and patronage to subsidize river and harbor improvements.[3]

Cities of the Countryside

There was a third obstacle to southern economic and urban development that few southerners acknowledged openly because it questioned the basic institutions of their society. Urbanization is a process that depends on the interaction of the city and the surrounding countryside. Eventually, connections with other cities, other regions, and other countries enhance the process, but, initially, it is the city-hinterland connection that provides the foundation for all future development.[4]

Southern cities were ill-served by their hinterlands. Cotton and tobacco were the two major staple crops of the South. Neither crop required significant marketing, storage, or processing that would generate urban growth and in turn other economic activities that would induce further growth. Soil and climate dictated that mixed farming, with grains the dominant crop, would characterize the agricultural Northeast. As cities grew in size, hinterland towns began to take on specialized functions, even manufacturing for the expanding urban demand. Reciprocal trade increased, profits mounted, and investments in diverse economic activities and internal improvements followed.[5]

The southern countryside had none of these advantages. Cotton and tobacco cultivation required huge territories of land because of the rapid soil erosion. Travelers often commented on the wasted aspect of a rural South pockmarked by deep gullies, barren old fields, and fallow land held for a future that would come too quickly. So when southern cities built railroads, they ran through a mostly empty countryside rather than connecting with prosperous towns and cities. Charlestonians built the longest railroad in the world in the 1830s and nothing happened. As one disappointed investor explained, it was a railroad "which ran into uninhabited wilderness in the absurd and chimerical expectation that [it] would create commerce and build New Yorks in a day."[6]

Beyond the wasted tracts of South Carolina lay the fertile fields of the Black Belt, of Alabama and Mississippi, of land but once removed from the wilderness where wealthy pioneers and their slave armies created a cotton empire. The profits from cotton trickled into the cities of the South in the form of railroad subscriptions, hotels and market houses, and industrial enterprises. But it was not enough. The planters were not ideologically adverse to manufacturing or to occasional investments in such activities. Like most investors, they preferred the sure things—land and slaves—where returns were steady and tested. Controlling capital and labor, planters controlled the southern economy. And the cities experienced chronic shortages of both workers and investment capital.[7]

The shortcomings of antebellum southern urbanization would not have been easily apparent to the casual observer. Just pick up a newspaper and the columns would be crowded with development schemes, current price lists, the latest news from the northeastern commercial centers, and advertisements for a variety of enterprises. The editor's rhetoric would be snappy and upbeat, sometimes too much so for a visitor accustomed to more sophisticated journalism. Alexander

MacKay, a Scottish sojourner in Richmond in 1846 offers his perspective on editorial puffery:

> Richmond . . . is a small, but certainly a very pretty town, if its people would only content themselves with having it so. It is a weakness of theirs to be constantly making the largest possible drafts upon the admiration of the visitor, by extorting his assent to the fidelity of comparisons which would be amongst the very last to suggest themselves to his own mind. He is reminded, for instance, that the prospect which it commands is very like the view obtained from the battlements of Windsor Castle; . . . He is also given to understand that it occupies more hills than imperial Rome ever sat upon, and if the number of hills on which the capital rested was an essential element of Roman greatness, this is one way of proving Richmond superior to Rome.[8]

Such extravagance was undoubtedly jarring to the Scotsman, but quite common in antebellum America. Equally surprising to European visitors was the diversity of people in southern cities. Blacks and whites mingled on the streets, in residential areas, and in the raucous taverns down by the wharves. Whether the blacks were slave or free, it was impossible to tell. Such was the nature of the urban milieu that distinctions of caste became less distinct. Slaves often hired out their own time, found their own lodgings, and participated in black institutions, especially the church. Urban work also held out the possibility of freedom. Although few slaves were able to purchase their freedom, the occasional examples were well known enough in the black community to establish the cities of the Old South as places of opportunity, however limited.[9]

There were opportunities as well for European immigrants. Although immigrants did not flood southern cities as they did in the major urban centers of the North, their presence was evident, especially in the work force. The further south one traveled, the greater the proportion of immigrants in the free work force. They comprised a majority of free labor in several southern cities, including more than 60 percent in Mobile. Except for the Irish, immigrants concentrated in skilled labor positions, with slaves and free blacks primarily occupying unskilled jobs. Apparently, slavery did not inhibit the migration of foreign-born labor; to the contrary, immigrants tended to depress the occupational status of blacks, slave and free.[10]

The nativism that peaked in the mid-1850s was generally mild in the South. Roman Catholics and Jews not only practiced their religions without interference, but also rose to positions of public prominence. Gustavus Myers, one of Richmond's leading Jewish citizens, was elected to the state legislature and the city council, helped to found the Virginia

14

Historical Society, and supported numerous economic development projects including a publishing house and a railroad. William Thalhimer, Myers's co-religionist, opened the South's first department store in Richmond in 1852. In fact, assimilation may have been too easy for some immigrants. A common complaint of the older generation was that their children were losing their cultural heritage.[11]

Although relatively little is known about immigrant life in the Old South, it seems apparent that the attention focused on the color line—and segregation, however informal, emerged in the cities of the Old South—deflected attention from distinctive groups of whites. Because most of the immigrants provided important work and entrepreneurial skills, their presence was an advantage to cities struggling to keep up with the growing national economy.

Alas, that struggle fell short. Southern cities were unable to shake their role as agricultural marketing way stations. Their residents followed the seasonal cycles of farming. Life coursed through the streets of southern cities from October to April. But once the warm weather set in and the crops began their long growing seasons, urban residents left. The episodic nature of rural time may have suited farm life, but it left cities bereft of year-round leadership and direction. A visitor to Mobile in 1840 summarized the effects of these migrations: "Mobile might be made a delightful place in Winter and a pleasant one in Summer, but unfortunately like too many of the Southern Towns & Cities but little attention is paid to it by the authorities . . . [so] many of the inhabitants leave there in the Summers, that their erratic life forbids them making improvements or paying much attention to these little conveniences & comforts without which any life & especially a city one is unpleasant."[12]

The inconsistent quality of services, especially streets, reflected the seasonal nature of urban life, as did the general inattention to such common public responsibilities in northern cities as education and poor relief. Intellectual life was limited (especially after 1840 when the sectional debate restricted the list of appropriate topics for public discussion), and social life was carried on in private clubs and associations. The common denominator in discourse was cotton or tobacco, and the health of these crops determined the success or failure of the city. A visitor to Mobile in 1858 expressed this propensity as follows: "Mobile—a pleasant cotton city of some thirty thousand inhabitants—where people live in cotton houses and ride in cotton carriages. They buy cotton, sell cotton, think cotton, eat cotton, drink cotton and dream cotton. They marry cotton wives, and unto them are born cotton children."[13] Simply put, antebellum southern cities were adjuncts to the countryside.

Identities were derived from roles in marketing a crop. There were considerable profits in these roles, but northeastern mercantile houses, bankers, and shippers secured an increasing share. In spatial terms, no sharp edges delineated the country from the city. Many urban residents kept farm animals and planted garden crops through the 1850s, and the larger plantations assumed industrial and marketing functions normally reserved for cities. Most streets were unpaved, and services were haphazard. Visitors often commented on the natural beauty of southern cities, even more striking amid the slovenly appearance of streets and alleys. But, beneath it all there was a sadness, of falling behind in an age of progress, of being different in a national culture of conformity, and of trying to reconcile a heritage of greatness with an indifferent present.

The sadness would deepen and spread with the Civil War. Southern cities, like southerners, would cope with defeat in different ways. Some would bury it quickly with an obligatory offering to the Old South; others would linger at the grave, deny the present, and embrace a vision of their history that bore little resemblance to that past. All would remain connected to agriculture, for better or for worse. And all would experience the strain of existence in a society that demanded the separation and exclusion of races from each other.

Stars and Scars in the Piedmont Crescent

Atlanta dusted off the ashes and went quickly to work establishing itself as the paragon of what came to be called the New South. Henry W. Grady, a stocky, boyish-looking newspaperman, became the city's prophet for the new creed. "As I think of it, a vision of surpassing beauty unfolds to my eyes," he exclaimed in typical understatement. "I see a South the home of 50 millions of people; her cities vast hives of industry; her countrysides the treasures from which their resources are drawn; her streams vocal with whirring spindles . . . sunshine everywhere and all the time, and night falling on her gently as wings of the unseen dove."[14]

For northerners equally eager to forget the past and invest in the future, Grady's words were comforting indeed. Although relatively little northern capital flowed into southern cities, agents, bank notes, and railroads did. And, as important for Grady and his colleagues, the North was content to adopt an attitude of political laissez-faire so that the Atlantas of the South could get on with the business of business.

Atlanta also became the symbol for a major shift in the pattern of southern urbanization. The Georgia capital was an offspring of the

16

railroad, and its strategic location astride a middle land known as the Southern Piedmont ensured its prominence in carrying the wealth of the South into the coffers of the North. Atlanta became a regional capital as the Piedmont developed after 1870 along the route of the Southern Railway and dozens of small branch lines. By 1880, ten towns came into existence along the rail corridor from Charlotte to Atlanta. Sleepy courthouse and market towns such as Greenville and Spartanburg, South Carolina came alive with the railroad.[15]

As the railroad crossed the Piedmont, so did industry. It had long been the dream of Old South entrepreneurs to develop an indigenous textile industry. But not until the 1880s did the right combination of transportation (the railroad), capital (from the growing urban merchant class), expertise (from northern-trained engineers and technicians), and a labor surplus (released by an agricultural depression) occur to encourage industrial enterprise. Like dark flecks in a landscape of white grits, mill villages became a new and distinctive type of urban settlement across the rural South.[16]

Mill owners typically erected their new towns in unincorporated rural areas, often adjacent to larger existing towns. The village included worker housing, leased from the mill owner, churches whose ministers served at the pleasure of the owner, social facilities, and schools that provided enough education for younger operatives to master the techniques of textile production, but not enough to open their minds to the possibilities of a life away from the mill. Judging, however, by the large outmigration from the South, the high turnover rates, and the periodic attempts at labor organizing, job dissatisfaction ran high.

The spatial configurations of the mill village reflected the lines of authority in much the same way as the big house and slave quarters denoted particular work and living arrangements on the antebellum plantation. The three-story brick factory with an ornate facade and "stair tower, corbelled cornice, quoined stucco corners, and heavily stuccoed window labels" stood in contrast to the simple vernacular clapboard structures that comprised the workers' housing. The modest homes often had garden patches, even pens for farm animals. A church, a company store, and a small schoolhouse completed the physical landscape of the mill village. The foremen or supervisors typically resided in the largest of the frame houses at the head or top of the street, specifying a status within the operative community.[17]

The mill village, like the antebellum town or city, was close to the countryside. The boundaries between village and countryside were permeable. Workers moved in and out of the village from their farms. The so-called public work offered by the mills was, for many, the only way to maintain an unprofitable farming life. Mill workers were often commuters, especially after 1910 when automobile use spread across the rural South. They traveled not only from farm to village, but also between villages up and down the Piedmont. Journalist Arthur W. Page noted in 1907 that the Piedmont was "one long mill village." Kinship, shared work experiences, and popular culture wove these villages together.[18]

Although the mill villages themselves were not major urban centers, their appearance generated urban specialization in the Piedmont region. Until the 1920s, most of the capital and entrepreneurial expertise for Piedmont industry came from surrounding areas. Places such as Greensboro and Charlotte, North Carolina and Greenville, South Carolina became financial and administrative centers for the textile industry. These cities boasted affluent neighborhoods where the textile barons and their banking colleagues resided. One-quarter of South Carolina's spindles were controlled by sixteen mill presidents who lived within a single ward in Greenville.[19]

The growing urban specialization reflected a growing social separation between mill and town, more specifically between mill workers and town residents. Mill operatives were "lint heads," and town dwellers alternately feared and despised them. Town parents warned their children against mingling with mill offspring; the children attended separate schools; and merchants set aside special shopping days for mill workers as they did for blacks. Social gaps had always existed between white southerners, of course. But, in a rural society, such differences were not constantly and readily apparent. In an urban setting, distinctions were likely to be more evident.

The stigma of mill villages and the workers' culture that evolved in them lent a particular identity to mill operatives. A similar self-consciousness emerged among middle-class residents of the town. Although historians disagree over whether these were new men or merely old landed elites in new environments, it is clear that their attitudes favoring economic development were similar to their antebellum urban predecessors. The major differences, however, were that their numbers were greater after 1880, their role in the postbellum economy was more crucial—they supplied goods and credit to planters—and they and their wives possessed the spiritual, financial, and organizational means to effect a wide range of reforms in southern society.

The Urban South in the Age of Reform

The urban middle class was not, of course, confined to the southern Piedmont. Railroads, marketing arrangements, migration, and modest efforts at industrial enterprise spawned towns throughout the South, particularly after 1880. Between 1880 and 1910, the number of urban places in the South nearly quadrupled from 103 to 398. The former figure represented 11 percent of the nation's urban places compared with 17 percent for the latter figure. The urban population had grown from 280,000 in 1870 to nearly two million by 1910. Only 8.7 percent of the South's population resided in urban places in 1880; thirty years later, that proportion jumped to 20 percent.[20]

This period, 1880 to 1910, coincided with the rise of organized urban reform efforts, which often grew out of church groups. Middle-class women were especially prominent in these activities, which focused on child labor, education, and city beautification. It is uncertain whether the movement represented a particularly novel innovation for southern women or whether the concern about children in the factory and in the school, and the interest in providing an esthetic urban environment, were extensions of the traditional domestic role for southern women, a role that southern men were glad to concede. Their public statements frequently drew the connection between domesticity and reform. In 1896, for example, the newly formed Atlanta Woman's Club announced that its work would "prove to the world that women could mean even more in their homes by participating in the civic, philanthropic and legislative interests of their growing city and in standing side by side with the development of the times they could aid in the progress of a great city. . . ."[21] It is not clear whether this public statement was a carefully crafted effort to defuse potential male opposition, or whether it was a heartfelt statement of ideology. It is clear, however, that once women attempted to transform some of these objectives—particularly child labor, lynching, and city planning—into public policies, civic leaders often intervened to short-circuit their efforts.

Civic leaders developed their own reform agenda which often diverged from the reform objectives of women. Good government was a major target of urban reformers. The idea was to provide efficient, business-oriented administration, but this idea had been extant since the antebellum era. The new feature was the desire to shield public officials as much as possible from the vagaries of partisan electoral politics. Cities would be managed, not governed. The South pioneered two major administrative innovations in the early 1900s, the commission form of government (which premiered in the wake of a devastating hurricane in Galveston in 1900) and the city manager system inaugurated in Staunton, Virginia in 1910. In the commission system, each commissioner was responsible for specific administrative tasks, such as waste disposal, street repair, and police and fire services. The city manager was an appointed official whose role was to administer the city and its services on a day-by-day basis. The council and mayor would make the policies, but the manager would carry them out, presumably in an efficient and nonpartisan manner.

Urban southerners were not unique in their desire for efficient local government; a major thrust of progressive urban reform was changing the structure of city politics. But in the context of the South, where recent constitutional revisions eliminated much of the black vote and placed potential restrictions on the white electorate, the move to reduce public participation in government took on other implications. The development of cities, industrialization, the increase in class divisions, and the growth of the urban black population created anxieties. Codified segregation was one response to these urban changes; governmental reforms from the commission system to disfranchisement were other responses. In the meantime, business leaders could harness local government to work for economic development objectives without threatening social relationships.

Within the prevailing racial and social frameworks, urban progressivism accomplished some important objectives. Expenditures for educating blacks and whites increased significantly during the first two decades of the twentieth century. City planning to order the chaotic and often unhealthful urban environment became an integral part of urban administration. And, major construction projects, including the paving of streets, the laying of sewer and water lines, and the erection of public buildings added to the health and efficiency of southern cities. Urban leaders also became a more cosmopolitan group. The emergence of public utilities and the technologies to support them; the growth of federal defense expenditures during and after the Spanish American War; and national innovations in teaching methods and curriculum filtered into the South over the telegraph wires, via the railroad, and through countless advertisements in national magazines and the ubiquitous Sears catalog.[22]

Dancing as Fast as They Could

The contact with the outside world led to some perceptual changes as well. Some small towns with big ambitions demonstrated their seriousness by changing names. Harmony Grove, Georgia became Commerce, and Big Lick became Roanoke, Virginia. Impressed by the value of national advertising, civic leaders launched promotional schemes to enhance their city's image. The exposition became a common enterprise in the larger cities, building on a theme and showing off new buildings (such as the Parthenon in Nashville's centennial exposition of 1897), or new technology such as Atlanta's 1909 fair featuring the automobile, or even new Negroes (Booker T. Washington presented his famous "Atlanta Compromise" speech as part of the festivities connected with the 1895 cotton exposition in that city).

The hyperbole that had emerged in the cities of the Old South became an art form in the decades after 1900, the major difference being that latter-day civic leaders acted on their rhetoric, often with silly results. The skyscrapers erected in the early 1900s by the civic leaders of Greensboro and Charlotte were notable less for their architectural merit than for the fact that, as Charlotte journalist W. J. Cash noted, these cities had as much need for such structures "as a hog has for a morning coat."[23] Atlanta's leaders, concerned that the 1930 census would not support their boasts of dramatic population gains, took in pieces of surrounding counties as "autonomous boroughs." Census-takers were not taken in, however. Atlantans compounded their antics by filing an unsuccessful lawsuit against the United States Census Bureau.[24]

Occasionally, the promotions paid off. Atlanta's successful technology exposition of 1909 led to automobile distributorships. A booster organization known as "Forward Atlanta," organized in 1925, initiated a million-dollar national advertising campaign. Between 1926 and 1929, the city received more than $34,500,000 in new investments. In Nashville, the appropriately named Joel O. Cheek founded the Nashville Coffee and Manufacturing Company and, beginning in 1892, experimented with blending various high-quality coffee beans. The results were successful, but the blend was expensive. In order to promote his up-scale product, Cheek persuaded the elegant Maxwell House Hotel in Nashville to serve his coffee, and he used the hotel's name on his label. In 1907 President Teddy Roosevelt visited Nashville and stayed at the Maxwell House. Cheek served the coffee to the president, and as he drained his cup, Roosevelt declared that the coffee was "good to the last drop," thus coining a national advertising slogan.[25]

The growth ethic espoused by the leaders of the New South's new cities (and many of these cities, such as Atlanta, Greenville, and Charlotte were not major urban centers in the antebellum era, and Birmingham did not exist prior to 1870) had several benefits quite apart from its sometimes dubious value as an economic development tool. First, growth prompted few dissenters. In a society increasingly troubled by racial and class distinctions, by problems attendant upon urban growth from crime to service delivery, and by issues that ignited fierce if often irrelevant debate such as prohibition and evolution, the ability to generate a consensus on anything was a major attribute. Second,

21

although the gap between rhetoric and accomplishment was great, the achievements of southern cities in the half century after Reconstruction were sufficient to stimulate a considerable degree of pride. Here were places that had overcome the burdens of poverty and defeat, even of destruction. They were taking their places in the national pantheon of cities. They were drawing outside investments, visitors, and tourists. If the South was finally an integral part of the nation again, the southern city was perhaps the greatest symbol of that integration.

But even in the prosperous places, there was a crassness that implied inferiority. The boisterous boosterism and the frenzied construction were less examples of progress than witnesses to an aimless desire to be something else. The results were ugliness and emptiness. Witness Rock Hill, South Carolina, one of the instant communities of the growing Piedmont region, at the turn of the century: "Rock Hill has no pleasure grounds, few gardens for flowers, no pretty public park with gushing fountains and shaded walks. There seems to be a dearth in the social atmosphere of sentiment and song, and lack of poetic shadings in the constituted nature of things. The town seems to have been built, not in a day, but hurriedly, and for business."[26]

Perhaps even sadder were those places once lovely that had succumbed to the fever of what leaders called progress. Thomas Wolfe offers a thinly veiled critique of Asheville's destruction in the 1920s in *You Can't Go Home Again*:

> A spirit of drunken waste and wild destructiveness was everywhere apparent. The fairest places in the town were being mutilated at untold cost. In the center of town there had been a beautiful green hill, opulent with rich lawns and lordly trees, with beds of flowers and banks of honeysuckle, and on top of it there had been an immense, rambling, old wooden hotel. From its windows one could look out upon the panorama of mountain ranges in the smoky distance. It had been one of the pleasantest places in the town, but now it was gone. An army of men and shovels had advanced upon this beautiful green hill and had leveled it down to an ugly flat of clay, and had paved it with a desolate horror of white concrete, and had built stores and garages and office buildings and parking spaces— all raw and new and were now putting up a new hotel beneath the very spot where the old one had stood. It was to be a structure of sixteen stories of steel and concrete and pressed brick. It was being stamped out of the same mold, as if by some gigantic biscuit-cutter of hotels, that had produced a thousand others like it all over the country.[27]

Some cities sought to obliterate the present, not the past. They could not or would not forget; they did not follow the Yankee way. Whether in shock or in mourning, these southern cities withdrew from the economic competition, seeking solace in a vision of the past that, however false, was comforting and secure. There was Richmond, the once-great Confederate capital, now stumbling, its commerce eroded by the railroad and by large ships that could not navigate the James River. Richmond became a shrine. In historic Hollywood Cemetery, citizens unveiled a statue of General J. E. B. Stuart—"Dead, yet Alive—Mortal, yet Immortal."[28]

Shortly after the war, Charleston settled into a comfortable negligence, allowing its beauty to seep through the ruins but showing little else to a hostile world. John T. Trowbridge, a northern correspondent, surveyed the desolation in 1865: "Broad semi-circular flights of marble steps, leading up to once proud doorways, now conduct you over cracked and calcined slabs to the level of high foundations swept of everything but the crushed fragments of superstructures, with here and there a broken pillar, a windowless wall." Still, Trowbridge admitted, Charleston's "ruins are the most picturesque of any I saw in the South."[29] A decade later the melancholy scene had scarcely changed, although the beauty was more difficult to discern. One foreign visitor found people constantly talking about life "before the war." All around her were "the battered walls, and broken pillars of churches standing in desolate dignity . . . and the stagnation reigning over a city once so beautiful, wealthy, and full of vitality, could not but strike the stranger with a sense of desolation, and even of awe. . . ."[30]

The New South of Henry W. Grady was a stranger to Charleston, and strangers were likely to be ignored in that city of ancestry and tradition. An editorial in the Charleston *News and Courier* in 1898 declared: "There is no 'New South' in the sense of a departure from and a protest against an old South. The New South is a phantom. Its prophets are fakirs and fanatics." History was what mattered. An anecdote of the time went, "Inquiring of a young stranger, it is asked in Boston 'How much does he know?'; in New York, 'How much is he worth?'; in Charleston, 'Who was his grandfather?' " As one chronicler of the city's past noted, "it was almost bad form to be rich." Charleston did not court commerce or outside investment; it cultivated history. When a prominent resident built a home in the decades after the war, he did not follow the design fashions of New York or Chicago. Rather, according to artist Willis John Abbot, who visited the city in 1896, "he builds it in all architectural essentials exactly like the house which the oldest banker . . . built some 150 years ago."[31]

It is hardly surprising then that the formal beginning of the historic preservation movement in the United States occurred in Charleston in 1910 with the formation of the Charleston Art Commission dedicated to preserving the "city historic." A decade later, a small group of elite Charlestonians organized the Society for the Preservation of Negro Spirituals. DuBose Heyward, one of the organizers, explained that this was "not a gesture of patronizing superiority, but a natural and harmonious collaboration wrought in affection and with a deep sense of reverence." In other cities, Heyward continued disapprovingly, blacks "will be taken from our fields, fired with ambition, and fed to the machines. . . ." But in Charleston, "where isolation and time have retarded the process," old relationships and cultures would be maintained.[32]

Charleston also held fast to its antebellum spatial arrangements. While other New South cities such as Atlanta, Nashville, and Charlotte experienced an increasing social and racial residential segregation, Charleston did not. The former sprouted streetcar suburbs by the early 1900s, some elegant like Druid Hills in Atlanta, and some for the rising middle class, as Dilworth in Charlotte (Frederick Law Olmsted, Jr., planned both communities), but Charleston's elite remained steadfastly a downtown group, with their black servants casually interspersed between them.[33]

Charleston was not alone in its pursuit of the past, although its dedication was perhaps singular. All over the urban South, in cities large and small after 1880, city dwellers immortalized war heroes and common soldiers with statues, parades, conventions, and memorials. Part of this outpouring of reverence resulted from the natural evolution of the grieving process. The period of pain and humiliation had passed, but it was important to hand down the memory to the next generation. There was also the growing realization, almost as painful as the memory itself, that recovery was not a simple matter of will. The South was a very poor region. Although the cluster of bumptious Piedmont towns and cities spoke to a new South, most southern cities shared the misery of the countryside, especially those places located along the coast away from major rail connections. A few New York *Tribune* reporters who toured the South in 1879 found Mobile "dilapidated and hopeless"; Norfolk "asleep by her magnificent harbor"; and life in Wilmington and Savannah "at a standstill."[34]

But the New South failed not necessarily because of what it did not do, but for what it did. In many respects the prosperous cities of the New South inherited the worst of both worlds, of the Old and the New South. They eschewed the progress that could come with investments in human capital, embracing instead aggrandizement and monumentality while at the same time casting off the sense of noblesse oblige and grace that marked the old order and retaining its bitter race and class distinctions.

Still, life for most urban southerners in the half century after Reconstruction moved slowly if at all. The small town, the county courthouse town, and the one-gin-general-store-railroad-depot town—more than the larger city—characterized the urban South. The town square was usually the focus of activity. Horses and wagons and automobiles and blacks and whites and children and grown-ups mingled about, gossiping, ogling, whittling, and shopping. This was not the New South, nor the Old South, merely the South, "familiar and familial" as one historian put it.[35] It was the South of soft talk on long porches, of twilight suppers, and of screen doors closing, of the wake-up scent of collards, and of stillness. Were these places passing, "drowned," as Thomas Wolfe asserted, "beneath the brutal flood-time, the fierce stupefaction of that roaring surge and mechanic life which had succeeded it?"[36] Or, were they holding fast, neither buried by the past, nor lured by the promises of a false future?

On the Move: Depression and War

Holding fast would be difficult after 1930. First depression and then war transformed southern cities and towns because they transformed the South. It was not the purpose of the New Deal to alter the South's social and political traditions, but its policies set the stage for changes in succeeding decades. The Agricultural Adjustment Act solved the problem of declining staple prices and overproduction, but it also resulted in the displacement of thousands of sharecroppers and tenants. They moved to Memphis, Little Rock, Jackson, and Birmingham. They moved up North. Southern cities soon found their limited resources strained, and only federal bailouts from agencies such as the Federal Emergency Relief Administration, the Public Works Administration, and the Works Progress Administration stemmed a potential social disaster. Federal officials were shocked by the apparent indifference of local government to the basic needs of its citizens. One official called Houston "parasitic" for its refusal to take on some responsibility for relief; others expressed dismay when Memphis cotton brokers protested the presence of WPA projects in the city because they drained needed labor from the cotton fields. Racial discrimination was rife in dispensing relief. In Atlanta, blacks received $19.29 per month compared with $32.66 for whites. Southern cities were merely following an old southern custom of absorbing change while maintaining the status quo.[37]

Southern cities managed to obtain sewer and water systems, public buildings, roads, power plants, and public housing. But this was only a prelude to the boom that occurred during World War II. Two things happened to the urban South during the war. First, following a policy of defense dispersal, as well as the persuasion of powerful congressional committee heads and the attractions of a moderate climate, the federal government awarded more than $8 billion in defense contracts and related work to southern cities. For the first time in decades, and possibly ever, southerners had money to spend, and consumer demand which had been a negligible factor outside the major cities soared despite wartime shortages. A reporter for *Fortune* magazine interviewed an erstwhile sharecropper, now a defense worker in Panama City, Florida, whose newfound affluence created an unanticipated dilemma: "Hit's got me right bothered how I'm a-goin to spend it all."[38]

The second impact of war on southern cities was the crush of population. The South's farm population declined by 20 percent between 1940 and 1945, while southern cities gained nearly 30 percent, exceeding the national rate of increase. Between 1940 and 1943, Mobile was the fastest-growing city in the nation, with a 61 percent population increase, while Norfolk was right behind with a 57 percent jump. Smaller communities experienced proportionally greater increases, such as Pascagoula, Mississippi which was a small town of four thousand residents in 1940, and a small city of thirty thousand four years later. The poor service and fiscal tradition of the urban South meant that many cities were unprepared for the population onslaught. Agnes Meyer, a reporter for the Washington *Post*, entitled her 1943 tour of the urban South "Journey Through Chaos." Mobile collapsed under the pressure, and the federal government had to assume many essential services.[39]

The flow of money and people carried over in the decade following the war. Defense contracts diminished, but with the emergence of the cold war and the continued power of southern Democrats in Washington, defense plants and shipyards hummed profitably away. And the cities continued to attract newcomers. The southern countryside emptied and poured its ambitions into the cities. During the 1950s, most of the croppers and tenants who had worked the cotton fields of South Carolina—150,000 of them—were gone to such cities as Columbia, Spartanburg, and Greenville. And most of the cotton was gone as well. In 1950, South Carolina still produced more than seven hundred thousand bales; by 1960, cotton cultivation had virtually disappeared as the white fields receded before the green wave of pasture, soybeans, and corn.[40]

Coming of Age: Cities and Civil Rights

Of greater portent for the future of the urban South was the fact that a growing proportion of these newcomers were blacks. Within the confines of the South's biracial society, cities were havens for blacks. In the antebellum era, cities offered slaves a limited mobility and the possibility, however remote, of eventual freedom. And free blacks could learn, if not practice, occupational skills and accumulate modest amounts of property. During the last months of the Civil War, and for a half decade after the conflict, blacks flocked to southern cities. They came to seek family, jobs, and above all freedom. They associated slavery with agriculture, not with urban life. A black Baptist minister recalled the scene in Richmond after the war, where the black population had doubled since 1860 to thirty thousand. "The colored people from all parts of the state," he said, "was crowding in at the capital, running, leaping, and praising God that freedom had come at last. It seems to me that I can hear their songs now [1893] as they run through the air: 'Slavery chain done broke at last; slavery chain done broke at last—I's goin' to praise God till I die.' "[41]

The conditions that confronted the freedmen soon tempered their enthusiasm. Regardless of skill levels, they discovered that only the menial, low-paying occupations were available. Where blacks and whites toiled at similar work, black wages were lower. As cities expanded and distinctive residential areas emerged, blacks invariably occupied the most unhealthy, least desirable locations, devoid of city services and prone to vice and crime. Their daily lives provided constant reminders not only of their distinction, but also of their inferiority. The segregated streetcars, the segregated schools, the forbidden parks, hotels, and restaurants, and the narrow futures became fixtures of black urban life in the South. Historians have noted that in some ways, the decades after the Civil War represented an advance for blacks. They moved from exclusion to segregation. But, the distinction may be more semantical than real. Segregation *was* exclusion. It meant exclusion from a competitive education, regardless of the presence of schools; it meant exclusion from meaningful participation in the political process and in economic development; and it meant exclusion from the dignity and self-worth that accompanies the free and equal intercourse between citizens.[42]

But exclusion held open a few possibilities, and urban blacks made the most of them. They built communities, however fragile and subject to whims of law, violence, and economic upheaval. The black church was the centerpiece of black urban life in the South. Much more than a religious institution, it served as a welfare collective, as an educational center (most southern cities refused to build black schools), and as a leadership training facility. Although not entirely independent of the white community, the black church was a bulwark of black culture and identity. Segregation also meant the development of black businesses to serve black customers and black real estate to satisfy the property-holding and residential demands of a growing black middle class. By 1900, distinctive black communities with some degree of affluence were emerging across the urban South. Their names—"Slippery Log Bottoms" and "Queen Bee Bottoms" in Memphis; "Beaver Slide" in Atlanta; "Elm Thicket" in Dallas; and "Tuxedo Junction" in Birmingham— reflected both a geographical poverty and a richness of life. The main business street of the black district indicated the growth of black enterprise since the Civil War. "Sweet Auburn" (Auburn Avenue) in Atlanta and East Hargett Street in Raleigh were among the more famous black middle-class shopping districts in the South. On East Hargett by 1915, there was an office building for professionals, barber shops, beauty parlors, a hotel, a bank, and numerous retail stores. East Hargett was also a social center, as one habitué recalled: "Anyone who wanted to pass the time away and just generally 'shoot the breeze' made his way [there]."[43]

These communities provided the foundation in terms of leadership, financial support, and inspiration for the mass protests that would occur in the 1950s and 1960s. The civil rights movement was, primarily, an urban phenomenon. The leaders were urban middle-class blacks—ministers, attorneys, and college students—who used the built-in organizational networks of churches, schools, and political groups and who chose urban venues—parks, lunch counters, courthouses, and the streets—to forge a movement. In an era of visual media, cities provided the opportunity for the massing of large numbers of people in discrete areas to maximize the impact of a demonstration. Protests that occurred in rural areas, even the Mississippi Freedom Summer of 1964, rarely moved national public opinion or Congress. The key locales of the civil rights movement were not the farms of the Mississippi Delta, but the cities and towns of the South—Little Rock, Albany, Birmingham, Selma, and Montgomery. The scenes that lingered in the public mind were the screaming mob at Central High in Little Rock, Bull Connor's dogs and hoses in Birmingham, and Sheriff Jim Clark's posse poised by the Edmund Pettus Bridge in Selma.[44]

The civil rights movement marked an important coming of age for southern cities. The successes of the crusade were directly related to the urbanization of black southerners and to the urban institutions they patronized. In 1940, roughly one out of three blacks in the South lived in the region's cities. By 1960, better than one out of two blacks had an urban address. A critical mass existed to wage massive, organized protests. In addition, the changing political climate in the urban South facilitated civil rights accommodations. After World War II, a new generation of urban political leaders emerged. Although they were just as dedicated to economic development as their predecessors, they were also aware that racial moderation and increased service levels were essential to sustained development. While southern businessmen were hardly in the forefront of the civil rights movement, their eventual support was important in gathering a community consensus for racial change. They had reached the conclusion that racial turmoil was bad for business, and that racial harmony was profitable. Atlanta, for example, received much favorable national publicity after its peaceful desegregation of schools and public accommodations in 1961. Atlanta was "a city too busy to hate."[45]

By the mid-1960s, the urban South was not only riding a crest of racial accommodation while the rest of the nation was in the process of exploding in a series of long, hot summers, but was also in the process of outdistancing northern rivals in terms of economic development. Although the term *Sunbelt* was coined only in 1969, and not employed very much until a series of New York *Times* articles in 1976, the urban South was clearly an economic phenomenon before the general public knew about it. The phenomenon resulted from a remarkable juxtaposition of circumstances.[46]

Cities in the Sun

Racial accommodation was one important element of an improved urban economy, of course. The improvement in race relations enabled black southerners to become more active participants in the political and economic life of cities. The rise of the black middle class, especially since the mid-1970s, and the growing numbers of black elected officials contributed to the image of a chastened and prosperous South, an image that often translated into economic development. A second factor involved national trends that favored the urban South. As the economy moved from an industrial to a service base, northeastern and midwestern cities declined. Southern cities which had little in the way of an industrial infrastructure were well positioned to take advantage of the change. Unlike the situation in the nineteenth and early twentieth centuries, the economy no longer centered almost exclusively on New York. Wash-

29

ington was now a power in its own right, the federal reserve system regionalized finance to some degree, and technological innovations in transportation and communications no longer required high degrees of resource concentration. The urban South offered cheaper land, cheaper labor, lower taxes, fewer racial problems, and perhaps most important, growing demand. Although relatively few firms picked up lock, stock, and briefcase, the South became a favorite location for branching. The ability of the urban South to attract high-class industry was underscored by the success of the Research Triangle Park straddling an urban region comprised of Raleigh, Durham, and Chapel Hill in North Carolina.

A third factor in the urban economic renaissance was the changing life-style patterns of Americans. People were retiring earlier. They were also concerned about an elusive concept called "quality of life." Long commuting trips, air and water pollution, crime, crowding, the breakdown of services, the decline of public school systems, the taxes and high property costs, and the disappearance of open spaces characterized the lives of many northerners. To them, the urban South offered many of the advantages of urban living with few of the drawbacks. In the 1960s, for the first time in over a century, more people moved into the South than moved away. Historically, the southerner has been the major export of the South; not so any longer. In 1950, about one out of twelve southern residents was born in the North; by 1980, that figure had climbed dramatically and one out of five southerners had Yankee roots. Ratios were even higher—better than one out of four—in the states of the peripheral South—Virginia, North Carolina, Florida, Texas, Arkansas, and Tennessee. Perhaps even more significant, a growing number of these migrants are black. In the 1970s for the first time since the end of the slave trade, more blacks moved into the South than left.

By the early 1970s, a cycle of development had been established. As more jobs were created in the urban South, more people came. In turn, these new residents increased the demand for consumer goods and for services, which generated more employment, which attracted more people. As with any other major event in southern history, the economic revival spread unevenly across the South indicating the persisting diversity of the region and its cities. In the antebellum era, the seaports were the favored urban centers, replaced by interior cities, especially in the Piedmont crescent in the New South era. After World War II, the pattern changed again. Economic development is no longer confined to a specific geographic region; a more dispersed pattern prevails, not only in the region as a whole, but also within metropolitan areas and within cities.[47]

In the early 1970s, a persistent question that emerged whenever more than two urban southerners met was, How can we avoid northern mistakes in a southern setting? It was the wrong question for at least three reasons. First, the problems of the urban North—eroding tax bases, white flight, racial tensions, rising social service costs, deteriorating housing stock and infrastructure—resulted less from conscious local decision making than from national demographic and economic trends and from federal policy initiatives with good intentions but bad results. Second, whatever contribution northern cities had made to their own decline, by the early 1970s, southern cities were well on their way to imitating them. The question was less one of avoidance than of minimizing the damage. Third, even if local officials were to follow the northern policy course, the results would be different because of demographic, economic, geographic, and cultural distinctions in the urban South.

Fringe Benefits and Central Costs

Southern cities discovered in the 1970s that the Sunbelt contained numerous shadows. The same national trends that had worked against northern cities began to appear in the South. A historical combination of cheap and available land on the urban periphery, a broad middle-class affluence, and the cultural preference for single-family homes had made suburban residence attractive to families since the nineteenth century. Pent-up demand from more than a decade of depression and war, as well as federal subsidies in the form of tax breaks and mortgage guarantees, fueled a major exodus from cities in the decades after World War II. The 1970 census confirmed what most observers had already surmised: we were a suburban nation. Southern cities, growing more slowly than their northern counterparts, did not experience a significant land rush until the late 1950s. Even then, liberal annexation policies masked the decline of central cities. Atlanta, for example, declined in population at a faster rate than both Newark and Detroit between 1970 and 1975. New Orleans and Norfolk lost population faster than New York and Detroit. The growth of the Sunbelt was primarily a growth of the urban periphery, of the metropolitan area as a whole, but not the central city. During the 1960s, Atlanta's population increased by 1.9 percent, while its metropolitan area was growing at a rate of 36.7 percent. More ominous, 80 percent of new jobs in metropolitan Atlanta between 1975 and 1984 were located in the suburbs.[48]

A walk through some of the major southern urban downtowns in the 1970s confirmed the statistics. A Memphis resident described his downtown perspective in 1978: "You can stand on Main Street now and see to where the city limits were fifty years ago and it's all vacant land." Retail establishments were closing and moving to the suburban shopping malls. Downtown Memphis accounted for only 5 percent of the metropolitan area's retail sales.[49]

Some cities saw the trend early and began to plan for it, assisted by federal urban renewal policies that encouraged the destruction of dilapidated residential properties and the construction of tax-rich office high-rises, expensive condominiums, and hotel and entertainment complexes. Atlanta, as a result of the promotional guile of architect-developer John Portman, became a national leader in downtown revitalization. Rocket-style elevators, spinning roof-top restaurants, atrium lobbies, and cocktail lounges in lagoons returned some excitement to central Atlanta, but it was an environment more for conventioneers and tourists than for residents. In the evenings downtown turned into a ghost-town with dark and looming office towers and an ominous sea of empty parking lots. While the downtown glittered, elsewhere in the city the public school system deteriorated and neighborhoods choked on traffic congestion and neglect.[50]

Urban Revival: Back to the Future

By the mid-1970s, new and more effective urban revival strategies emerged. Pressures from minority groups recently energized by the 1965 Voting Rights Act and from neighborhood organizations, angered that downtown development projects and service commitments in annexed areas meant neglect and decline for their areas, transformed the priorities and the personnel in local government. Changes from at-large to district representation enhanced the possibilities for black candidates who, once in office, let more city contracts to minority firms and hired blacks for administrative positions. Atlanta was a prototype of the new emphasis in local government as a coalition of blacks and neighborhood groups elected Maynard Jackson as the city's first black mayor in 1973.

One strategy adopted by the new governments was to lessen the focus on downtown and concentrate on what southerners are best at—remembering. Charleston made a career of it, and New Orleans, Savannah, and Richmond soon followed. These were cities that had either no taste for Yankee-style boosterism, or had the ill-fortune to be on the backwater of American economic development in the century after Appomattox. One circumstance may have generated the other. In any case, after the orgy of obliteration, history emerged by the 1970s as a major tool to revitalize southern cities. Aside from the growth of neighborhood coalitions and black voters, the approaching bicentennial and the churning up of the southern past by the civil rights movement also contributed to a renewed sense of the past. The sense manifested itself in preserving inner-city neighborhoods such as Ansley Park and Inman Park in Atlanta and Dilworth and Myers Park in Charlotte. Civic leaders also sought to preserve or even re-create traditional city centers such as Beale Street in Memphis and Pack Square in Asheville, whose destruction Thomas Wolfe chronicled in the 1920s.

And just as the Civil War produced an outpouring of shrines and holy places in southern cities, so the civil rights movement began to penetrate the historic sense of civic leaders. Tours of historic Selma proceed along the route of the famous voting rights march of 1965, terminating at the newly restored Edmund Pettus Bridge. Birmingham is restoring the jail cell in which Martin Luther King, Jr., wrote his famous letter in April 1963. A metal street marker stands down the block from where the first sit-ins occurred in Greensboro, North Carolina, in February 1960. Museums such as the Valentine in Richmond and the state museum in Jackson, Mississippi, devote generous space to the story of the black struggle for freedom. And reenactments abound. The sit-ins, the Selma-Montgomery march, and the Birmingham demonstrations have been the Confederate veterans' parades of the late twentieth century. Although these commemorations and restorations undoubtedly make white people feel good about themselves, symbols and shrines are important in the South, a region that for decades had only symbols and shrines to which to cling.[51]

It was natural that southern cities should become the region's memory. Smaller places, especially in rural areas, were losing the strength to carry on, and the new fringe communities had few traditions on which to draw other than wanderlust. But the central cities continue to play an important role in the multicentered metropolis because the banking, insurance, and government apparatus that have grown with the metropolitan South have a strong stake in maintaining the vitality of the center. Although a young girl from Greenwood, Mississippi, no longer dreams of her before-school shopping trip to Memphis, there is still an excitement about downtowns in the South—the grand old hotels, such as the Peabody in Memphis and the new-old Tutwiler in Birmingham, the museums, the symphonies, and, yes, even the retail shopping. Taking a page from the suburban shopping mall, cities such as Norfolk, Savannah, and New Orleans have returned to their watery heritage and developed specialty shops and restaurants along neglected waterfronts. Although some of the history is ersatz, it at least reminds visitors and residents alike that this is a place, a place with its own roots, its own story, and its own connection to the South. It is a way to pass on traditions to the children.

While southern urban policymakers have brought the past to present tense, they have maintained a steady pace of megaprojects such as coliseums, hotel-entertainment complexes, and convention centers. The difference from earlier iterations is that these projects are part of a broader and more balanced strategy. Economic development remains a major priority at city hall. And in southern city halls, governing without the support of downtown banking and commercial interests is difficult. Andrew Young, who succeeded Maynard Jackson in Atlanta, was especially adept at courting the traditional economic elite in that city and in traveling far and wide to deliver the message of what one journalist called, "Andynomics." Business leaders discovered the considerable good-will that a black mayor can generate on the investment front.[52]

The role of a southern urban political leader is considerably more complex than when he (and it was always *he*) could call up the chairman of Coca-Cola or meet the bank directors for lunch at the City Club. In some respects his role is more similar to urban leaders in other parts of the country in that he must practice consensus and coalition politics. For one thing, southern cities are more diverse than at any time since the antebellum era. In addition to assorted Yankees, the urban South is hosting considerable numbers of immigrants. The Hispanic presence and influence in Texas and southern Florida cities is well known, but there are, for example, fifty thousand Hispanics in the Atlanta metropolitan area. There is also a like number of Koreans, Chinese, Indians, Laotians, and Vietnamese. Every major southern city now includes these groups—just look at the supermarket shelves and the restaurants for confirmation.[53]

Southern urban leaders also face different national and economic realities from their predecessors. Economic competition is global. Very few mayors of major southern cities have not been abroad touting the attributes of their city to foreign investors. In addition, it is no longer morning in the so-called Sunbelt. The reported demise of northeastern and midwestern cities was premature. Cities in New York and Ohio in particular have revived to offer stiff competition to southern upstarts. Cheap land and cheap labor are no longer the main and only attractions. In the post-industrial economy and with the late-twentieth-century American life-style, an educated work force, a high-quality school system, and cultural and recreational amenities have become important considerations for firms seeking to move or branch in new areas. Education and service amenities have traditionally not been the strong suits of southern urban governments. Local officials have had to build new coalitions of consensus, including business, universities, and citizens' groups to both upgrade the business climate and devise new development strategies.[54]

Urban Regions

Urban leaders have also had to take their coalition-building expertise beyond the city line. Although southern cities have managed to reverse or at least halt the erosion of their influence within the metropolitan area, the periphery continues to outpace the central city across the South, but they are facing some problems that require regional cooperation. In particular, the migration of northerners fueled the outward drive. It was more a suburb-to-suburb migration than a city-to-city movement. It stood to reason that newcomers would want to reconstruct the positive aspects of their old environment as much as possible—single-family homes, easy access to multipurpose shopping malls, and good school systems. These and other services drove up the tax rates and drastically changed the landscape of rural areas and small towns in the path of metropolitan development. Because southern cities had grown up in the age of the automobile, suburban development went wherever the automobile could go, and that meant hither and yon in areas that had not seen so many people since General Sherman's tour more than a century ago. And some viewed the newcomers as little better than the earlier northern visitors with the added disadvantage that the twentieth-century invaders were staying.

Gwinnett County, Georgia, was a quiet, sparsely settled farming area in the 1960s. Lawrenceville, the county seat, is thirty-two miles northeast of Atlanta. By 1985, Gwinnett held the distinction of being the fastest-growing county in the country. The county's population grew 38 percent between 1980 and 1984 to a total of 230,000 residents. In another decade the county should approach the half-million mark. In the meantime, county officials must build new sewage treatment facilities as the old one is beyond capacity. Traffic is a nightmare in the southern part of the county, and as yet, Gwinnett does not have a land use plan.[55]

Rural areas all over the South are being thrust into the suburban age with little preparation. The results can be especially jarring to long-time residents, now challenged for political office, burdened with higher taxes, and confronted by a declining quality of life. Counties in the middle of transition offer an interesting juxtaposition of separate lifestyles. Journalist Mary Hood recounted a 1987 visit to her home in Cherokee County, Georgia. Although it is even further away from Atlanta than Gwinnett, the metropolitan spread has oozed into Cherokee.

Hood relates that the county has become three places, each defined by a Wal-Mart discount store. In the traditional portion of the county where residents still drink well water and pay cash, the Wal-Mart has clerks named Delma, Edna, or Bud Jr., and the shoppers are mostly from nuclear families. The radio is turned to the local country station and the booths at the snack bar are the major media centers. Nine miles to the southeast there is a four-lane highway, shopping plazas, and water towers. The ball fields, speedway, and churches of the old community persist, but the Wal-Mart in this part of the county does not contain a snack bar, and few people loiter. As Hood notes, "These are busy people, involved in PTA and soccer and tennis camp. They shop in their crisp Realtor's blazer, nurse's or policeman's uniform; everyone has somewhere else to be, and soon." The radio is tuned to 96-ROCK, and the customers' names are Brandon, Angie, Kim, Scott, and Dawn.[56]

Driving (always driving) toward the interstate, apartments and homes have replaced the horse barns and oak trees. "The road names and mall stores," Hood writes, "make no claim on native loyalties and sympathy." At this Wal-Mart "we are all newcomers, all strangers, and I shop in the same anxiety and alienation as everyone else. . . . I shop here in that anonymity attained more often in large cities." The clerks "are chic, worldly." Yet, despite the very real physical and life-style changes she witnessed in traveling across her county, Hood concludes that the important things have not been lost: "the purest things, and the everlasting springs, run deep."[57]

Living in three different time zones, past, present, and future, is nothing special for southerners. They have been doing it for a long time, even if a good deal of it is unconscious. As with the gentleman I met in Richmond, there is nothing incongruous about referring to long-dead people, long-past eras, and long-gone places in the present tense. Southerners, as the most mobile Americans, have learned that there is no country but the heart, and they have often worn that heart on their sleeve, carrying it through major upheavals. And the beat goes on. Even in the established cities, and even apart from the conscious efforts to compress time zones, it is still not difficult to find the easy mingling of past and place. Jim Cobb has found "cracklin's and caviar" within two blocks in Atlanta.[58] And even above the hum of the air-conditioner, which, not so incidentally has made much of the urban South possible, conversation for conversation's sake and the courtesies of casual social intercourse in shops, restaurants, and other public places, persist.

But the terms on which southern culture persists clearly depend on the metropolitan frame of mind as more of the countryside becomes part of the southern urban daily orbit. For urban leaders it is not simply reaching out to suburbs within an easy commute of downtown, it is reaching further and further out to what are becoming new cities in new regions. The major urban development of the 1980s was the growth of urban regions. The metropolitan ooze has advanced far enough for metropolitan areas to grow together. Interstate highways have been major facilitators for regional urban growth. The I-85 corridor from Raleigh to Atlanta is host to a growing diversity of manufacturing and retail enterprises. Excellent trucking and air access, the participation of high-quality higher education institutions, and active promotional activities undertaken on behalf of urban regions, rather than merely towns and cities, have enabled the textile belt to more than recover lost employment. Winston-Salem, for example, has gained three times more jobs than it lost since 1983. These positions came from small businesses, service industries, health care, and higher education. Spartanburg caught the drift of a declining textile industry a decade ago and went after foreign investment—a relatively new feature in the southern metropolitan economy. Today, Spartanburg has more investment from abroad—$1 billion—than any other American city of its size. The stretch of I-85 that runs past the city is called "the Autobahn," in recognition of the number of German and Swiss firms in the area.[59]

There is a growing concentration within these urban regions, especially on their peripheries, that reflects a new urban form emerging nationwide. These are the "out-towns," the new concentrations of high-rise office buildings, shopping malls, hotels, and residential neighborhoods that are quite different from the traditional suburban bedroom communities of the post-World War II era. Developers promote them more as villages than as suburbs. Las Colinas, west of Dallas, is a model of the out-town. Corporate giants, including Xerox, DuPont, and A.T.&T. have offices there; there are strict architectural controls, generous park space, canals, a 125-acre lake, a shopping mall, and residences. Its daytime population is roughly forty thousand and its attractions rival downtown Dallas. Few of the out-towns are as structured as Las Colinas. Most evolved out of a major regional shopping mall, such as River Chase outside of Birmingham, the Cumberland-Galleria complex on the outer edge of the Atlanta metropolitan area, and a massive Edward De Bartolo project outside of Miami. What they offer, according to urban consultant Christopher Leinberger, are places where "people can work, live, shop and play in close proximity, thereby enjoying many advantages of urban density but avoiding its high costs and problems."[60] These communities are the urban South of the twenty-first century. They are the new downtowns, and they conform to the relatively low-density residential traditions of southern urban history.

Both the leaders of these new towns and the central cities are seeing themselves less as rivals than as partners in service provision and economic development. Regional airports, waste treatment facilities, and technical training programs are some of the cooperative efforts underway. Regional coalitions have been successful in putting together economic development programs, recognizing that increasing competition from other parts of the country requires the pooling of resources and expertise. Intra-regional competition was fierce and nasty in the Atlanta metropolitan area until the formation of the Metropolitan Atlanta Council for Economic Development (MACFED). The council is a cooperative effort of the chambers of commerce in Atlanta and the surrounding suburban and semi-suburban counties of Clayton, Cobb, DeKalb, Douglas, and Gwinnett.[61]

There is a danger, of course, in the constant contemplation of growth—how to get it, how to manage it, and how to profit from it. Although southern urban governments are more inclusive and have greater social and historical awareness than they have ever had, economic development has the greatest political rewards. It is the most easily visible success of an urban administration and business community. Less visible, both in terms of urban policy and media attention, are the imbalances in the metropolitan economy and areas beyond. Although they are easy to ignore, these imbalances are difficult to address. But they are as much a part of the urban present and future as the regional shopping malls and the downtown office towers. More seriously, these imbalances can threaten the economic and social vitality of the South's metropolitan regions.

The Last Picture Show

As southern metropolitan areas sprawled outward and as central cities began to recover from the problems of withdrawal, the towns and small cities of the South, especially those away from growth areas, were also undergoing changes. The 1970s and early 1980s were difficult years for the Piedmont textile region. Foreign competition and mechanization struck hard. Because most textile communities were one-industry towns, the closing of the mill meant the closing of the town. The Riegel Textile Corporation created Ware Shoals, South Carolina, on the banks of the Saluda River in 1906. The company shut down its plant at the end of 1984, throwing nine hundred people out of work. Young people have moved to find work elsewhere, and 60 percent of the population is retired. Riegel provided 60 percent of the tax base and 20 percent of the school budget. Mayor Hugh Frederick tried to put a brave face on the situation: "Riegel built the town. They built all the homes around the mill. They provided the water, electricity and the company store. It looks bad, but we've got a lot of assets. . . . We're pretty gritty people."[62]

In other Piedmont communities, death did not come so suddenly, but the long decline has set in. Vacant storefronts dot downtown Chester, South Carolina. In Whitmire, South Carolina, as the textile giant J.P. Stevens cut its work force, a department store, a drugstore, and a clothing store have left the downtown. Beauty shops and churches remain, and young people leave. For some of these towns, their new centers have become the highways or the interstate, where shopping malls have sprouted like chickweed. It is here that the K-Marts and Wal-Marts flourish.[63]

The small towns face a difficult prospect. Many, like Woodville, Mississippi, list welfare as their major industry. Their populations are dependent, highly skewed toward the elderly, and offer little attraction for outside investment and little inspiration for indigenous entrepreneurship. They once may have hosted prosperous industries, but they now are competing against third-world nations, a competition they will obviously lose despite a long history of mortgaging their people and their land for dubious short-term gains. These are the towns that would love the problem of a traffic jam and overtaxed infrastructure, but all they are likely to see are roads leading in one direction and structures rotting from disuse. These are the places of high dropout rates, high infant mortality, and high unemployment—37 percent higher than in larger cities. The development coalitions of government, business, and education are considerably beyond the resources and capabilities of these communities. Historically, the fate of the countryside has been inextricably linked to the fate of the city in the South. The depopulation of the rural and small-town South will create burdens on metropolitan areas, the likely destination of rural migrants.

Metropolitan Imbalances

Although urban-rural distinctions are relatively obvious, there are considerable imbalances both within cities and within metropolitan regions. The service and high-tech economy has created a two-tiered work force of high-skilled, well-educated, white-collar personnel and poorly educated, low-skilled workers who have little hope of upward mobility in salary and responsibility. In addition, the majority of low-skill-level jobs are opening on the metropolitan periphery, where few of the lower-income people live. The inadequacy of public transit in the metropolitan South exacerbates disjunction between work and residence for the poor.

The two-tiered metropolitan economy raises issues of equity. Given the traditions of southern local government and the expectations of many of its constituents there is little likelihood that higher taxes and increased social services will emerge as urban policies. Black political leaders such as Atlanta's Andrew Young and Birmingham's Richard Arrington have shuttled some city contracts to minority firms, but on the whole they have adopted the entrepreneurial priorities of their white predecessors. An added difficulty is that environmental concerns have emerged as powerful issues in urban politics. As metropolitan areas march across the southern landscape, they bring air and water pollution, the destruction of farm land, and the obliteration of historic structures. Growth management has replaced economic development as the key policy phrase in many southern cities, and states such as Florida and North Carolina are supporting such efforts with statewide growth controls. But, will it be more difficult to address equity issues in an economy held in check?

There are also persisting imbalances between central city and out-towns. Suburban and out-town communities are overwhelmingly white, as are their school districts and their occupational networks. There is little sentiment to change this situation, and the unwillingness of Atlanta's suburbs to participate in the extension of the city's subway system suggests that race is still an important factor dividing the metropolitan South. The division is especially evident in the separate city and county school systems in most metropolitan areas. City systems are becoming overwhelmingly black, while suburban districts are predominantly white. The deliberate resegregation of some public schools in Norfolk and Little Rock is designed to curb white flight. Although metropolitan cooperation has become part of a regional strategy in recent years, such efforts are typically confined to economic development and services. Housing and schools remain off the agenda.

The Promise of the Urban South

As urban southerners attempt to deal with these imbalances, they have several strengths upon which to draw. First, they have the benefit of scale. Although the South contains roughly the same number of metropolitan areas as other regions, there are very few large ones. The largest southern metropolitan area is Dallas, but it ranks only eighth nationally; Houston is ninth, and Atlanta is sixteenth. There are no other southern metropolitan areas in the nation's top twenty, and only three others (Miami, Tampa, and New Orleans) are in the top forty. Smaller scale should mean easier management. It also means that the historical connection with the land is never very far from the doorstep of the metropolitan southerner. In fact, the Southeast interior region (bounded by Nashville in the west and Birmingham and Atlanta in the south, and extending up the Piedmont to the Virginia border), one of the nation's six urban regions designated by the Urban Land Institute, is the least city-dominated, with only 29 percent of its population in central cities. Of the six regions, it has the lowest number of people per square mile, about two hundred. Although growth has overwhelmed some of the smaller places within this region, others have been able to maintain their semirural character. These are, as termed by demographer J. C. Doherty, "countrified cities"—spread-out, low-density communities.[64]

Another positive feature of southern urbanization is the tradition of volunteerism. Private agencies, especially churches, have taken up many activities ordinarily associated with government. Reform movements in the South from the antebellum era through the civil rights movement have typically originated in churches, black and white. New organizations are emerging from the churches across the urban South to address housing, job training, and counseling needs. In 1980, for example, a church-based organization, Strategies to Elevate People (STEP) formed in Dallas. STEP mobilized five hundred volunteers from its member churches which, by the rules of the organization, include both black and white congregations, and renovated a black housing project in Dallas. In addition, STEP has established a college assistance fund for children from low-income families. By 1987, STEP ministries had appeared in Fort Worth, Richmond, Norfolk, Nashville, and Charlotte. Other STEP services include pairing adults with low-income elementary school children and operating joint programs with local community colleges to provide adult education. STEP churches have succeeded in leveraging business assistance in the form of supplies, funds, and additional voluntary help. The religious institutions of the urban South represent a moral reservoir that can serve both the region's traditions and its future.[65]

Perhaps the strongest tradition the urban South has in its favor is southern history. Unlike the rest of the country, history in the South has not been a straight-line progression upward. There have been major detours. Only recently, and thanks primarily to southern blacks, has the South shown a willingness to accept its past—not just the good parts, or the parts clouded over by myth—but all of it. The willingness is especially noticeable in the urban South, among the black middle class, at city hall, and especially in the new shrines and symbols that have become part of the urban iconography as much as the glass skyscrapers and the salad bars. Americans have generally been uncomfortable with the past. Memories are excruciatingly short. Perhaps metropolitan southerners, whom sociologist John Shelton Reed identifies as the new gatekeepers for southern culture, can teach a lesson or two in this regard, that the past, present, and future are all part of the same seamless fabric, and that time zones are not only irrelevant, but they are also barriers to a better understanding of self, of others, and of the environment.[66]

The Madison County, Alabama, Tourism Board sends out a promotional package entitled "Instant Huntsville." The package contains five plastic capsules. Drop the capsules in a bowl of warm water and suddenly bobbing to the surface are an astronaut, an antebellum mansion, a space shuttle, a southern belle, and the state of Alabama. The promotion covers all time zones and appeals to a wide variety of taste. It also underscores how much the urban South has become, simply, the South. This does not necessarily mean that we are apt to see gun racks in the backs of BMWs or frog-leg nuggets, but we may. These are no less ironic than the fact that the police chief of Charleston, South Carolina, is black and Jewish or that a black woman is mayor of Little Rock. This is the South of the 1990s, and this is the urban South.[67]

The identity between city and region is not surprising given a historical perspective. Although a minor element in the Old South civilization in terms of population and culture, the antebellum southern city was the focal point for a region's dreams of economic parity. The city's failure was the South's failure. After the Civil War, urbanization required a reorientation of race relations. If "segregation" and "South" became synonymous, then the southern city made it so. It was here also, in diverse ways, that the New South Creed battled with scarred traditions resulting in few victors and many losers. No longer merely an adjunct to the countryside, the urban South was now a partner, sometimes a dominant one. The fact that Scarlett O'Hara moved to Atlanta after the war and established a business was of more than symbolic import.

In depression and world war, the urban South became the repository of regional hope again. People left the countryside, and money flowed from Washington. And the city became a battleground again, for the bodies of blacks and the souls of whites. This time, the winners outnumbered the also-rans. Finally, the urban South, for all its remaining difficulties, now not only offers to lead the region, but also has the opportunity to set an example for the rest of the nation in race relations, in economic development, in the value of traditions, and maybe even in equity. It is a heady role, and perhaps George Tindall is right in saying that if history is any guide "the South will blow it." But the strengths of the city today are the strengths of the region, and both city and South are connected more intimately than ever before. As Judge Reuben Anderson noted in a 1980 Southern Growth Policies Board report, "the future of the South cannot be separated from the future of Southern cities."[68]

NOTES

1. William Faulkner, *Intruder in the Dust* (New York, 1948), p. 194.

2. Frederick Law Olmsted, *A Journey in the Back Country* (New York, 1860), pp. 279–80.

3. For a discussion on the relationship between sectionalism and urban development in antebellum Virginia, see David R. Goldfield, *Urban Growth in the Age of Sectionalism: Virginia, 1847–1861* (Baton Rouge, 1977). See also, Allan R. Pred, *Urban Growth and City-Systems in the United States, 1840–1860* (Cambridge, 1980), on the South's weakening position within the national economy.

4. The crucial nature of city-hinterland relations in the process of urbanization is best explicated by Diane Lindstrom, *Economic Development in the Philadelphia Region, 1810–1850* (New York, 1978). See also, Roberta Balstad Miller, *City and Hinterland: A Case Study of Urban Growth and Regional Development* (Westport, 1979).

5. The literature on the relationship between crop type and patterns of urbanization is extensive. Three of the more recent and more helpful works are Carville Earle and Ronald Hoffman, "The Foundation of the Modern Economy: Agriculture and the Costs of Labor in the U.S. and England, 1800–60," *American Historical Review* 85 (December 1980): 1055–94; Thomas M. Doerflinger, *A Vigorous Spirit of Enterprise: Merchants and Economic Development in Revolutionary Philadelphia* (Chapel Hill, 1986); and Frederick F. Siegel, *The Roots of Southern Distinctiveness: Tobacco and Society in Danville, Virginia, 1780–1865* (Chapel Hill, 1987).

6. Quoted in William H. Pease and Jane H. Pease, *The Web of Progress: Private Values and Public Styles in Boston and Charleston, 1828–1843* (New York, 1985), p. 219.

7. Considerable debate exists on whether or not southern planters invested in land and slaves because they perceived such investments as providing the highest rates of return, or whether noneconomic factors motivated them. Gavin Wright, *The Political Economy of the Cotton South: Households, Markets, and Wealth in the Nineteenth Century* (New York, 1978), chapter 3 (pp. 43–88), supports the view presented in this chapter, while Eugene Genovese argues the opposite case in several works, most notably, *The Political Economy of Slavery: Studies in the Economy and Society of the Slave South* (New York, 1965).

8. Alexander MacKay, "The People of Richmond Are a Peculiar People," in *A Richmond Reader, 1744–1983*, ed. Maurice Duke and Daniel P. Jordan, (Chapel Hill, 1983), p. 87.

9. Richard Wade argued the incompatibility of slavery and cities in *Slavery in the Cities: The South, 1820–1860* (New York, 1964), but most of the more recent work has challenged that view. See especially, Claudia Dale Goldin, *Urban Slavery in the American South, 1820–1860: A Quantitative History* (Chicago, 1975).

10. Ira Berlin and Herbert G. Gutman, "Natives and Immigrants, Free Men and Slaves: Urban Workingmen in the Antebellum American South," *American Historical Review* 88 (December 1983): 1175–200.

11. Myron Berman, *Richmond's Jewry: Shabbat in Shockoe, 1769–1976* (Charlottesville, 1979).

12. Quoted in Harriet E. Amos, *Cotton City: Urban Development in Antebellum Mobile* (University, 1985), p. 78.

13. Quoted in Amos, *Cotton City*, p. xii.

14. Quoted in Lawrence H. Larsen, *The Rise of the Urban South* (Lexington, Ky., 1985), p. 15. The definitive work on Atlanta's recovery is James M. Russell, *Atlanta, 1847–1890: City Building in the Old South and New* (Baton Rouge, 1988).

15. David Carlton, *Mill and Town in South Carolina, 1880–1920* (Baton Rouge, 1982), pp. 21–24. Carlton's book is the most important work to date on the socioeconomic implications of urbanization in a portion of the Piedmont. Although there have been studies on a few individual cities of the Piedmont such as Atlanta and peripheral places such as Richmond and Birmingham, there has not yet been a comprehensive analysis of the Piedmont as an urban region.

16. There is a considerable literature on mill villages and workers. One of the most important contributions to this literature in recent years is Jacquelyn Dowd Hall et al., *Like a Family: The Making of a Southern Cotton Mill World* (Chapel Hill, 1987).

17. Jacqueline Dowd Hall et al., "Cotton Mill People: Work, Community, and Protest in the Textile South, 1880–1940," *American Historical Review* 91 (April 1986): 255.

18. Hall, "Cotton Mill People," p. 261.

19. Carlton, *Mill and Town in South Carolina*, p. 106.

20. Don H. Doyle, *New Men, New Cities, New South: Atlanta, Nashville, Charleston, Mobile, 1860–1910* (Chapel Hill, 1989).

21. Doyle, *New Men, New Cities*, p. 323. On the role of southern women in urban reform during the late nineteenth and early twentieth centuries, see also James L. Leloudis II, "School Reform in the New South: The Woman's Association for the Betterment of Public School Houses in North Carolina, 1902–1919," *Journal of American History* 64 (March 1983): 886–909; Darlene R. Roth, "Feminine Marks on the Landscape: An Atlanta Inventory," *Journal of American Culture* 3 (Winter 1980): 673–85.

22. The literature on southern progressivism is extensive, and there are disagreements concerning the origins of progressives and the true extent of their reforms. The most balanced perspective is Dewey W. Grantham, *Southern Progressivism: The Reconciliation of Progress and Tradition* (Knoxville, 1983). His article, "Review Essay: The Contours of Southern Progressivism," *American Historical Review* 87 (December 1981): 1035–59, provides a fine historiographical analysis. For a dissent from Grantham's even-handed treatment, see J. Mor-

gan Kousser, "Progressivism—for Middle-Class Whites Only: North Carolina Education, 1880–1910," *Journal of Southern History* 46 (May 1980): 169–94.

23. W. J. Cash, *The Mind of the South* (New York, 1941), p. 219.

24. Roger Biles, "The Urban South in the Great Depression," unpublished manuscript in author's possession, p. 21.

25. On the New South promotional efforts of Nashville and Atlanta, see Don H. Doyle, *Nashville in the New South, 1880–1930* (Knoxville, 1985), p. 43, and Howard L. Preston, *Automobile Age Atlanta: The Making of a Southern Metropolis, 1900–1935* (Athens, 1979), pp. 21–29. The classic work on the southern urban growth ethic of the early twentieth century is Blaine A. Brownell, *The Urban Ethos in the South, 1920–1930* (Baton Rouge, 1975).

26. Quoted in Carlton, *Mill and Town in South Carolina*, p. 28.

27. Thomas Wolfe, *You Can't Go Home Again* (New York, 1934), pp. 111–12.

28. Quoted in Mary H. Mitchell, *Hollywood Cemetery: The History of a Southern Shrine* (Richmond, 1985), p. 71. For a detailed discussion on the postwar decline of Richmond, see Michael B. Chesson, *Richmond after the War, 1865–1890* (Richmond, 1981).

29. John T. Trowbridge, *The Desolate South, 1865–66*, ed. Gordon Carroll (New York, 1956), pp. 274–75.

30. Quoted in Doyle, *New Men, New Cities, New South*, pp. 82–83.

31. Ibid., pp. 159, 336–37, 332.

32. Ibid., pp. 329, 446–47.

33. The rise of the urban middle class and the new technology of the electric trolley combined to create a suburban movement by the late nineteenth century. Although not of great proportions compared with the major urban centers of the North, the movement was significant enough to attract the nation's most prominent suburban planners. See Catherine W. Bishir, ed., *Early Twentieth-Century Suburbs in North Carolina* (Raleigh, 1985) and Dana F. White and Victor A. Kramer, eds., *Olmsted South: Old South Critic/New South Planner* (Westport, 1979).

34. Quoted in Larsen, *Rise of the Urban South*, p. 11.

35. Robert C. McMath, Jr., "Community, Region, and Hegemony in the Nineteenth-Century South" in *Toward a New South? Studies in Post-Civil War Southern Communities*, ed. Orville Vernon Burton and Robert C. McMath (Westport, 1982), p. 284.

36. Thomas Wolfe, *Of Time and the River* (New York, 1935), p. 898.

37. Roger Biles has written extensively on the New Deal and southern cities. He has completed a manuscript on the subject, "The Urban South in the Great Depression." See also, his book, *Memphis in the Great Depression* (Knoxville, 1986). For the regional context of urban change during the 1930s, see James C. Cobb and Michael V. Namorato, eds., *The New Deal and the South* (Jackson, 1984).

38. "The Deep South Looks Up," *Fortune* 28 (July 1943): 100.

39. Quoted in David R. Goldfield, *Promised Land: The South since 1945* (Arlington Heights, 1987), p. 8. See also, David R. Goldfield, *Cotton Fields and*

Skyscrapers: Southern City and Region, 1607–1980 (Baton Rouge, 1982), pp. 182–84. The urban South during World War II is a major historiographical frontier. So far, we have had only indirect evidence of the war's importance: Morton Sosna's essay, "More Important than the Civil War? The Social Impact of World War II on the South," in *Perspectives on the American South,* vol. 4, ed. James C. Cobb and Charles R. Wilson (New York, 1987), 145–58; and Pete Daniel, *Breaking the Land: The Transformation of Cotton, Tobacco, and Rice Culture since 1880* (Urbana, 1985), which provides a thorough account of the exodus from the rural South.

40. Goldfield, *Cotton Fields and Skyscrapers,* pp. 142–43.

41. Quoted in Peter J. Rachleff, *Black Labor in the South: Richmond, Virginia, 1865–1890* (Philadelphia, 1984).

42. The definitive work on urban life for southern blacks during the generation after the Civil War is Howard N. Rabinowitz, *Race Relations in the Urban South, 1865–1890* (New York, 1978). Rabinowitz develops the exclusion-to-segregation model in the book, challenging C. Vann Woodward's argument, put forth in *The Strange Career of Jim Crow* (New York, 1955), that segregation occurred relatively late in the nineteenth century.

43. Quoted in Thomas C. Parramore, *Express Lanes and Country Roads: The Way We Lived in North Carolina, 1920–1970* (Chapel Hill, 1983). Although blacks became increasingly urban during the first half of the twentieth century, we know more about their antebellum counterparts. There are a few exceptions such as Lester C. Lamon, *Black Tennesseans, 1900–30* (Knoxville, 1977), and George C. Wright, *Life Behind a Veil: Blacks in Louisville, Kentucky, 1865–1930* (Baton Rouge, 1985).

44. For a discussion on the relationship between urbanization and the civil rights movement in the South, see David R. Goldfield, *Black, White, and Southern: Race Relations and Southern Culture, 1940 to the Present* (Baton Rouge, 1990).

45. For a discussion on how southern businessmen handled desegregation in the urban South, see Elizabeth Jacoway and David R. Colburn, eds., *Southern Businessmen and Desegregation* (Baton Rouge, 1982). Generally, business leaders in those cities that were growing and had good prospects for future economic development were more inclined to agree to a racial accommodation in the early 1960s.

46. On the origins of the Sunbelt concept and its application to the South, see Carl Abbott, "New West, New South, New Region: The Discovery of the Sunbelt" in *Searching for the Sunbelt,* ed. Raymond A. Mohl (Knoxville, 1990).

47. Although there is no comprehensive treatment of southern urban economic development since World War II, and especially since 1965, there are several helpful works that provide historical context for that development. See, for example, Richard M. Bernard and Bradley R. Rice, eds., *Sunbelt Cities: Politics and Growth since World War II* (Austin, 1983); Bernard L. Weinstein and Robert E. Firestine, *Regional Growth and Decline in the United States: The Rise of the Sunbelt and the Decline of the Northeast* (New York, 1978). For a debunking view of the Sunbelt phenomenon, see George B. Tindall, "The Sunbelt Snow Job," *Houston Review* 1 (Spring 1979): 3–13. James C. Cobb's two books, *The Selling*

of the South: The Southern Crusade for Industrial Development, 1936–1980 (Baton Rouge, 1982) and *Industrialization and Southern Society, 1877–1984* (Lexington, Ky., 1984), contend that some traditional characteristics such as exploitation of land and labor persist alongside Sunbelt hyperbole.

48. Goldfield, *Cotton Fields and Skyscrapers*, p. 193.

49. Roger Biles, "Epitaph for Downtown: The Failure of City Planning in Post-World War II Memphis," *Tennessee Historical Quarterly* 44 (Fall 1985): 267–84.

50. For a discussion of Portman's work and its consequences, see Goldfield, *Cotton Fields and Skyscrapers*, pp. 156–57.

51. On neighborhood revitalization and the urban uses of history, see Goldfield, *Promised Land*, pp. 208–11.

52. On the effective use of "Andynomics" in Atlanta, see Art Harris, "Atlanta, Georgia: Too Busy to Hate," *Esquire* 102 (June 1985): 129–33.

53. Historians have only recently begun to analyze and describe the increasingly pluralistic populations of the urban South, see Raymond A. Mohl, "Miami: New Immigrant City," Ronald H. Bayor, "Race, Ethnicity, and Intergroup Relations in the Sunbelt South: Patterns of Change," and Elliott Barkan, "New Origins, New Homelands: Immigration into Selected Sunbelt Cities since 1965," in Mohl's edited volume, *Searching for the Sunbelt*; Randall M. Miller and George E. Pozzetta, eds., *Shades of the Sunbelt* (Westport, 1988).

54. For a discussion of this competition and its relation to questions of equity and quality of life, see David R. Goldfield, "Economic Development in the South: Education, Equity, and the Quality of Life," in *Education, Environment and Culture: The Quality of Life in the South*, ed. Commission on the Future of the South, (Research Triangle Park, 1986), pp. 13–17.

55. William E. Schmidt, "Georgia County Knows Beauties, Burdens of Fast Growth," New York *Times*, June 4, 1985.

56. Mary Hood, "Of Water and Wal-Mart: The Demographics of Progress in a Georgia Community," *Southern Magazine* 1 (January 1987): 22.

57. Hood, "Of Water and Wal-Mart," p. 23.

58. James C. Cobb, "Cracklin's and Caviar: The Enigma of Sunbelt Georgia," *Georgia Historical Quarterly* 58 (Spring 1984): 19.

59. "Winston-Salem Moves to Temper A.T.&T.'s Blow," Charlotte *Observer*, January 24, 1988; David Treadwell, "Gloom to Boom: Spartanburg Saw Textiles' Future Early," Los Angeles *Times*, November 10, 1985.

60. Quoted in Neal Peirce, "Can Urban Villages Become Real People Places?" Washington *Post*, August 17, 1985. See also, Peter O. Muller, "The Suburbanization of the Sunbelt City: Metropolitan Restructuring in the South and West," presented at Conference on the Sunbelt, Miami, November, 1985.

61. Bradley R. Rice, "Searching for the Sunbelt: An Update," in *Searching for the Sunbelt*, ed. Mohl. Although MACFED dissolved, cooperation on economic development persists in the Atlanta region.

62. "Mill's Closing Cuts to the Heart, Soul of an SC Town," Charlotte *Observer*, November 4, 1984.

63. "Shopping 'bah, Humbug!' in Small Towns," Charlotte *Observer*, December 20, 1987.

64. On the low-density character of southern metropolitan development and its costs and benefits, see "Development Threatens Farmers," Charlotte *Observer*, May 31, 1987. See also, Robert G. Healy, *Competition for Land in the American South: Agriculture, Human Settlement, and the Environment* (Washington, 1985), chapter 5. On "countrified cities" see, "Census Statistics Don't Reflect Rural Growth," Charlotte *Observer*, May 31, 1987.

65. "A Giant STEP," Charlotte *Observer*, May 10, 1987.

66. John Shelton Reed, *Southerners: The Social Psychology of Sectionalism* (Chapel Hill, 1983).

67. Journalist Linton Weeks discusses these "ironies" in "The Real South," *Southern Magazine* 1 (May 1987): 8.

68. Commission on the Future of the South, ed. *The Future of the South* (Research Triangle Park, 1981), p. 22.

2

The Future of Southern Politics: New Directions for Dixie

ALEXANDER P. LAMIS

By practically any measure of overall political change, the South has far outstripped the other regions of the country over the last twenty-five years. Therefore, this attempt to peer cautiously forward and glimpse southern politics in the year 2000 begins with a look backward.

Politics in the twentieth-century South breaks distinctly into two eras with the dividing line coming during the Second Reconstruction of the middle 1960s. Following the failure of the Populist upheavals at the end of the nineteenth century, the southern one-party system took shape and persisted in virtually unchallenged fashion for the next six decades.[1] The system was rooted in the desire to preserve white supremacy. The argument, in its most basic form, went as follows: If whites remained united in the Democratic party, blacks would be unable to bargain between competing partisan groups of whites in an effort to change their position as second-class citizens.

The arrangement left the South with an odd political process, one that required white regional unity to guard against outside attempts to force change in the racial status quo and one that left the region without the benefits, small as they may sometimes seem, of organized competition for public office between two established political parties.

The southern Democracy of the one-party era received its most penetrating analysis in 1949, when V. O. Key, Jr., with the assistance of Alexander Heard, published the classic *Southern Politics in State and Nation*. Key stripped the region's politics of its many myths and bore in on a few harsh realities. He knew that what he would have to say would not be pleasing to many white southerners. Seeking to dissuade Roscoe Martin of the University of Alabama from "forcing him" to take on the southern politics project, Key wrote an associate: "Of the significance of the study there can be no doubt. One thing that bothers me . . . is how one could do an honest job without being ridden out of the South on a rail."[2] Early in his 675-page study, Key asserted that "In its grand outlines the politics of the South revolves around the

49

position of the Negro. It is at times interpreted as a politics of cotton, as a politics of free trade, as a politics of agrarian poverty, or as a politics of planter and plutocrat. Although such interpretations have a superficial validity, in the last analysis the major peculiarities of southern politics go back to the Negro. Whatever phase of the southern political process one seeks to understand, sooner or later the trail of inquiry leads to the Negro."[3]

In addition to the obvious result of keeping blacks isolated and powerless, the one-party system relegated politics in the South to a ceaseless struggle among transient, highly personalized factions of whites within the Democratic party. It was a strange system, one poorly understood by outsiders. The antics of the region's more flamboyant politicians gave it an air of "comic opera," a phrase Key used in the delightful opening pages of *Southern Politics*. Key wrote: "That not all the actors in the southern political drama have been clowns or knaves may be dismissed as a detail obscured by the heroic antics of those who were. That the South's spectacular political leaders have been indiscriminately grouped as demagogues of a common stripe, when wide differences have actually separated them, may likewise be regarded as an excusable failing of the Yankee journalist insensitive to the realities of southern politics."[4]

Despite the confusing and, at times, hilarious surface action, there existed the "deadly serious" side of things: the ubiquitous operation of the political process as it distributed the benefits of government to some and denied them to others, always working amid a sea of competing powerholders caught up in the very human process of advancing their many varied interests. And in whose interest did the southern politics of the era operate? It is a complicated question not easily answered. Key approached it through his analysis of Democratic factional arrangements that existed in each of the eleven southern states. In such a disorganized system of "pulverized factionalism," Key concluded in his famous chapter 14, "Nature and Consequences of One-Party Factionalism," that the chief losers are "those who have less." To capture fully the argument, it is best to quote Key's marvelous phraseology, which can rarely be conveyed by paraphrase:

> Politics generally comes down, over the long run, to a conflict between those who have and those who have less. In state politics the crucial issues tend to turn around taxation and expenditure. What level of public education and what levels of other public services shall be maintained? How shall the burden of taxation for their support be distributed? . . .
>
> It follows that the grand objective of the haves is obstruction, at least of the haves who take only a short-term view. Organization is not always necessary to obstruct; it is essential, however, for the promotion of a

sustained program in behalf of the have-nots. . . . It follows, if these propositions are correct, that over the long run the have-nots lose in a disorganized politics. They have no mechanism through which to act and their wishes find expression in fitful rebellions led by transient demagogues who gain their confidence but often have neither the technical competence nor the necessary stable base of political power to effectuate a program.[5]

Although Key did not explicitly exclude blacks from his category of "those who have less," the nature-and-consequences chapter is focused on the outcome among whites. After all, the one-party system existed, almost by definition, to keep blacks at the bottom of society. So, for the one-party South described by Key, the big losers in governmental terms were the less prosperous whites and practically all blacks. I return shortly to the critical question of winners and losers in southern politics, but first it is necessary to recount how and why the one-party system collapsed and sketch the nature of the two-party structure that arose in its place.[6]

There is loose in the land the notion that political change chiefly results from economic and social factors. Uncritical acceptance of this notion—which at a very general level certainly contains a grain of truth— can lead to serious misunderstanding of the nature of political change, and it has done so in regard to the tremendous transformation of southern politics that resulted when the one-party era gave way to a new order during and after the Second Reconstruction. What caused the great changes that led to the current era in southern politics? Economic changes? Societal changes?

No one can deny that southern society has undergone tremendous change since World War II. From a predominantly agricultural region that lagged far behind the rest of the country in urbanization and industrialization, the South has been playing catch-up with a vengeance (Table 2.1). The changes visible in Table 2.1 are all part of the southern political environment, and they have certainly contributed significantly to making the South's political environment resemble more closely that which is found outside of the region. (Although the settlement of Yankees in Dixie is sometimes put forward as a major factor in southern political change, most people who have studied the matter have concluded that the impact of northern migrants is negligible except in South and Central Florida, the Virginia suburbs of Washington, and several very large metropolitan areas.)[7] For example, do Cleveland's ubiquitous shopping malls and suburban sprawl differ that much from similar developments in Charlotte or Columbia? Of course not, and it would be futile to discount or ignore the very real socioeconomic nationalization

Table 2.1. Southern Changes in Per Capita Income, Urbanization, and Persons Employed in Manufacturing, 1940–80

	1940	1950	1960	1970	1980
Per Capita Income as Percentage of U.S. Average Income:					
Alabama	47.4	58.1	68.6	73.6	78.6
Arkansas	43.0	54.0	61.7	70.3	76.3
Florida	86.2	86.4	89.1	95.8	94.5
Georgia	57.1	68.1	74.7	84.2	84.8
Louisiana	61.0	73.0	75.0	77.1	88.8
Mississippi	36.6	48.9	54.3	64.8	69.1
North Carolina	55.1	67.7	71.6	81.6	82.1
South Carolina	51.6	59.1	63.4	75.4	76.3
Tennessee	57.0	66.7	71.6	78.5	81.1
Texas	72.6	89.9	86.1	89.6	100.3
Virginia	78.3	82.0	85.5	94.1	98.6
Urbanization (Percent):					
Alabama	30.2	43.8	54.8	58.4	60.0
Arkansas	22.2	33.0	42.8	50.0	51.5
Florida	55.1	65.5	73.9	80.5	84.3
Georgia	34.4	45.3	55.3	60.3	62.4
Louisiana	41.5	54.8	63.3	66.1	68.7
Mississippi	19.8	27.9	37.7	44.5	47.3
North Carolina	27.3	33.7	39.5	45.0	48.0
South Carolina	24.5	36.7	41.2	47.6	54.1
Tennessee	35.2	44.1	52.3	58.8	60.4
Texas	45.4	62.7	75.0	79.7	79.6
Virginia	35.3	47.0	55.6	63.1	66.0
United States	56.7	64.0	69.9	73.5	73.7
Employed Persons Engaged in Manufacturing (Percent):					
Alabama	19.0	21.9	26.5	27.1	26.1
Arkansas	11.0	13.9	20.1	24.7	25.1
Florida	13.7	10.9	13.1	13.1	12.6
Georgia	18.4	23.1	26.3	25.6	24.1
Louisiana	14.9	15.3	15.6	14.9	14.4
Mississippi	9.9	12.7	19.2	24.4	24.6
North Carolina	25.1	28.0	31.7	33.6	32.8
South Carolina	23.7	28.0	32.0	34.2	32.6
Tennessee	17.7	21.2	26.0	28.8	26.7
Texas	11.0	13.6	16.3	17.4	17.9
Virginia	20.2	20.6	22.4	21.4	19.0
United States	24.2	26.0	27.1	26.0	22.4

Source: U.S. Census of Population for appropriate years.

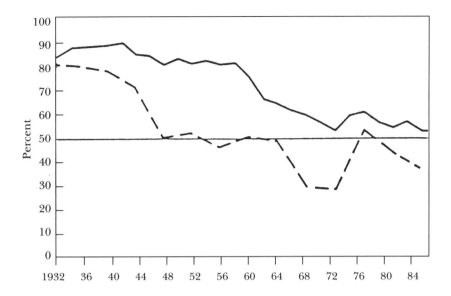

Figure 2.1. Democratic Party Strength in the South, 1932–86

——— Paul David's index of Democratic party strength for the South (composite of the vote for governor, U.S. senator, and U.S. representative)

— — — Democratic presidential vote in the South

Source: Alexander P. Lamis, *The Two-Party South,* exp. ed. (New York, 1988), p. 42.

that has occurred in the South in recent decades. Still, after examining carefully the major political changes that have transformed the region, one realizes that they did not occur in any gradual sequence directly propelled by and linked to the major socioeconomic changes alluded to previously.

Rather, they were tied to actions by politicians on political issues that went to the heart of the political arrangements underpinning the solidly Democratic South. When the national Democratic party moved off of dead center on the question of equal rights for blacks, starting slowly with Harry Truman and ending momentously with Lyndon Johnson, the southern rationale for white unity in the Democratic party collapsed and the region's politics underwent a massive restructuring that is still not complete.

The broad outline of what transpired is portrayed in Figures 2.1 and 2.2, although the illustrations are from opposite partisan perspectives. Figure 2.1 charts the decline of Democratic party strength as measured by voter support for candidates at several ballot levels. The lower broken

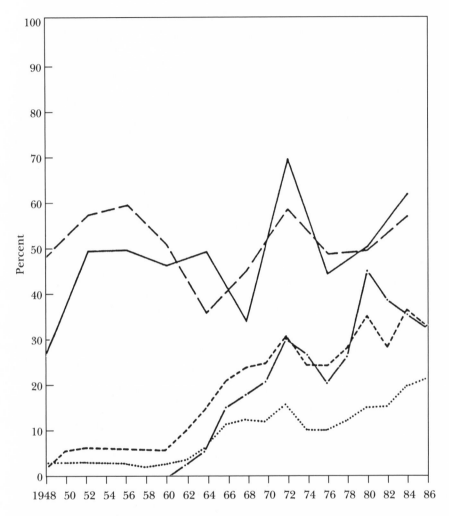

Figure 2.2. The Uneven Growth of the Republican Party in the South, 1948–86.

———— Republican presidential vote in the South

— — — Republican presidential vote in the North

•—•— U.S. Senate seats and governorships held by Republicans after each election

- - - - - U.S. House seats won by Republicans in each election

·········· State legislative seats held by Republicans after each election

Source: Alexander P. Lamis, *The Two-Party South,* exp. ed. (New York, 1988), p. 22.

line pinpoints the initial break—at the presidential level—and depicts the bottom falling out of southern Democratic voting for president in 1968 and 1972 prior to a partial recovery under Jimmy Carter. Figure 2.2 depicts the uneven growth of the Republican party in the South and highlights the mid-1960s take-off period for contests below the presidential level, when the region's GOP was energized by Barry Goldwater's triumph in the Deep South following his opposition to the Civil Rights Act of 1964.

The rest of the 1970s after Richard Nixon's sweeping reelection in 1972 witnessed a reversal of the subpresidential trends, which is shown in both figures. The nascent southern Republicans suffered a dip, and Dixie's post-civil-rights-era Democrats underwent an upward surge in strength. There was more to these reversals than merely voter disgust with Watergate and the recession of 1974, or even southern pride that the party of George McGovern could nominate a Georgian for president. Unraveling why these twin reversals occurred takes us a long way toward understanding the nature of contemporary southern politics.

After the southern Democractic party was forced to abandon white supremacy, there occurred one of those remarkable ironies that frequently punctuate human affairs: the former party of segregation—the Democratic party—become the home of the region's newly enfranchised blacks. Clever white Democratic politicians shrewdly sized up what was happening and in state after state put together a potent coalition of nearly all blacks and those whites who had weathered the integration crisis with their Democratic voting inclinations still intact. The potency of this coalition was surpassed only by its volatility, which was greatest where it was most potent, where there were proportionally more blacks to team up with the white wing. Mississippi, the southern state with the largest percentage of blacks and with the deepest tradition of racial strife, illustrated the point in its 1978 U.S. Senate race. In that election a black independent candidate split the Democratic coalition, and the Magnolia State elected its first Republican to statewide office since Reconstruction.[8]

In general, the Democratic coalition has held its own since the 1970s. To list its beneficiaries is to produce an honor roll of southern Democratic politicians: Dick Riley of South Carolina; George Busbee and Joe Frank Harris of Georgia; Reuben Askew, Lawton Chiles, and Bob Graham of Florida; Charles Robb of Virginia; William Winter and Wayne Dowdy of Mississippi; and Jim Hunt and Terry Sanford of North Carolina, among scores of others. They are known as "southern moderates," which, although imprecise, does differentiate them from Huey

Long Democrats, who are in short supply these days below the Mason-Dixon line.

In order to hold together their ideologically diverse biracial coalition, southern moderates need to be skilled practitioners of the art of the political straddle, and they certainly are. Consider, for example, the testimony of U.S. Representative David R. Bowen, a Mississippi Democrat elected to the House in 1972. Bowen represented the state's 45 percent black Second Congressional District until January 1983; he chose not to run for a sixth term in 1982 after a federal court, responding to two decades of racial gerrymandering, had dismembered his district to create a Delta district with a black majority. In a 1982 interview I asked Bowen how he was able to accommodate the sharply divergent components of his coalition. His response is instructive:

> I think I just didn't do anything to alienate either of those two blocs that I had put together. Obviously, there were a lot of white votes I didn't get. Because if my high-water mark was 70 percent of the votes and I was getting maybe 90 percent of the black votes, there were a lot of white votes I was not getting. But my voting record was often on the conservative side, but it varied across the middle of the board. It was not far right or far left. In all these national organizations that rate you, I might range from 35 to 85. . . . My ADA and liberal-type votes were usually in the low numbers. The conservative organizations were more often in the high numbers, but usually in the middle ranges somewhere.
>
> So it was not a very doctrinaire sort of pattern. You could look at it and you could say, "I don't know whether it falls under liberal or conservative." That's pretty much the way it was. No one could really stamp me as a liberal or a conservative. I never did anything to alienate the black support that I had. I never did anything to alienate the business support that I had. There were never very many issues that came along which were kind of no-win issues where you would totally outrage half the people whatever you did. . . .
>
> Take things like food stamps. . . . Theoretically, a lot of the people who do not receive food stamps are against them. Of course, almost all the black community is for them as well as a lot of the whites. I'm on the Ag[riculture] Committee and I have to write food stamp legislation. Of course blacks stayed with me because I voted for food stamps. And [to] the whites, I was able to explain that I was tightening up the legislation, improving it. And it would have been a lot more costly and a lot less efficient if I were not in there trying to put amendments in there to improve it—conditions that require recipients to register for work and accept work if it is offered and to make sure that people don't draw food stamps who are able-bodied and unwilling to work. So, generally those conservatives who would cuss and holler about food stamps all the time would say, "Well, David's doing a good job trying to improve the program.

They are going to pass the thing . . . anyhow. He's in there trying to improve it, trying to tighten it up, trying to cut out the fraud, the waste." But I would certainly vote for the program after I got through tightening it up.[9]

The performance, to put it mildly, irritated the Republicans, as illustrated by the remarks of a Georgia GOP leader: "So what catches us is that you find the conservative rural vote going in voting the straight party ticket, and by the same token you find the urban blacks voting the straight party ticket. And they'd be considered a liberal element, with the South Georgia farmer voting conservative. And yet they're voting hand in hand, and when they do, they're squeezing the lives out of us. And yet there's no tie-in between the two at all. Ideologically, they're as far apart as night and day."[10]

The GOP has had its greatest success in breaking the coalition at the presidential level. Walter Mondale of Minnesota and Michael Dukakis of Massachusetts came up woefully short of white Democratic votes against, respectively, Ronald Reagan in 1984 and George Bush in 1988, and even Jimmy Carter had a substantial drop-off in white support in 1980 over his 1976 showing, although he came close to victory in six of the ten southern states he lost to Reagan that year.

But below the presidential level, the Democratic black-white coalition is alive and, if not totally well, is far from on its death bed. The key to the coalition's success is the absence of issues that split its potentially antagonistic wings. Consider the effect of Jesse Jackson on the southern electoral scene; he energizes black voters, but for many whites the result is quite different. As Ernest F. Hollings, the South Carolina Democrat, says of the Jackson impact: "When Jesse stood up and said, 'My time has come' and 'We want it all,' they went in droves and as a result we got a Republican governor in South Carolina [in 1986]." And a black Georgia Democratic state representative, Tyrone Brooks, added: "I believe Jackson's candidacy may in fact contribute to the further alienation of conservative whites and Democrats, who will go and vote Republican in the general election."[11] A full assessment of Jackson's forceful role in southern and national politics must await events; what Jackson would call "the economic common ground,"[12] where he foresees future Democratic successes, will be addressed later. But before attempting to gaze into the future, it is wise to get as close to that forward-moving line as possible and thus to examine the electoral developments of 1988.

No southerner of whatever partisan affiliation could complain about a lack of attention from the national parties during the 1988 presidential election season. Both national conventions were held in the South—the Democrats in Atlanta and the Republicans in New Orleans. Both national presidential standard-bearers had southern strategies, George Bush's being endemic to his political roots, and Michael Dukakis's demonstrated by his selection of Lloyd Bentsen of Texas as his running-mate. (In the end Dukakis's seemed misplaced, but the hindsight of November is of no value in July.) And, of course there was that unprecedented event of March 8—Super Tuesday—in which virtually the entire South (South Carolina being the lone exception) and the border states, along with a handful of Western and New England states, chose their convention delegates.[13]

After sewing up the nomination before the Atlanta convention, Dukakis made a three-day campaign swing in June through seven southern states, meeting with various Democratic politicians, including Alabama's George Wallace. The Massachusetts governor declared in Montgomery: "I'm serious . . . about campaigning hard in the South, working hard in the South and winning the South."[14] In introducing the candidate at an outdoor rally, Lieutenant Governor Jim Folsom, Jr., of Alabama, exclaimed: "Mike Dukakis believes in the same things Alabamians believe in. He believes in a strong defense, a strong family, a strong economy that provides jobs for all its citizens."[15] Throughout his southern tour, Dukakis emphasized his record as a battler against crime and drugs. As Robin Toner of the New York *Times* reported: "He attended a flag-raising ceremony with police cadets in Miami. He preached the dangers of drug abuse to youngsters in Florence, S.C. He met with sixty criminal justice officials from around the country, accepted their endorsement and kicked off their efforts as 'crime fighters for Dukakis.' "[16]

Foreshadowing what was to come, Republican orators preceded Dukakis at each stop, branding him a "Teddy Kennedy liberal" who is soft on crime. Dukakis brushed off the GOP surrogates. To quote from Toner's account:

> "They sent some guy from Arizona [Senator John McCain] into Florida who doesn't know beans from brown bread," he said in Biloxi. "I don't think that's a particularly helpful or frankly winning campaign. I say that because I think the American people are tired of this stuff."
> Mr. Dukakis, who was also assailed by Vice President Bush last week as a Harvard liberal, indicted that he was not yet ready to fight back. "If I'm attacked there may come a time when I have to respond," he said. "I hope not."[17]

Of course, Dukakis's slowness to respond to Republican attacks against him on a variety of emotional issues became a central controversy in the fall campaign. These issues—among them his management of a Massachusetts prison furlough program that released Willie Horton, a black convicted murderer who went on to commit further crimes; his veto of a Massachusetts bill imposing penalties for public school teachers who refused to lead their students in the Pledge of Allegiance; and his opposition to the death penalty—dogged his campaign in the region and in the nation. The headline on a New York *Times* article about a Dukakis campaign rally in Hawkinsville, Georgia in late October conveyed the state of affairs: "Dukakis Fights Negative Image in South."[18] In a television appeal broadcast at the time of this rural Georgia rally, Dukakis lashed out at the GOP "campaign of distortion and distraction, of fear and smear."[19] The Georgia visit was one of the Democrat's rare southern forays in the last part of the campaign, when the hope of a successful Democratic southern strategy had evaporated. The southern front was abandoned to the nominee's running-mate, Senator Bentsen.[20]

While Willie Horton and the Pledge of Allegiance were "smears" to the Democrats, for Republicans they were simply symptomatic of what the public gets from "traditional liberals," as Bush labeled his opponent during a visit to Memphis. "If we are successful in getting the truth out there, they (Democrats) will be unsuccessful in drawing the traditional Southern Democrats and Southwest Democrats back into the fold," the vice president said at a rally held on a site near the Mississippi River.[21]

In a visit to Raleigh, Ronald Reagan boosted his former running-mate with a powerful dose of Democrat-bashing, at which he is the recognized master: "The opposition can say that ideology and values don't matter. The opposition can try to hide what they believe. Wasn't George Bush right when he said the opposition is over there in left field . . . and their policies can only be described by the dreaded L-word—liberal, liberal, liberal." The president asserted that the Republican party is now the party of Franklin D. Roosevelt and Harry Truman: "It is often said that the once-proud Democratic Party of FDR and Harry Truman is dead and gone. The party of FDR and Harry Truman couldn't be killed. . . . The secret is that when the left took over the Democratic Party leadership, we took over the Republican Party."[22] Throughout the campaign, the Republican orators repeatedly stressed the economic growth and prosperity with low inflation that occurred during President Reagan's two terms, the strengthening of America's military forces, and the improvement of relations with the Soviet Union. They warned of the dire consequences to economic and defense policies if the "Democratic wrecking crew" of the late 1970s—the Carter years—returned to power.

When the votes were counted, it was a decisive Republican victory nationwide, 53.4 percent to 45.6 percent. Bush handily carried all eleven southern states (Table 2.2) and twenty-nine others. Dukakis won

Table 2.2. 1988 General Election

	Bush (Percent)	Dukakis (Percent)	Percent Black 1980
Deep South:			
Mississippi	59.9	39.1	35.2
South Carolina	61.5	37.6	30.4
Louisiana	54.3	44.1	29.4
Georgia	59.8	39.5	26.8
Alabama	59.2	39.9	25.6
Rim South:			
North Carolina	58.0	41.7	22.4
Virginia	59.7	39.2	18.9
Arkansas	56.4	42.2	16.3
Tennessee	57.9	41.5	15.8
Florida	60.7	38.5	13.8
Texas	56.0	43.3	12.0
Dukakis's States:			
Rhode Island	43.9	55.7	2.7
Iowa	44.5	54.7	1.4
Hawaii	44.8	54.3	1.8
Massachusetts	45.4	53.2	3.8
Minnesota	45.9	52.9	1.3
West Virginia	47.5	52.2	3.3
New York	47.5	51.6	13.7
Wisconsin	47.8	51.4	3.9
Oregon	46.6	51.3	1.4
Washington	48.5	50.0	2.6

ten states in the northern tier of the country from Massachusetts to Oregon and Washington.

Bush's southern margin of victory far exceeded his vote in the rest of the nation. In the eleven states of the South—which account for a quarter of the popular votes—Bush had 58.3 percent to 40.9 percent for Dukakis; elsewhere, the percentages were 51.7 to 47.1. The demographics of the various partisan categories of voters did not differ greatly from those in the two Reagan elections. Dukakis improved on Mondale's support among southern whites, going from a regional average of 28 percent in 1984 to 32 percent in 1988.[23] There were, of course, variations in white support among the southern states; these are suggested in Table 2.2, which lists the percentage of the population that is black in each state next to the Democratic vote. Because blacks voted in the high 80 percent range for Dukakis, Dukakis obviously received a higher proportion of white votes in such states as Texas and

Tennessee than he did in Mississippi and South Carolina. By way of contrast, the lower portion of Table 2.2 shows Dukakis's vote in the ten states he won along with the relatively low percentages of blacks in those states.

The result of seeing the sharp racial polarization in the black-white southern voting patterns spurred yet another round of hand-wringing over "white flight" from the Democratic party by national commentators whose quadrennial focus on the southern situation seems always to be accompanied by outbursts of amazement at patterns well established for more than two decades. For example, Tom Wicker, the veteran New York *Times* writer, began a widely circulated post-election column as follows:

> A fundamental reason why Democratic nominees have lost five of the last six Presidential elections . . . is that in these national contests Republican victories have been very nearly lily-white. . . .
>
> Why has this happened? Unquestionably because the Democratic Party has become associated in the public mind with blacks—partly because blacks have been voting heavily Democratic . . . ; partly because the Democrats in their eight years of Presidential power since 1964 sponsored most of the programs that many whites think benefit blacks disproportionately; and partly because of recurrent campaign phenomena like Jesse Jackson's high visibility in the Democratic Party and Willie Horton's in this year's Republican television appeals.
>
> Michael Dukakis would have lost the 1988 election in any case, because peace, prosperity and patriotism—all embodied in Ronald Reagan—were working for Bush. But white flight into the Republican Party, in all regions of the country but most spectacularly in the South, will be a palpable, continuing, virtually fatal problem for the Democrats as far ahead as a poll-taker can see.
>
> This is not racism in a sheet and a hood; it is a race consciousness in a white as well as a blue collar. It is the dominant, underlying fact of modern national elections, year after year. Republicans who deny that they exploit it are disingenuous; Democrats who pretend that they can win anyway are whistling past the graveyard.[24]

No one could deny that Republicans have made subtle racial appeals in the Reagan era. Roger Ailes and Lee Atwater's effective use of Willie Horton[25] had its counterparts in earlier campaigns, such as in Reagan's "welfare queen" of 1980. The point was driven home to me during an interview with a political official in the Reagan White House who was expounding on the "new southern strategy" of Ronald Reagan, to use the official's phrase. When asked if Reagan was appealing to the racist side of the Wallace voter with efforts to slash domestic programs such as food stamps and legal services for the poor, the official responded:

You start out in 1954 by saying "Nigger, nigger, nigger." By 1968 you can't say "nigger"—that hurts you. Backfires. So you say stuff like forced busing, states' rights, and all these things you're talking about are totally economic things and a by-product of them is [that] blacks get hurt worse than whites. And subconsciously maybe that is part of it. I'm not saying that. But I'm saying that if it is getting that abstract, and that coded, that we are doing away with the racial problem one way or another. You follow me—because obviously sitting around saying, "We want to cut this," is much more abstract than even the busing thing and a hell of a lot more abstract than "Nigger, nigger."[26]

Obviously, how much one is doing away with the race issue in this context is debatable.

Still, to argue that race was a factor in Bush's southern victory is not the same thing as saying it was *the* factor. I am convinced that the North-South disparity in white Democratic support would have lessened significantly had the public's attention in the campaign been focused on economic issues and not on highly charged social issues. Southern and northern whites hold similar views on economic and domestic role-of-government matters, but southern whites are more conservative than northern whites on racial and public morality issues (the famed Social Issue, as this cluster has been effectively dubbed) and on foreign and defense matters. It is the hope of national Democrats that they can turn a presidential campaign on the questions that unite their white supporters across regions while continuing to attract nearly solid support among America's blacks.

Shifting below the presidential level in the 1988 election season, one finds a partisan environment that is evolving along lines quite familiar to students of recent southern politics. The 1988 extensions of Figures 2.1 and 2.2 summarize the trends. At the least visible level—state legislative races—Republicans continued their glacial upward movement, occupying 25.4 percent of the region's legislative seats after the election compared with 22.7 percent following the 1986 balloting; the bulk of the gains came in North Carolina, where the GOP surge was unprecedented, but other states contributed here and there. The partisan balance in U.S. House seats remained the same, thirty-nine of the 116 seats (or 33.6 percent) won by Republicans in 1988. The GOP picked up two seats in Florida while losing two in Texas, and a Democratic success in Georgia was offset by a Republican gain in Louisiana. (In February 1989, a U.S. representative in Florida switched to the GOP; an Arkansas congressman made a similar move in July 1989. Neither shift is reflected in the post-election totals.)

High-visibility statewide races were scarce in 1988; only five U.S. Senate seats were up for election in the region, and there was a lone gubernatorial contest in North Carolina, the only state still "brave" enough to elect its major state offices in a presidential election year. Governor Jim Martin, the popular moderate Republican, handily won reelection. The only two incumbent U.S. senators running for reelection in 1988, both Democrats, were easily returned: Jim Sasser of Tennessee and Senator Bentsen, who followed Lyndon Johnson's 1960 example and wisely chose an "insurance" campaign in case of national defeat. Virginia's former Democratic governor, Charles Robb, effortlessly claimed a seat left open by the failure of a first-term Republican incumbent to seek reelection.

The remaining two Senate elections were the only really interesting southern statewide battles of 1988—open seats being vacated by a pair of retiring Democrats, Lawton Chiles of Florida and John Stennis of Mississippi. Hard-fought Republican victories in each gave the GOP a boost in the category of major statewide offices, with the party holding twelve of the region's thirty-three governorships and U.S. Senate seats, or 36.4 percent, after the 1988 elections, compared to eleven after the 1986 voting.

In Florida, U.S. Representative Connie Mack, a conservative Republican, edged out U.S. Representative Buddy MacKay, 50.4 percent to 49.6 percent. Mack hammered at MacKay as too liberal for Florida, ending his many television spots with the refrain, "Hey, Buddy, you're liberal!" MacKay countered by calling Mack "an extremist" and placing himself in the mainstream. "Anyone who wants to call me liberal is having to defy the facts in order to do that," MacKay said.[27]

In Mississippi, U.S. Representative Trent Lott, the polished, aggressive, conservative House Republican whip, defeated U.S. Representative Wayne Dowdy, a folksy moderate Democrat who related well to rural and small-town whites and who cultivated strong ties with blacks. Lott received 53.9 percent to Dowdy's 46.1 percent. Lott's well-financed campaign, according to *Congressional Quarterly Weekly Report*, quickly took the offensive to blunt any possible attacks on Lott's conservative record. "He was on the air early with ads touting himself as a leader in strengthening the Social Security system, pledging his allegiance to student loans and showing his concern for bringing in federal money to improve Mississippi's roads." *CQ* also noted that Lott sought support among rural and low-income whites by pointing out that "his father farmed cotton and drove a school bus [while calling] Dowdy, whose family owns a number of radio stations, a millionaire, country-club type."[28]

As usual when examining a multiplicity of partisan elections below the high-visibility presidential contest, it is not always easy to find a dominant pattern. A useful statistic is Paul David's index of Democratic party strength, a composite of the vote for governor, U.S. senator, and U.S. representative, which is plotted from 1932 to 1986 in Figure 2.1. The trend-line graphically portrays the demise of the solidly Democratic South, starting in the early 1960s. Then in the mid-1970s a clear resurgence is depicted as the transformed Democracy led by Jimmy Carter and his fellow "New South" Democrats assembled the potent black-white coalition that I have referred to at various points previously. When the Reagan era began in 1980, Southern Democratic strength stood at 56.1 percent. It rose to 59.5 percent during the recession of 1982, but moved more favorably to the GOP—at 55.2 percent—as Reagan was winning a smashing reelection victory in 1984. The Democratic index remained at the same 55.2 percent following the complex 1986 midterm election.[29] After the 1988 elections the figure again went up for the Democrats—to 58.3 percent—pointing once more to the stubborn staying power of the ideologically diverse black-white Democratic coalition. (The coalition, of course, still comes up woefully short of white support for national nominees, although even that situation improved to a limited extent in 1988.)

This consistently strong Democratic party-strength figure should give pause to anyone taking the view that the 1988 elections in the South contained something strikingly new. The recent balloting should be placed within the context of an ongoing regional transformation that is at least two decades old. Such an exercise in taking the long view focuses attention squarely on Dixie's still dominant—if harried—black-white Democratic coalition. It has cracked repeatedly at the presidential level and in more than a few statewide elections. But, overall this key biracial alliance remains in place, and wrapped up in its uncertain future is to be found the future of southern Republicans as well.

Toward the Future

Four political trends are likely to evolve in the years leading from the present into the next century, although I lay no claim to having a crystal ball stashed away in my office, nor do I believe that my current residence north of the Ohio River, despite the crispness of the air, gives me special powers. In the hackneyed phrase of an old newspaperman, "This is just one man's opinion."

1. The black-white Democratic coalition will persist, but it will grow weaker as the deep tensions in that party drive portions of the white wing into the waiting arms of the Republicans. The broad-based nature of the resurgent southern Democratic party of the 1970s resulted from

a historical anomaly. The coalition faces formidable odds as we move further and further from the Solid South era. In addition to its tensions, the coalition must contend with the three other future trends, all of which support at least a short-term weakening of Democratic strength. These three are the inevitable growth of the GOP in "down-ticket" contests; the continuing nationalization of southern politics; and the remaking of the southern Democratic party into a party committed to the interests of "those who have less" of both races.

Before the effects of these trends are outlined, I will explore some interesting data that have never before been published and that quantitatively capture the divisions Democrats must confront. In early 1981, Alan I. Abramowitz mailed questionnaires to state legislative candidates in the South and the North (the northern sample is smaller and served primarily as a reference point for the southern data).[30] Candidates were asked about the strength of their party identification, both to the national party and to their state party; about their support for their party's presidential candidate in 1980; their ideological self-identification; and their positions on fifteen issues, which were used to construct a liberalism-conservativism issue scale. Southern results were broken down by the venerable Deep South and Rim (Outer) South divisions (Table 2.3). Then, the southern Democratic figures were further subdivided into rural, urban, and mixed districts (Table 2.4).

The results bring a degree of precision to what one senses to be true through examination of more impressionistic data. First, and of less importance here, the Republican party exhibits remarkable unity across

Table 2.3. Partisanship and Ideology of State Legislative
Candidates by Regions

	Democrats			Republicans		
	Deep South (n = 43)	Rim South (n = 77)	North (n = 69)	Deep South (n = 61)	Rim South (n = 111)	North (n = 74)
Strong national identification	21%	50%	61%	70%	74%	74%
Strong state identification	44	68	63	62	72	74
Supported presidential candidate	30	61	61	82	81	86
Ideological liberalism	29	42	62	5	6	14
Issue liberalism	36	46	66	15	19	25

Source: Alan I. Abramowitz, "Party Leadership, Realignment, and the Nationalization of Southern Politics," delivered at the annual meeting of the Southern Political Science Association, Memphis, November 5–7, 1981, composite of Tables 1, 2, and 4.

Table 2.4. Partisanship and Ideology by Degree of Urbanization and
Subregion for Democratic State Legislative Candidates

	Deep South			Rim South		
	Urban Areas (n = 15)	Mixed Areas (n = 11)	Rural Areas (n = 16)	Urban Areas (n = 27)	Mixed Areas (n = 26)	Rural Areas (n = 24)
Strong national identification	33%	18%	12%	59%	46%	44%
Strong state identification	47	64	31	85	69	48
Supported presidential candidate	47	27	12	70	65	46
Ideological liberalism	48	27	12	56	46	23
Issue liberalism	40	39	30	62	46	32

Source: Abramowitz, "Party Leadership, Realignment, and the Nationalization of
Southern Politics," Table 6.

the nation, although there are a few minor but interesting differences.
For example, southern Republicans are a little more conservative than
their counterparts in the North. By comparison, however, the divisions
among the Democrats are gigantic.

Democratic legislative candidates in the Deep South, and particularly
those in rural areas, have very distinct differences with their counterparts in the North. For example, only 12 percent of the rural Deep
South Democratic candidates had a strong national party identification
or were ideological liberals, and only a similar percentage of them supported Carter in 1980. This contrasts sharply with the overall northern
figures, which are in the 60 percent range. Even within the Deep South,
city and country showed significant differences on these questions. Is
there little wonder that Michael Dukakis found the going tough in the
southern rural and small-town expanses?

Although intra-Democratic cleavages are real and portentous, it does
not follow that these divisions will translate into automatic GOP gains.
The next sections treat other factors likely to be involved in the future
process.

2. One prediction about the future is clear: The scene of competition
will shift from the statewide level, where two-party politics is firmly
rooted now, to lower positions on the ballot, to what David Sturrock
calls the "down-ticket" arena. The state legislative level is a good one
to examine; to move to even less obscure offices—those at the county
and municipal levels—is extremely difficult because of the lack of comprehensive data. The bottom trend-line in Figure 2.2 traces Republican

state legislative successes. In the 1980s, the GOP movement was slow but gradually upward. Table 2.5 gives the percentages by state, using once again the Deep South and Rim South divisions. Arkansas has an atypically weak GOP Rim South presence at this level, and South Carolina is particularly strong for the Deep South category. Detailed examination of the factors peculiar to each state should suggest reasons for these differences, but the overall future trend is what is of interest. Sturrock, who has investigated the southern "down-ticket" process thoroughly, is at work testing a series of hypotheses concerning the process. His propositions are:

A. Republican legislative strength will be greatest in:
   1. Counties that are urban, suburban, or are dominated by small cities (population of twenty thousand or more).
   2. Counties that regularly voted Republican before 1950, primarily mountain counties that opposed secession in the 1860s.
   3. "Interstate" counties containing small but rapidly growing population centers, often situated on or near the periphery of major metropolitan areas and usually traversed by an interstate highway.

B. Republican legislative strength will be least in:
   4. Historically Democratic, rural, non-interstate counties.
   5. Predominantly black areas, both rural and urban.

C. General characteristics of Republican legislative strength:
   6. Significant numbers of legislative candidacies (25 percent or more of the total number of seats in a state) and victories (10 percent of that total) will not be attained until after Republican victories have occurred in high-visibility races (both presidential and either gubernatorial or U.S. Senate) in a given state.

Table 2.5. Republican Share of Legislative Seats, by State, as of January 1988

State	GOP Seats	Total Seats	GOP Percent	State	GOP Seats	Total Seats	GOP Percent
Arkansas	13	135	9.6	Alabama	21	140	15.8
Florida	60	160	37.5	Georgia	38	236	16.1
N. Carolina	45	170	26.5	Louisiana	23	144	16.0
Tennessee	48	132	36.4	Mississippi	16	174	9.2
Texas	62	181	34.3	S. Carolina	45	170	26.5
Virginia	45	140	32.1				
Outer South	273	918	29.7	Deep South	143	864	16.6
Entire South	416	1782	23.3				

Source: David E. Sturrock, "Legislative Elections and the Two-Party South," delivered at the 1988 Citadel Symposium on Southern Politics, Charleston, March 3–4, 1988, p. 7 (Table 3).

7. Legislative strength will grow slowly and incrementally, will be only modestly affected by strong Republican showings in high-visibility elections, and can be affected by significant state-specific political events or trends.[31]

In a preliminary report based on partial case studies in five states, Sturrock concludes that these propositions held up fairly well. The completion of Sturrock's project will provide a full view of "down-ticket" dynamics, both at the state legislative level and at the other out-of-the-limelight elective levels.

My own best guess is that by the turn of the century there will have occurred a spread of competition to these lower ballot levels that will have no counterpart in post-Reconstruction southern political history. Areas that have known only intra-Democratic competition for local office will become hotbeds of two-party politics. Perhaps the Palmetto State will come to be viewed as a Deep South pacesetter in this process as Florida has been for the Rim South. Local politics rarely contains the ideological divisions that are pervasive at the national level, and the variations found in local politics are absolutely dizzying. It is hard to imagine how our localities could be worse off by having another organized vehicle for the contest of public office—the general election. In that sense alone, we can take comfort that the cause of democracy in the South will likely be well served in the emerging new era.

3. The destruction of the one-party Democratic South and the rise of two-party competition have made southern politics more closely resemble politics outside of the region. This nationalization of southern politics is a powerful phenomenon that will continue. The causes of the transformation are fundamental and irreversible; more than a century after the Civil War, the South is fast on the way to rejoining completely the national political mainstream.

To predict a continuing nationalization of politics in Dixie is not to say that regional political features tied to the peculiar southern experience will disappear. For some years to come, the viability of the black-white Democratic coalition will form the key to partisan developments in the region. We know that such will not be the case, for example, in Minnesota, Wisconsin, Iowa, Oregon, or Connecticut. These states share political similarities with southern states; after all, we are part of the same country. But the dynamics of politics in the North revolve around different considerations. In northern industrial states with sizable black urban concentrations, southern analogies are present and will persist. In fact, as the race issue moved north in the late 1960s, it was partially correct to point to a "Southernization of America," as John Egerton did in his book with that subtitle.[32]

Still, in general, the next century will find fewer commonalities across Dixie as the region slips more and more into the mainstream. Perhaps in the next century political commentators will look at Alabama, Georgia, and South Carolina as they look at Illinois, Indiana, and Ohio. Certainly, it is agreed, these three midwestern states share common features in their electoral politics. Yet it also is well recognized that they are distinctive political entities with different political traditions generated by various demographic, social, economic, and historical differences. And, before too long, similar types of differences in their Dixie counterparts may likewise stand out.[33]

Occasionally an indicator of the ongoing nationalization of southern politics surfaces and causes the rest of the country to stand up and take note of a "New South." This occurred in the fall of 1987, when every southern Democratic senator save one (South Carolina's Hollings) voted against confirmation of the Supreme Court nomination of Robert Bork. Ronald Reagan's choice was vigorously opposed by civil rights groups, and opposition in the Senate was led by several of the party's prominent northern liberals. Although the Bork fight was a dramatic, high-visibility episode, recent studies of congressional voting records have revealed growing cohesion among Democrats, North and South. Before the Bork vote, for example, *Congressional Quarterly* published a cover story on what it called the "fading alliance" of southern Democrats and Republicans, the famed Conservative Coalition: "What is clear right now is that Southern Democrats simply are not casting many votes with Republicans anymore."[34] The full impact of the ongoing nationalization of southern politics both on our national political institutions and on the region is yet to be fully played out.

4. By the next century the southern Democratic party will have made major strides toward becoming an organization that faithfully champions the interests of "those who have less" of both races. This development, if it materializes, will have important implications for the future course of left-of-center domestic politics and policy at the national level, as well as within the region. The short-run effect of this trend may very well be a sharp decline in southern Democratic strength, but the purified and unified party that emerges could, in league with a compatible Democratic party in the rest of the country, lead to a return of the Democrats to a position of dominance in presidential elections, a position they have not held in more than two decades. Although this prediction is tinged with philosophical hope, it is also supported—at least tangentially—by hard data.

The other three trends I have identified are supportive of the outcome I am suggesting here. A weakened southern black-white Democratic coalition, slowly drained of its more conservative elements, faced with increasing opposition at the lower ballot levels, and subjected to strong nationalizing tendencies, will be forced to abandon its current centrist, straddling posture and become a party with serious policy content and a meaningful program for its adherents. Such a posture will not be right of center; the Republicans have that ground staked out clearly in the region, as they have had generally in the rest of the country since the New Deal.

If what I am predicting occurs, in essence, "those who have less" of both races will finally have attained the vehicle that Professor Key predicted in 1949 would flow from a dissolution of the one-party South. The consequences of such an outcome for southerners who have less is simply that they will begin to win on the great questions of taxation, expenditure, and those concerning in whose interest the government should function. Such has not been the case in the current era.

From time to time, critics have pointed to Key's prophesy and declared that he was wrong. I think results in the twenty-first century will show that Key was on target. He simply miscalculated the length of time needed for the complete dismantling of the one-party system. He also discounted the extent to which the race issue would linger on as a barrier to the coming together of blacks and whites to form a meaningful political force for the promotion of the interests of "those who have less" of both races. I am reminded of a famous quotation from "The Negro Question in the South," written in 1892 by Tom Watson, the Georgia Populist. Watson predicted that the Populist party would settle the race question by offering whites and blacks "a rallying point which is free from the odium of former discords and strifes. . . . by presenting a platform immensely beneficial to both races and injurious to neither . . . by making it to the interest of both races to act together. . . . Now the People's Party say to these two men [one black and one white], 'You are kept apart that you may be separately fleeced of your earnings. You are made to hate each other because upon that hatred is rested the keystone of the arch . . . which enslaves you both.' "[35]

Today in the South and in the nation the race question is rarely an overt element in political discourse, but it lingers on and remains a barrier to the fulfillment of the trend outlined above. The barrier will be overcome only when leaders openly confront the problem and explain to their adherents of both races that they are, as Watson so powerfully asserted, kept apart so that they can be "separately fleeced" of their earnings. Some analysts point to surveys of public attitudes in the South and see only a region suffused in a sea of conservatism that makes impossible the success of the biracial coalition I am concerned with here.[36] I read the survey information differently. On the critical economic class and role of government questions, the attitudinal base exists in the region to support the future trend I am predicting. A brief venture into the world of survey analysis supports the point.[37]

So often what is missing in a discussion of southern conservatism (or liberalism, progressivism, populism, or whatever term is applied to left-of-center positions) is the recognition that the use of such shorthand labels masks several distinct dimensions into which these concepts logically divide. Three such dimensions are (1) economic class and role of government questions; (2) foreign policy and defense questions; and (3) a cluster of social questions that include public morality issues, race relations, and women's rights.[38] Table 2.6 examines the responses of southern and northern white voters in 1984 on a variety of issue questions grouped under these three dimensions.

Overall, the various panels of Table 2.6 confirm once more Key's observations in *The Responsible Electorate* concerning voter rationality.[39] "[V]oters are not fools," Key reminds us, because against all odds—or so it sometimes seems—they show a remarkable inclination to line up their votes with their policy preferences.[40] "From our analyses the voter emerges as a person who appraises the actions of government, who has policy preferences, and who relates his vote to those appraisals and preferences. One may have misgivings about the data and one can certainly concede that the data also indicate that some voters are governed

Table 2.6. Attitudes on Various Public Policy Issues and the Vote for
President in 1984

| | 1. Economic Class and Role of Government Questions Cut Services to Save Money | | | | | |
| | Southern Whites | | | Northern Whites | | |
	Cut	Neutral	More Services	Cut	Neutral	More Services
Reagan	90%	59%	47%	85%	60%	38%
Mondale	10	41	53	15	40	62
	100%	100%	100%	100%	100%	100%
N	113	91	77	297	262	249
	(40%)	(32%)	(27%)	(37%)	(32%)	(31%)

Question: Some people think the government should provide fewer services, even in areas such as health and education, in order to reduce spending. Suppose these people are at one end of the scale at point number 1. Other people feel it is important for government to provide many more services even if it means an increase in spending. Suppose these people are at the other end, at point 7. And, of course, some other people have opinions somewhere in between. . . . Where would you place yourself on this scale . . . ? [Points 2 and 3 were combined with point 1 for ease in handling; points 5 and 6 went with point

Table 2.6. (Continued)

7. Point 4, the middle slot, was labeled neutral. All seven-point scales in the table were handled in this manner.]

| | Health Insurance | | | | | |
	Southern Whites			Northern Whites		
	Gov't	Neutral	Private	Gov't	Neutral	Private
Reagan	63%	66%	78%	49%	67%	76%
Mondale	37		22	51	33	24
	100%	100%	100%	100%	100%	100%
N	46	29	63	136	78	169
	(33%)	(21%)	(46%)	(36%)	(20%)	(44%)

Question: There is much concern about the rapid rise in medical and hospital costs. Some people feel there should be a government insurance plan which would cover all medical and hospital expenses for everyone. Others feel that all medical expenses should be paid by individuals and through private insurance plans like Blue Cross or other company-paid plans. Where would you place yourself [on a seven-point scale]?

| | Role of Government on Jobs and Standard of Living | | | | | |
	Southern Whites			Northern Whites		
	Gov't Do It	Neutral	Self Help	Gov't Do It	Neutral	Self Help
Reagan	40%	64%	83%	42%	53%	76%
Mondale	60	36	17	68	47	24
	100%	100%	100%	100%	100%	100%
N	62	66	156	199	203	502
	(22%)	(23%)	(55%)	(25)	(25%)	(50%)

Question: Some people feel the government in Washington should see to it that every person has a job and a good standard of living. Others think the government should just let each person get ahead on his own. Where would you place youself [on a seven-point scale]?

2. Foreign Policy and Defense Issues
Level of Defense Spending

	Southern Whites			Northern Whites		
	Decrease	Neutral	Increase	Decrease	Neutral	Increase
Reagan	40%	70%	79%	37%	70%	83%
Mondale	60	30	21	63	30	17
	100%	100%	100%	100%	100%	100%
N	63	92	135	280	282	272
	(22%)	(32%)	(47%)	(34%)	(34%)	(33%)

Question: Some people believe that we should spend much less money for defense. Others feel that defense spending should be greatly increased. Where would you place yourself [on a seven-point scale]?

Table 2.6. (Continued)

Involvement in Central America					
Southern Whites			Northern Whites		
More	Neutral	Less	More	Neutral	Less
Reagan 84%	72%	52%	77%	75%	47%
Mondale 16	28	48	23	25	54
100%	100%	100%	100%	100%	100%
N 85	53	100	175	176	412
(36%)	(22%)	(42%)	(23%)	(23%)	(54%)

Question: Some people think that the United States should become much more involved in the internal affairs of Central American countries. Others believe that the U.S. should become less involved in this area. Where would you place yourself [on a seven-point scale]?

Proper Approach to the Russians					
Southern Whites			Northern Whites		
Cooperate More	Neutral	Get Tougher	Cooperate More	Neutral	Get Tougher
Reagan 47%	68%	80%	39%	72%	77%
Mondale 53	32	20	61	28	23
100%	100%	100%	100%	100%	100%
N 83	63	133	311	185	331
(30%)	(23%)	(48%)	(38%)	(22%)	(40%)

Question: Some people feel it is important for us to try to cooperate more with Russia, while others believe we should be much tougher in our dealings with Russia. Where would you place yourself [on a seven-point scale]?

3. Cluster of Social Questions
A. Race Relations Questions
Pace of Civil Rights Effort

Southern Whites			Northern Whites		
Too Fast	About Right	Too Slowly	Too Fast	About Right	Too Slowly
Reagan 67%	70%	54%	81%	56%	36%
Mondale 33	30	46	19	44	64
100%	100%	100%	100%	100%	100%
N 64	74	13	141	257	36
(42%)	(49%)	(7%)	(33%)	(59%)	(8%)

Question: Some say that the civil rights people have been trying to push too fast. Others feel they haven't pushed fast enough. . . . Do you think that civil rights leaders are trying to push too fast, are going too slowly, or are they moving at about the right speed?

Table 2.6. (Continued)

Government Help for Minorities

	Southern Whites			Northern Whites		
	Gov't Should Help	Neutral	Should Help Selves	Gov't Should Help	Neutral	Should Help Selves
Reagan	52%	64%	78%	43%	63%	75%
Mondale	48	37	22	57	37	25
	100%	101%	100%	100%	100%	100%
N	67	85	134	239	286	293
	(23%)	(30%)	(47%)	(29%)	(35%)	(36%)

Question: Some people feel that the government in Washington should make every effort to improve the social and economic position of blacks and other minority groups. Others feel that the government should not make any special effort to help minorities because they should help themselves. . . . Where would you place yourself [on a seven-point scale]?

B. Public Morality Questions
Prayer in Schools

	Southern Whites		Northern Whites	
	Allow Prayer	Keep Prayer Out	Allow Prayer	Keep Prayer Out
Reagan	67%	50%	74%	46%
Mondale	33	50	26	54
	100%	100%	100%	100%
N	202	44	422	247
	(82%)	(18%)	(63%)	(37%)

Question: Which do you think—schools should be allowed to start each day with a prayer or religion does not belong in the schools?

Abortion

	Southern Whites				Northern Whites			
	Never	Only Rape, etc.	Clear Need	Always	Never	Only Rape, etc.	Clear Need	Always
Reagan	67%	64%	66%	68%	75%	71%	66%	51%
Mondale	33	36	34	32	25	29	34	49
	100%	100%	100%	100%	100%	100%	100%	100%
N	43	104	65	101	85	237	200	355
	(14%)	(33%)	(21%)	(32%)	(10%)	(27%)	(23%)	(41%)

Question: There has been some discussion about abortion during recent years. Which one of the options on this page best agrees with your view?

1. By law, abortion should never be permitted.

74

Table 2.6. (Continued)

2. The law should permit abortion *only* in case of rape, incest or when the woman's life is in danger.
3. The law should permit abortion for reasons *other than* rape, incest or danger to the woman's life, but only after the need for the abortion has been clearly established.
4. By law, a woman should always be able to obtain an abortion as a matter of personal choice.

C. Women's Rights Questions
Place of Women in Society

	Southern Whites			Northern Whites		
	Equal Role	Neutral	Place in Home	Equal Role	Neutral	Place in Home
Reagan	64%	66%	70%	56%	75%	77%
Mondale	36	34	30	44	25	23
	100%	100%	100%	100%	100%	100%
N	157	67	63	548	171	124
	(55%)	(23%)	(22%)	(65%)	(20%)	(15%)

Question: Recently there has been a lot of talk about women's rights. Some people feel that women should have an equal role with men in running business, industry, and government. . . . Others feel that women's place is in the home. . . . Where would you place yourself [on a seven-point scale]?

Government Help for Women

	Southern Whites			Northern Whites		
	Gov't Should Help	Neutral	Should Help Selves	Gov't Should Help	Neutral	Should Help Selves
Reagan	53%	69%	78%	41%	67%	78%
Mondale	47	31	22	59	33	22
	100%	100%	100%	100%	100%	100%
N	88	88	104	279	262	260
	(31%)	(31%)	(37%)	(35%)	(33%)	(32%)

Question: Some people feel that the government in Washington should make every effort to improve the social and economic position of women. Others feel that the government should not make any special effort to help women because they should help themselves. Where would you place yourself [on a seven-point scale]?

Source: National Election Study, 1984. Center for Political Studies, University of Michigan, as presented in Alexander P. Lamis, *The Two-Party South,* exp. ed. (New York, 1988), pp. 244–47.

by blind party loyalty and that some others respond automatically to the winds of the environment of the moment. Yet the obtrusive feature of the data is the large number of persons whose vote is instrumental to their policy preferences."[41]

Given the positions of Ronald Reagan and Walter Mondale on the issues of the day, the voters—South and North—demonstrated a pronounced tendency to cast their presidential ballots for the candidate who came closer to sharing their issue preferences. For example, those who favored cuts in government services were much more likely to vote for Reagan, whose reputation as one who preferred reducing the role of government certainly stood higher than Mondale's. Those who favored a role for the federal government in providing jobs and a good standard of living were much more likely to back Mondale, whose fondness for positive governmental action in these areas was undisputed and far outstripped the president's. Perusal of the other issues in Table 2.6 generally produces similar findings. While it is comforting to affirm again that voters are not fools, the table reveals more than merely this.

The percentages at the bottom of each cross-tabulation in Table 2.6 allow for comparison of voter opinions in the South and the North on all these issues. When the responses of southern whites are compared with those of northern whites, noticeable sectional differences are evident among the issues grouped under two of the three conservatism-liberalism dimensions: foreign-defense policy issues and social issues. On the economic class and role of government dimension, however, the South-North differences were quite small indeed. Thirty-three percent of southerners and 36 percent of northerners preferred some sort of governmental medical insurance system as opposed to leaving the matter to the private sector. On the question of cutting services in fields such as health and education to reduce government spending, there was again virtually no difference between the regions. And the third question used to tap this dimension—involving the role of government in providing jobs and a good standard of living—revealed similar agreement across regions. Thus, on this important dimension a picture emerges of a white South sharply divided and far from monolithically conservative—and scarcely more conservative than the white North.

On the other two dimensions, the South-North differences were more sizable. In the national security arena, white southerners were far more willing to favor increased defense spending, more United States involvement in Central America, and a tougher stance toward the Russians. On the six questions that fall under the social-issue cluster, the differences between the North and South were closer to those in the national security area, but there were exceptions. Forty-two percent of white southerners found civil rights leaders pushing too fast, compared with 33 percent of white northerners; a similar difference was found on the question concerning government help for minorities. On whether women should play an equal role with men in society, there was a gap of 10 percentage points, with weaker support for an equal role found in the South. On abortion, the responses were somewhat the same in the two parts of the country except that the pro-choice position had support from 41 percent of white northerners compared with 32 percent of white southerners. Whether prayer should be allowed in the public schools produced the sharpest North-South divergence. Eighty-two percent in the South favored allowing prayer, as compared with 63 percent in the North.

The preceding was meant to demonstrate—in addition to arguing for the value of more dimensional reasoning in electoral analysis—the weakness in viewing southern whites as merely a bastion of undifferentiated conservatism and using such a conclusion to explain or predict the South's voting patterns. The southern reality reflected in responses to these survey questions is far more complex. In fact, as Table 2.6 illustrates, the attitudinal basis exists in the region for a two-party competition not unlike that found in the rest of the nation, although the South's historical and cultural legacy will continue to give it certain singular characteristics.

It remains only to link this constellation of southern public opinion to a useful theory that explains how public attitudes are related to what government does. For such a formulation we are indebted once more to V. O. Key, Jr., who, in his other great masterpiece, *Public Opinion and American Democracy*, concludes that public opinion rarely controls political action. Instead, Key wrote, it operates "as a system of dikes which . . . fix a range of discretion within which debate at official levels may proceed," and the responsibility for exercising that discretion rests with political elites.[42] The southern dikes of opinion, if one views them correctly, that is, comparatively and through their logical dimensions, are plenty broad enough to offer the promise of the southern political future sketched here.

I view the future as open-ended, but ultimately its course is directed by those who do battle in the political arena. And if the cause is just—and the creation of a vehicle in the South for the promotion of the political interests of "those who have less" of both races is a just and long-overdue cause—it ought to be worth embracing. It is my hope and my expectation that by the next century effective leaders will have arisen who will offer the region this promising and exciting course of action.

NOTES

1. For an excellent panoramic overview of more than a century of southern political history, ranging from the Redeemers to the Reaganites, see Dewey W. Grantham, *The Life and Death of the Solid South: A Political History* (Lexington, Ky., 1988).

2. Alexander P. Lamis and Nathan Goldman, "V. O. Key's *Southern Politics:* The Writing of a Classic," *Georgia Historical Quarterly* 71 (Summer 1987): 263.

3. V. O. Key, Jr., *Southern Politics in State and Nation* (New York, 1949), p. 5.

4. Key, *Southern Politics*, pp. 3–4.

5. Ibid., p. 307.

6. Various works cover this period or a part of it, including Numan V. Bartley and Hugh D. Graham, *Southern Politics and the Second Reconstruction* (Baltimore, 1975); William C. Havard, ed., *The Changing Politics of the South* (Baton Rouge, 1972); Jack Bass and Walter DeVries, *The Transformation of Southern Politics* (New York, 1976); Earl Black and Merle Black, *Politics and Society of the South* (Cambridge, 1987); and Alexander P. Lamis, *The Two-Party South*, exp. ed. (New York, 1988). See especially the excellent bibliographical essays in Bartley and Graham, *Southern Politics*, and Grantham, *Life and Death of the Solid South.*

7. Black and Black, *Politics and Society in the South*, p. 17.

8. Lamis, *The Two-Party South*, pp. 52–54.

9. Interview with David R. Bowen, July 28, 1982.

10. Lamis, *The Two-Party South*, p. 99.

11. Ibid., p. 299, for both the Hollings and Brooks quotations.

12. Jackson's perspective is worth quoting at length: "The issues of segregation have been overcome and it is time to move from the racial battleground to the economic common ground. Slavery, legal and social segregation, school segregation, public accommodation and the right to vote—these troubles have finally been overcome and conquered. . . . We need an economic agenda that can meet human needs, have more commitment to quality education, stopping slave labor jobs from being exported abroad, enfranchising women, stopping the South from being used as a toxic waste dump. . . . These are not black-white issues." Jackson made these 1984 comments to reporters after meeting with southern Democratic state chairpersons and Mondale campaign officials to plan strategy for the fall campaign, Washington *Post*, September 1, 1984.

13. Super Tuesday offered a fascinating group snapshot of southern partisan life in a rare, non-general-election setting, a veritable treasure-trove of southern political information. Among the topics worth exploring are the different approaches of the candidates to the diverse southern electorate, the divisions among the voters (including the choice of which party's primary to participate in), and the various decisions by state and local influentials about which national politicians to support.

14. Associated Press dispatch carried in the Charleston *News and Courier*, June 20, 1988. For more on the 1988 elections, see Lamis, *The Two-Party South*, 2nd exp. ed. (1990).

15. New York *Times*, June 20, 1988.

16. Ibid.

17. Ibid., June 18, 1988.

18. Ibid., October 23, 1988.

19. Ibid.

20. Typical of Senator Bentsen's appeal to Dixie is the following quote from his remarks on a visit to Panama City, Florida. After declaring his pride in being a life-long "Southern Democrat," Bentsen told his audience: "This year, Michael Dukakis reached out to the South. He chose one of you. He took the extra step to bring us home again. He came here and listened to us. He campaigned among us. He asked a Southerner to join him on the ticket, and one reason I accepted was because I want to help bring Texas and Tennessee and Arkansas and Mississippi back into the Democratic Party," Warren Weaver, Jr., "Bentsen Plays Up Roots in His Tour of the South," New York *Times*, September 18, 1988.

21. Associated Press dispatch carried in the Columbia *State* July 24, 1988.

22. Charlotte *Observer*, October 22, 1988.

23. This figure is from the New York *Times*/CBS News exit poll and was reported in "Portrait of the Electorate," New York *Times*, November 10, 1988.

24. Wicker's column was carried in the Columbia *State*, November 20, 1988. After the 1984 election, similar comments came from Bill Moyers on CBS: "You know, the overwhelming reason [for Reagan's strength among whites] . . . is race. It's not white drift so much as it is white flight. . . . When they say in the South that the national Democratic party is too liberal, what they really mean is that Jesse Jackson is too powerful in the Democratic party." A fuller version of Moyer's remarks is found in Lamis, *The Two-Party South*, p. 239.

25. When asked on a network television program if the use of the Horton case represented "an element of Republican racist appeal," Senator Bentsen responded: "When you add it up, I think there is, and that's unfortunate, and I just don't want to see this election won on that kind of packaging and that kind of distortions," John Harwood, "Democrats Charge Bush's Campaign Using Racist Pitch," St. Petersburg *Times*, October 24, 1988.

26. Lamis, *The Two-Party South*, p. 26.

27. St. Petersburg *Times*, November 8, 9, 1988.

28. *Congressional Quarterly Weekly Report*, October 15, 1988, pp. 2912–13.

29. For a full state-by-state treatment of these elections, see chapter 17, "The 1986 Elections," in Lamis, *The Two-Party South*, pp. 265–97.

30. Alan I. Abramowitz, "Party Leadership, Realignment, and the Nationalization of Southern Politics," delivered at the annual meeting of the Southern Political Science Association, Memphis, November 5–7, 1981. Abramowitz, of Emory University, also surveyed local party officials.

31. David E. Sturrock, "Legislative Elections and the Two-Party South," delivered at the 1988 Citadel Symposium on Southern Politics, Charleston, March 3–4, 1988, p. 6. Sturrock's paper is part of his Ph.D. dissertation at the University of California, Riverside.

32. John Egerton, *The Americanization of Dixie: The Southernization of America* (New York, 1974).

33. This paragraph and the next two draw from Lamis, *The Two-Party South*, pp. 300–301.

34. *Congressional Quarterly Weekly Report*, August 1, 1987, p. 1699.

35. C. Vann Woodward, *Tom Watson, Agrarian Rebel* (New York, 1938), p. 220.

36. Black and Black, *Politics and Society in the South*, pp. 213–31.

37. This survey discussion comes from Lamis, *The Two-Party South*, pp. 242–48.

38. For a useful discussion of these dimensions, see James L. Sundquist, *Dynamics of the Party System: Alignment and Realignment of Political Parties in the United States*, rev. ed. (Washington, D.C., 1983), pp. 430–32.

39. V. O. Key, Jr., with the assistance of Milton C. Cummings, Jr., *The Responsible Electorate: Rationality in Presidential Voting, 1936–1960* (Cambridge, 1966).

40. To quote Key completely on the point: "The perverse and unorthodox argument of this little book is that voters are not fools. To be sure, many individual voters act in odd ways indeed; yet in the large the electorate behaves about as rationally and responsibly as we should expect, given the clarity of the alternatives presented to it and the character of the information available to it," *The Responsible Electorate*, p. 7.

41. Ibid., pp. 58–59.

42. V. O. Key, Jr., *Public Opinion and American Democracy* (New York, 1961), pp. 552, 558.

3

Variations on a Theme by Henry Grady: Technology, Modernization, and Social Change

ROBERT C. McMATH, JR.

"Of the making of books about the South there is no end." But of the making of books about technology in the South there is only a beginning. Much has been written about the forces which inhibited technological development in the region, about attitudes toward technology, and about the impact of particular technologies on the social fabric.[1] But of the machines and tools themselves, and the skills and methods employed to make them useful, we know relatively little.

The phrase "southern technology" is not an oxymoron, as anyone can plainly see by driving through the mill-crowded towns of the piedmont. Let us move beyond the question, Why so little technology in the South? to ask, Why have particular technologies been encouraged, by whom, and to whose benefit? and How have technology and community-building been related in the South? And finally, because technology is often cast as the villain in the story of the disappearing South, How will technology and culture be related in the future South?

But first, to name the beast. Following the political scientist Langdon Winner, I shall include under the rubric of "technology" three things: (1) Apparatus: the physical devices—tools, machines, gadgets, and the like used to accomplish various tasks. (2) Technique: the "skills, methods, procedures, and routines that people engage in to accomplish tasks." (3) Organization: social arrangements in which technique is applied to apparatus, such as factories, workshops, and research laboratories.[2] Technology, thus defined, is cultural and social as well as physical, and its history, therefore, is social as well as material.

Technologies do not just happen; they are chosen. From revolutionary times to the present, southern public officials and civic leaders have promoted technological innovation and diffusion. Early state legislatures offered bounties for the establishment of manufactures and for the development of new technologies, most notably the cotton gin. In

81

1780 the Georgia legislature enacted a law for "more speedy and effectually settling this state," which included the following provision:

AND WHEREAS it will tend greatly to the Interest and strength of the State to establish Manufactures of Iron, to the end thereof of encouraging able and proper persons to undertake the same[,] Be it Enacted by the authority aforesaid that any person or persons who will give approved security to his Honor the Governor and Council for erecting proper and effectual works for that purpose shall be entitled to a grant of two thousand acres for a forge and two thousand acres for a bloomery and two thousand acres for a furnace.[3]

Similarly, post-Civil War civic boosters lusted after northern technology, and their spiritual descendants have never stopped selling the South to those masters of technology, foreign and domestic, who seem to hold the key to community growth.[4]

Some economists and historians have explained this diffusion of technologies as a function of profit maximizing on the part of individuals or firms. Where, they ask, is the "threshold" at which a reasonable, profit-maximizing individual would adopt a particular technology?[5] But decision making about technologies can also be communal, and the calculus for such decisions based on something other than the slope of the economists' S-curve.[6] As David L. Carlton has demonstrated with regard to piedmont South Carolina, we need also to consider the introduction of new technologies as an exercise in community-building,[7] or as has often been the case, in dreaming about communities that might be: the eighteenth-century speculator in the Shenandoah Valley, surveying a tract of timberland underlain with iron ore while imagining the difference that a Pennsylvania iron master could make; the nineteenth-century merchant in the Carolina piedmont, viewing a falling stream with an eye to the impact of a Rhode Island spinner; and the twentieth-century booster on Atlanta's northern rim, looking at a stand of slash pine and envisioning a high-technology park.

All these visions may be understood as variations on a theme by Henry Grady, editor of the Atlanta *Constitution* from 1879 until his death in 1889 and patron saint of Atlanta. The theme is this: Add to the natural endowments of the South the magic ingredients of capital and technology, stir in a measure of public relations hype, and vibrant new communities will spring up across the piedmont landscape.

The distillation of Grady's vision can be found in his speech to the New England Society of New York, delivered in 1886. Flanked on the dias at Delmonico's by J. P. Morgan, Elihu Root, H. M. Flagler, and one William Tecumseh Sherman (whom he described as "an able man, but a kind of careless man about fire"), Grady proclaimed, "We have sowed towns and cities in the place of theories, and put business above politics. We have challenged your spinners in Massachusetts and your iron-makers in Pennsylvania. We have established thrift in city and country. We have fallen in love with work."[8] What sounded like a boast was in fact a sales pitch aimed at northern technologists as well as capitalists: "invest your skill and machinery in the South, and you won't regret it."

In Grady's time and since, there have been skeptics and critics. Without mentioning Grady by name, the agrarian leader Tom Watson thundered from the stump, "Shame to Southern men who go to Northern banquets and glory in our defeat."[9] A half-century later the Nashville Agrarians denounced "the capitalization of the applied sciences, [which] has enslaved our human energies to a degree now clearly felt to be burdensome." More critical of intrusive technology even than the Vanderbilt crowd was one T. J. Cauley, an economist who labored in the belly of the beast—Georgia Tech—from whence in 1935 he published a little book entitled *Agrarianism*, an appeal for the South to forsake manufacturing in favor of subsistence farming.[10]

Even southerners who embraced a technocratic vision of the newest New South have worried about the social impact of technological change. Witness another banquet in an American metropolis, where, like the one at Delmonico's, a visitor from afar was trying to charm the Yankees out of a little technical assistance. The year is 1979, and the setting is the East Room of the White House. The visitor is Deng Xiaoping, known before the Tiananmen Square massacre as the architect of China's "four modernizations." After this Henry Grady of the New China had flattered the locals and made his pitch, his host, a southern Yankee from Plains, rose to offer a toast: "Like you, Mr. Vice Premier, I am a farmer; and like you, I am a former military man. In my little farming community, when I grew up, our agricultural methods and way of life were not greatly different from those of centuries earlier. I stepped from that world into the planning and outfitting of a nuclear submarine. When I returned to the land, I found that farming had been transformed in just a few years by new scientific knowledge and technology. I know the shock of change, and the sometimes painful adjustments it can require—as well as the great potential for good that change can bring to individuals and nations."[11]

There's the rub. The tricky part for the South, as Grady well knew, was the same one that has faced underdeveloped nations the world over: how to appropriate new or imported technologies without destroying the very social fabric the modernizing campaign was designed to strengthen.

If we, like Deng Xiaoping, are to anticipate the impact of technology on our homeland in the twenty-first century, we might well begin, as did President Carter, with a look backward. Let us focus briefly on three epochs when southerners set out to create or import particular technologies: the nineteenth century with the importation of textile technology, the mid-twentieth century with the development of cotton harvesting machinery, and the last two decades with the promotion of research, development, and commercialization of high technology, particularly in electronics. Having then done what historians do best—predicting the past—let us probe the future of technology in the South, for that future is, after all, a part of southern history.

It is appropriate to begin with technologies related to textiles, for our word *technique* can be traced to the Indo-European root meaning *to weave*.[12] And in Spartanburg, stories of beginnings have naturally to do with Dexter Edgar Converse, who learned cotton manufacturing inside the mills of Vermont and New York in the 1840s, supervised factories in North and South Carolina in the 1850s, and gained recognition as a leading figure in the fledgling South Carolina textile industry.[13]

The contributions of men like Converse, George Makepeace in North Carolina, and Henry Merrell in Georgia are less well known than those of William Gregg of Graniteville fame, but they may well be more typical than Gregg of textile pioneers in the antebellum South. To paraphrase a modern jingle, when you say Gregg, you haven't said it all. These three men, like William Gregg, were northern born. Unlike him, all three had learned textile manufacturing in northern mills, more specifically in mills based on the "Rhode Island plan" of Samuel Slater, and it was the Slater system that they brought South. Slater-type operations tended to concentrate on spinning rather than develop integrated manufacturing; they adopted the family labor system with its attendant mill villages; and they were oriented toward local markets and typically combined manufacturing and mercantile operations.[14]

Thanks to James Skinner, who discovered and is editing for publication the autobiography of Henry Merrell, we know something about the transfer of textile technology to antebellum Georgia and how that technology fit into the community structure of the southern piedmont. Merrell learned textile manufacturing in Whitesboro, New York, from William Walcott, a Slater protégé. Upon being invited in 1838 to set in operation the Roswell Manufacturing Company in Georgia, Merrell tapped the Slater network to secure top-quality spinning equipment from the firm of Rogers, Ketchum, and Grosevner of Paterson, New Jersey, and personally supervised its construction before moving to

Georgia. However, when in the 1840s Merrell left Roswell to buy a small factory in nearby Clarke County, he found his new mill to be "made up of scraps of machinery picked up here and there . . . a perfect museum of old things."[15] We need more stories like Merrell's to determine which of his two experiences was more nearly typical of textile manufacturers in the antebellum South.[16]

Merrell's manufacturing operations fit comfortably into the rhythms of community self-sufficiency which marked the antebellum upcountry.[17] Textile manufacturing was, for such men, an extension of their mercantile operations, in which the objective was to maintain a strong trading presence in a limited market area.[18] Processing local cotton and bartering with local farmers for yarn and other trade goods, these early cotton manufacturers more nearly fulfilled the slogan of "bringing the cotton mills to the cotton fields" than would later cotton manufacturers more closely tied to national and world markets. To be sure, one can see in those early years the outlines of the modern networks linking southern mills to New York commission houses and New England machinery makers, but the mills of the Old South were, by and large, as locally oriented as the communities of which they were a part.

In the great cotton mill boom of the post-Civil War era, especially in the 1880s and 1890s, mill building and community building were still intimately related, but from a technological perspective there were substantial differences.

With regard to apparatus, southern mills became major buyers of the latest machinery offered for sale by the Lowell Shops, the Whitin Machine Works, and other northeastern manufacturers. In 1876, five years before Atlanta's International Cotton Exposition which supposedly triggered the cotton mill boom, the Lowell Shops filled a $100,000 order for the Atlanta Cotton Factory in order to make it "the showroom for Lowell Machinery in the South."[19] Regrettably, Lowell had to repossess its machinery when the company went belly up. Lowell's management threatened to cut off all credit sales to the South, but then thought better of doing so.

In 1882 a single train carried twenty-two car loads of machinery from Boston to southern mills, and three hundred car loads more were in the works. In every year between 1880 and 1905 southern mills were among the biggest buyers of machinery from both Lowell and Whitin, with the former concentrated mainly in South Carolina and Georgia, and the latter in North Carolina.[20]

The southern mill boom of the 1880s and 1890s coincided with significant innovations in textile technology, and many new mills in the South were able to leapfrog over their New England counterparts to acquire more efficient equipment, which, at the same time, required less skill to operate. The ring spinning frame, which had undergone significant improvements in the 1870s and required far less skilled labor than mule spindles, accounted for almost all spinning in the South. The Northrop automatic loom which was first marketed by the George Draper Company in the 1890s was technologically complementary to ring spinning, thus readily adoptable in the South, but less so in the North where mule spinning was relatively more common.[21]

Despite these advances in southern textile technology, the region remained primarily a *consumer* of technology rather than an *innovator* in machine design. Unlike Japan, which became a heavy importer of American and British textile machinery at roughly the same time, the South did not develop its own machine industry until much later, nor (unlike the Japanese) did southern textile leaders devote much energy to mechanical refinements which would take advantage of the region's particular mix of natural and human resources.[22] Far more typical of early southern technological leaders were the "mill engineers" and manufacturers' representatives like Charlotte-based Stuart W. Cramer, southern representative for the Whitin Works, who specialized in the application of off-the-shelf textile technologies to new mills in the piedmont.[23]

When one shifts the focus from "apparatus" to "technique" in the postbellum expansion of southern textiles, two distinct trends emerge. On the one hand, many of the skilled positions continued to be filled by northerners or by southern men who had been trained in northern mills. Northern machinists accompanied the machinery sent down from Lowell. The historian of the Lowell Shops was correct in arguing that "the great debt of the South to the North was not for capital but for skill."[24]

Southern efforts to gain control of this strategically important knowledge can be seen in the continuing stream of young southern men of prominent families who were packed off to New England to learn the secrets of the mill and in the drive to add textile engineering to the region's fledgling technological institutions.

An example of the first of these strategies can be seen in the brief career of William Greene Raoul, who in 1897 was put in charge of the spinning room at the same Roswell Manufacturing Company that Henry Merrell had set in operation sixty years earlier. Young Raoul, the son and grandson of Georgia railroad presidents, had made his way to Lowell and Lawrence in 1895 to learn textile mill management and had then returned in hopes of becoming a captain of southern industry. Unfortunately, young Raoul's technical expertise outstripped his ability to get along with southern mill operatives, and after several stormy confrontations in the mill his textile career came to a abrupt end.[25]

The second of these strategies was being implemented at precisely the time of Raoul's brief foray into textile mill management. Clemson's campaign to create a textile school in South Carolina spurred similar drives in North Carolina and Georgia. With Grady-like hyperbole, President Lyman Hall of Georgia Tech announced in 1898 that "when the first brick is laid in the textile department . . . the South declares war against New England."[26]

The outcome of that war turned not only on the locally trained captains of industry, but also on the privates. For while northerners continued to dominate the highly technical positions, the South was building up a sizable pool of experienced mill operatives who, by the end of the nineteenth century, were not only improving manufacturing efficiency but also influencing plant location. More and more mills located in the towns and cities of the piedmont, in part to have better access to that pool of experienced labor. By the turn of the century the new "low skill" machinery in southern mills was in fact operated by workers with considerable experience.

One striking example of this increased reliance on experienced textile workers is to be found in the records of the Fulton Bag and Cotton Mill, Atlanta's largest industrial employer at the turn of the century. By the first decade of the twentieth century, responses to advertisements for workers came not from Appalachian or piedmont farmers, but from families containing several experienced operatives and located in the towns and cities of the piedmont crescent stretching from Atlanta to Charlotte.[27]

The picture beginning to emerge of work inside the factories of the postbellum South and of life in the early mill communities suggests that industrialization at that early stage (before the 1920s) did not necessarily have the disruptive effect on a traditional sense of community usually associated with that process. Before the speed-up of production which accompanied electrification and the advent of industrial engineering, workers maintained relatively more control of work processes in the mill.[28] Furthermore, in the first flush of the town-building and mill-building crusade, the division between town people and mill people was not yet fully evident.[29] In this regard, southern mill communities of the 1880s and 1890s more nearly resembled their counterparts of a half-century before than of a half-century later.

If the technological changes associated with textiles in the nineteenth century did not immediately rend the social fabric of southern communities, the same cannot be said for the twentieth-century revolution in agricultural technology, despite the best intentions of the early modernizers. Henry Grady, the champion of manufacturing technology in the South, had also been an armchair advocate of agricultural modernization, but to the end of preserving rural life, not destroying it. In 1886 Grady's fellow enthusiast Richard Edmonds proclaimed, "Every manufacturing establishment planted in the South marks the progress towards the time when diversified agriculture will be the rule. . . ." The poet Sidney Lanier concluded, "The New South means small farming."[30] Crop diversification, coupled with scientific agriculture, would revive the dying world of the yeoman.

But the real history of science and agriculture in the twentieth century turned out differently, giving us an unintended variation on the theme by Grady. As Jimmy Carter observed, within the space of a generation the Old South of plantation and subsistence farm disappeared, agricultural mechanization came to Dixie, and the southern countryside was largely depopulated.[31] There were, of course, many technological revolutions in southern agriculture, but it was the transformation of the cotton South, beginning in the Mississippi Delta and the high plains of West Texas, that most profoundly altered the rural landscape. The key innovation was the successful development of machinery for harvesting the cotton crop: more precisely, for two innovations, one a cotton stripper suitable for removing the cotton boll from the stalk on the dry Texas plains and in the cotton fields of the arid Southwest, and the other a mechanical picker which, by means of two revolving cylinders, could perform the same task in the lush Mississippi Delta and the cotton belt of the Old South.[32]

Two questions loom large in the history of cotton mechanization. One is why it took so long to happen. The other is whether the accompanying social disruption could have been avoided or minimized.

Cotton mechanization lagged a full century behind the revolution in small grain harvesting. Not until after World War II did mechanized cotton picking begin in earnest. Most observers agree that the South's peculiar institutions—slavery and its successor, sharecropping—inhibited the development of labor-saving machinery, although some interpret this as merely a threshold problem for rational agribusinessmen (at what point does it make sense to replace sharecroppers with machines?), while others view it as proof that planters and planter values still ruled the southern countryside.[33]

Both views underestimate the technical problems associated with cotton mechanization. It took a "bundle" of tools to overcome the various bottlenecks in production. These tools included the general purpose tractor, chemical herbicides, and genetic alteration of the cotton plant, as well as the mechanical cotton picker itself. Unlike the case of textiles, there was no such bundle ready for export to the South. Tractors were not widely used in the South until just before World War II.[34] The herbicide 2,4-D, used in weeding and thinning the crop, was not marketed for agricultural purposes until after the war.[35] And although tinkerers and engineers had dreamed of a mechanical cotton picker since the 1850s, the perfection of such a machine was no simple feat. The cotton picker more nearly resembles the mechanical tomato harvester, developed in the 1960s, than it does the machinery which revolutionized grain harvesting before the Civil War.[36]

Infusion of capital into southern agriculture through the farm support programs of the 1930s, the *relative* scarcity and high cost of farm labor during World War II, and the serendipity of technological breakthroughs all contributed to the perfection and spread of cotton pickers in the 1940s and 1950s.[37] But before we can fully understand the technological revolution in cotton, someone must examine the interplay within a network of inventors, implement company executives, planters, and USDA scientists working at experiment stations in Texas and Mississippi. We need more study of this "community of interest," not only to understand the particular technology which emerged, but also to explore the blind alleys, near misses, and options considered and rejected. People made *choices* about which bundle of tools would prevail.

And that raises the second question about the technological revolution in cotton: could the collapse of rural life which accompanied it have been avoided? Perhaps not, but for reasons which were not fundamentally technological. By the 1930s the postbellum sharecropping plantation—the product of a rough compromise between planters and freedmen—was giving way to a raw new form of agribusiness. As the perfection of the cotton picker loomed in the 1930s and 1940s, the social scientists, labor leaders, and journalists who watched, Cassandra-like, found themselves helpless even to shape a federal policy for alleviating the suffering of those about to be pushed off the land.

But choices were made about the scale, complexity, and cost of the technologies which were actually adopted. There is a story yet to be told about the experiments with small-scale, low-cost pickers and tractors. In the 1920s smaller, simpler, less expensive technologies were no further from perfection than the behemoths which finally prevailed. Of course one can always make a case for the inevitable collapse of traditional community life in the face of modernization (How can you keep them down on the farm once they've seen Spartanburg?). But, without becoming, in Gilbert Fite's damning phrase, "agrarian fundamentalists,"[38] can we not also ask what might have been? Only if we can get beyond the point of equating "technological progress" with "labor-saving" mechanization.[39]

The mechanization of southern agriculture was the last chapter in a century-long story of decline for traditional, labor-intensive farming. Ironically, in the decade or so that followed, those who remained on the land as farm proprietors were, for the most part, free of the ancient curse of southern rural poverty. Farm owners shared in the region's general prosperity, or at least did not cause undue embarrassment for those singing the praises of the newly christened Sunbelt. Farmers, like the South as a whole, rode the crest of government largess to a new and relatively more prosperous South. "Our economy is no longer agricultural," lamented William Faulkner in 1956. "Our economy is the Federal Government."[40]

As with agriculture, the growth of high-technology industries in the South since World War II has floated on a sea of federal money. Defense- and space-related electronics research in southern universities, NASA facilities in Texas, Alabama, and Florida, and other federal projects in the late Confederacy have created a modest down-home version of the Massachusetts miracle.[41]

But the trend toward high technology in the South has not followed a straight line. It is the frantic race for high technology to which we turn for our last variation on a theme by Grady.[42]

In the 1970s and 1980s the South and the nation experienced a series of economic shocks almost as severe as those that racked the country in Grady's day. This time, however, the problems were not those of a colonial south, but rather of a mature industrial economy threatened by the escalating price of essential raw materials and by a loss of global mastery in industrial technology.

In the midst of the crisis, some analysts, taking a cue from Japan, called for a national industrial policy to revitalize the American economy by targeting specific industries for an infusion of research and development funds. For a time, the writing of books and articles on industrial policy itself became a flourishing minor industry.[43] But in the New Age of Supply Side Economics, the idea of a federal industrial policy sounded vaguely socialistic.[44] However, throughout the 1980s the *states* plunged right ahead with high-tech industrial policies of their own, nowhere more so than in the South.[45]

It was not a new idea in Dixie, for the southern states had behind them several decades of experience in promoting industrialization to overcome the region's legacy of poverty and underdevelopment. In the 1970s, and before, southern proposals for high-tech development came from interstate groups such as the Southern Growth Policies Board and from the iron triangle of business, university, and state development leaders in the various states. Under the leadership of "business progressive" governors from Luther Hodges to James B. Hunt, North Carolina took the lead in the high-tech quest, but other states soon followed. In every successful state initiative there was a foundation of federal support: aerospace boosted high-tech development in central Florida and the Huntsville, Alabama, area, as did federally induced electronics research in Atlanta, Austin, and North Carolina's Research Triangle.

This time, the South's search for the Holy Grail did not lead north to Boston or New York, but west to Silicon Valley. When North Carolina's Governor Jim Hunt made a well-publicized trip to Santa Clara County in 1980, he sounded for all the world like Henry Grady. To the homefolks he preached, "the microelectronics industry is our chance—perhaps the only chance that will come in our lifetime—to make a dramatic breakthrough in elevating the wages and per capita income of the people in this state."[46]

In 1982 Georgia's Governor George Busbee stood before a gathering of northern money men in an Atlanta hotel ballroom named for the sainted Grady (the mountain had come to Mohammed): "As we plan ways to escape the current economic contraction, I'm convinced that our state needs to concentrate on building a base of high technology employment. . . . I want to propose that the public sector in Georgia form an alliance with business to focus our best resources on finding and implementing solutions to our economic growth problems."[47]

What was all the hype about? The Silicon Valley model (which already had a budding southern counterpart in the Research Triangle) was the brainchild of Stanford University's Frederick Terman, who in an attempt to keep his brightest engineering graduates in the San Francisco Bay area fostered a "modern community of technological scholars," centered in universities "which have strong programs in engineering and science, surrounded by companies emphasizing research and development, under conditions where there is continual interaction among all of the components."[48] Some of his best students did stay, men with names like Varian, and Hewlett, and Packard. The rest, as they say, is history.

By looking to Terman's community of technological scholars and its counterpart along Boston's Route 128, southern officials were aiming for the mother lode of high technology. The South had once been willing to accept someone else's machine technology, but this time southerners were no longer content to have some of the golden eggs shipped down in box cars. They wanted the goose. This time around, to return to our original nomenclature, the emphasis was less on "apparatus" than on "technique," or knowledge. The region's universities, land grant colleges, and technical institutes would now be asked to fulfill the promise upon which many of them had been chartered a century before.[49]

University-industry collaboration, university-based "incubator" facilities for high-tech start-up firms, and state-aided technology parks sprang up all over the South. By 1983 six southern states had established such facilities, and more were in the works. States which fell behind in the race for research facilities felt the pinch. Said one Arkansas official, "high technology? By the time it gets here it is like any type of assembly industry."[50]

There was the rub. Unlike the textile and agricultural technologies of an earlier day, modern innovations in electronics held little promise for region-specific improvement. When high-technology initiatives filtered down from research and development to routine manufacturing technologies, regardless of whether the idea had come from Boston or Raleigh-Durham, high-tech industries produced low-tech jobs. Furthermore, as Arkansas illustrates, most of the high-skill, high-pay jobs clustered in a few metropolitan centers. By one estimate, in 1982, 55 percent of the jobs in high-tech industries in metropolitan areas were professional, technical, managerial, or skilled positions, whereas among similar industries located in rural areas, only 20 percent were.[51]

In such an environment, the southern states were, once again, put in a position of falling back on the old pattern of hustling for manufacturing jobs, which happened to be in high-tech industries, only this time the shoe was on the other foot with regard to labor.[52] Computer boards, like textile goods and apparel, can always be fabricated more cheaply elsewhere.

Has the high-tech hype run its course? Certainly there remains great promise for the high end of high tech, the research and development part, but the overall mix of job opportunities and the impact on research infrastructure has not lived up to expectations. In North Carolina, for example, while the great experiment in state-supported high-tech growth has produced many high-paying jobs, it has also given rise to a new term—*Research Triangle Park effect*—to describe the unhappy condition of high-tech gentrification in which high-income emigrés bid up the cost of everything at the expense of low-income natives.[53] Jim Hunt's super salesmanship played well with the business progressives and moderate corporate leaders, but lack of performance and a seeming disinterest in the state's "traditional" industries created a political backlash, not only among the conservative followers of Senator Jesse Helmes, but among the community activists and radicals as well.[54]

Three variations on a theme by Henry Grady—how might these chapters from the past and present inform our expectations of the future?

First, the South's traditional industries, including textiles, have been with us for more than a century and a half, and in some form they will be with us still, despite the talk about the demise of "smokestack" industries. They will survive, I expect, regardless of what Washington does about trade policies, in part through a blending of the old and the new. Electronically controlled equipment and robots are simply one step beyond the numerical control technologies, industrial engineering, and electrification which have been used to increase speed and reliability for decades. The compelling question facing the textile industry is not one of apparatus, but rather of organization. When one hears industry spokespersons speak with pride of "lights out" production (that is, peopleless manufacturing), one wonders if it is already too late to follow the location-specific path as the Japanese textile industry did and encourage job-promoting rather than job-destroying technologies. Machines will survive, but how many people will?

That answer to that may depend, in part, on how well the industry can learn a lesson from the South's textile pioneers of the early nineteenth century: look carefully for a niche in a particular market and be flexible enough to change with the times. But the answer may also depend, in part, on decisions that are as much political as they are technological. In the past, southern states have not shrunk from investing tax dollars in technical assistance and educational programs which were industry- and even firm-specific. The time may come when state governments and governmental agencies must ask themselves if there are not other ways in which technical and technically oriented educational assistance might flow to the people and communities of the South.

And what of agriculture? The mechanical revolution saved agribusiness but at great social cost. Another high-tech revolution now looming on the horizon may offer hope for a revival. The Hewlett and Packard of this newest revolution are named Watson and Crick. Their research into the mysteries of the double helix opened the age of biotechnology. The unraveling of genetic codes (a work still in its infancy) plus the development of powerful techniques in molecular genetics are giving humankind the ability to modify genetic structures in animals, plants, and microbes. The application of biotechnology may well reduce dependence on energy and water inputs and lessen our dependence on chemical pesticides, herbicides, and fertilizers. Furthermore, the products of biotechnology, unlike those of the mechanical revolution, are relatively scale neutral.[55] If the family farm is not quite dead yet, there may yet be hope in designer genes.

Perhaps. But when the urge comes to believe the latest panacea, lie down and remember Grady, Hall, Hunt, et al. Or, better yet, listen to a latter-day Tom Watson named Jim Hightower, the populist-sounding agriculture commissioner of Texas. Hightower has noted that although biotechnology holds the promise of reducing farmers' dependence on chemicals by engineering disease- and insect-resistant crops, agrichemical companies are now devoting much of their research efforts to the development of *herbicide*-resistant crops—herbicides marketed by those same companies. As Hightower notes, "we cannot afford to accept all new products or developments uncritically. Directions in new technology are never politically neutral. They are guided by all kinds of political, economic and social considerations."[56]

And what of microelectronics and computers? The fact of the matter is that the goose has not yet flown south. Even Austin, Texas, which won the sweepstakes in two national competitions for giant industrial- and government-sponsored research facilities in microelectronics, has not yet challenged Silicon Valley or competitors beyond the Pacific shore in real scientific breakthroughs, and the collapse of the "all bidness" [oil business to those who don't speak Texan] and real estate markets in Texas have more than offset the job-creating power of this particular form of high tech. Of course we should continue to support basic and applied research in these fields, as well as to foster the diffusion of electronics technologies, but we have a right to expect that such projects, financed in part with public funds, should be brought to bear on the problems of that other South still locked in poverty beyond the shiny suburban towers of Atlanta and Charlotte.

One of the most exciting moments of my own undergraduate experience was the discovery, through the works of C. Vann Woodward, George Tindall, and others, that the system of racial control which seemed then so immutably fixed had a beginning in choices made by human beings, and could therefore have an end. So too with technology. Throughout the long history of the South people have chosen some technologies and abandoned or ignored others. The notion that people can make their own history is heady stuff indeed. But we should claim that right rather than assuming that the South is to be bulldozed out of existence.

NOTES

1. A useful survey of the recent literature on these matters is to be found in James C. Cobb, "Beyond Planters and Industrialists: A New Perspective on

the New South," *Journal of Southern History* 54 (February 1988): 45–68. Cobb makes the useful suggestion that we stop arguing about whether planters or a new class of industrialists presided over the South's postbellum economic development, because the two groups shared a "central policy core" of conservative values. It is a reflection on the state of the literature, not Cobb's analysis, that technology is hardly mentioned in his treatment of southern industrialization.

2. Langdon Winner, *Autonomous Technology: Technics-out-of-Control as a Theme in Political Thought* (Cambridge, 1977), pp. 11–12.

3. Allen D. Candler, *The Colonial Records of the State of Georgia*, 28 vols. (Atlanta, 1904–16, repr. New York, 1970), vol. 19, pt. 2, p. 57, quoted in Stephen G. Hardy, "The Forgotten Industry: Georgia's Eighteenth Century Ironworks," unpublished manuscript, 1984, in possession of Robert C. McMath, Jr. On state efforts to encourage invention of a cotton gin, see Gavin Wright, *The Political Economy of the Cotton South: Households, Markets, and Wealth in the Nineteenth Century* (New York, 1978), pp. 13–14.

4. Paul M. Gaston, *The New South Creed: A Study in Southern Mythmaking* (New York, 1970); Patrick J. Hearnden, *Independence and Empire: The South's Cotton Mill Campaign, 1865–1901* (DeKalb, 1982); James C. Cobb, *The Selling of the South: The Southern Crusade for Industrial Development, 1936–1980* (Baton Rouge, 1982).

5. See, for example, Paul A. David, "The Mechanization of Reaping in the Antebellum Midwest" in *Industrialization in Two Systems: Essays in Honor of Alexander Gerschenkron*, ed. Henry Rosovsky (New York, 1966), reprinted in David, *Technological Choice: Innovation and Economic Growth* (New York, 1975), pp. 201–2; and Zvi Griliches, "Hybrid Corn and the Economics of Innovation," *Science*, July 29, 1960, pp. 207–13.

6. Among the economists who have taken a broader view of technological diffusion than the one described in this paragraph are William N. Parker and his students—most notably, with regard to the South, Gavin Wright. See especially Wright, *Old South, New South: Revolutions in the Southern Economy since the Civil War* (New York, 1986), and Wright, "The Economic Revolution in the American South," *Economic Perspectives* 1 (Summer 1987): 161–78.

7. David L. Carlton, *Mill and Town in South Carolina, 1880–1920* (Baton Rouge, 1982), chapter 2.

8. Henry W. Grady, *The New South: Writings and Speeches of Henry Grady* (Savannah, 1971), p. 8.

9. C. Vann Woodward, *Tom Watson, Agrarian Rebel* (New York, 1938), p. 126.

10. Twelve Southerners, *I'll Take My Stand: The South and the Agrarian Tradition* (New York, 1930), p. xi; George Tindall, *The Emergence of the New South, 1913–1945* (Baton Rouge, 1967), p. 581.

11. Toast at state dinner for Vice-Premier Deng Xiaoping and Madame Zhao Lin, Press/Powell, Box 81, Carter Presidential Library, Atlanta.

12. Winner, *Autonomous Technology*, p. 12.

13. *National Encyclopedia of American Biography*, vol. 6 (New York, 1896), p. 138; Gary R. Freeze, "Genesis of a Paternalistic Ethic: George Makepeace, North Carolina's Deep River Cotton Mills, and Some Antecedents of the New South Creed, 1839–1906," unpublished manuscript, undated, in possession of Robert C. McMath, Jr.; "Autobiography of Henry Merrell," edited typescript, undated, in possession of James L. Skinner.

14. On the spread of Slater-type mills into southern New England from Rhode Island, see Jonathan Prude, *The Coming of Industrial Order: Town and Factory Life in Rural Massachusetts, 1810–1860* (Cambridge, 1983).

15. Merrell Autobiography, pp. 158–59, 208–9.

16. Broadus Mitchell reports that in the early years of southern textile manufacturing, "Much machinery was made in local blacksmith shops, and must have been crude even for that period." Mitchell, *The Rise of Cotton Mills in the South* (Baltimore, 1921), p. 17. However, the evidence on source of machinery for this era is far more limited than the evidence on the men who brought knowledge of textile manufacturing techniques to the South.

17. Steven Hahn, *The Roots of Southern Populism: Yeomen Farmers and the Transformation of the Georgia Upcountry, 1850–1890* (New York, 1983).

18. Fred Bateman and Thomas Weiss, *A Deplorable Scarcity: The Failure of Industrialization in the Slave Economy* (Chapel Hill, 1981), pp. 39–41; Robert D. Mitchell, *Commercialism and Frontier: Perspectives on the Early Shenandoah Valley* (Charlottesville, 1977), pp. 200–204.

19. George Sweet Gibb, *The Saco-Lowell Shops: Textile Machinery Building in New England, 1813–1949* (Cambridge, 1950), pp. 249–53; Jack Blicksilver, "The International Cotton Exposition of 1881 and Its Impact upon the Economic Development of Georgia," *Atlanta Economic Review* 7 (June 1957): 1–5.

20. Thomas R. Navin, *The Whitin Machine Works since 1831: A Textile Machinery Company in an Industrial Village* (Cambridge, 1950), pp. 204–35; Gibbs, *The Saco-Lowell Shops*, pp. 241–54.

21. Irwin Feller, "The Draper Loom in New England Textiles, 1894–1914: The Study of the Diffusion of an Innovation," *Journal of Economic History* 26 (September 1966): 325–31; Feller, "The Diffusion and Location of Technological Change in the American Cotton Textile Industry," paper presented to the Southern Historical Association, 1973; Chen-Han Chen, "Regional Differences in Costs and Productivity in the American Cotton Manufacturing Industry, 1880–1910," *Quarterly Journal of Economics* 55 (August 1951): 556; Jacquelyn Dowd Hall et al., *Like a Family: The Making of a Southern Cotton Mill World* (Chapel Hill, 1987), pp. 46–51.

22. Wright, "The Economic Revolution in the American South," pp. 169–70; Gary Saxonhouse and Gavin Wright, "Rings and Mules Around the World: A Comparative Study in Technological Choice" in *Technique, Spirit and Form in the Making of the Modern Economies: Essays in Honor of William N. Parker*, ed. Saxonhouse and Wright (Greenwich, 1984), pp. 271–300.

23. Navin, *The Whitin Machine Works*, pp. 219–25.

24. Gibb, *The Saco-Lowell Shops*, p. 248. A major grievance in the 1886 millworkers' strike in Augusta, Georgia, was that "the overseers were all Yanks."

Marjorie W. Young, ed., *Textile Leaders of the South* (Anderson, SC, 1963), p. 448.

25. Robert C. McMath, Jr., "From Captain of Industry to Sergeant of Socialism: William Greene Raoul and the Management of Southern Labor," in *Looking South: Chapters on the Story of an American Region*, ed. Winfred B. Moore, Jr. and Joseph F. Tripp (Westport, 1989), 171–90. See also, Bess Beatty, "Lowells of the South: Northern Influences on the Nineteenth-Century North Carolina Textile Industry," *Journal of Southern History* 53 (February 1987): 57–58.

26. Lyman Hall to Clark Howell, March 7, 1898, correspondence of Lyman Hall, Georgia Institute of Technology Archives, Atlanta. Clemson's textile school opened in 1898, and Georgia Tech and North Carolina A&M followed suit in 1899.

27. Fulton Bag and Cotton Mill Papers, Georgia Institute of Technology Archives, Atlanta; see also, Wright, *Old South, New South*, pp. 142–43; Leonard A. Carlson, "Labor Supply, the Acquisition of Skills, and the Location of Southern Textile Mills, 1880-1900," *Journal of Economic History* 41 (March 1981): 65–73. Other factors besides the availability of experienced labor certainly contributed to the locational shift from countryside to town, including the conversion from water power to steam and then to electricity, and the town-building crusades that David Carlton has described.

28. Hall et al., *Like a Family*, p. 44.

29. Carlton, *Mill and Town*, chapters 2 and 3.

30. Gaston, *The New South Creed*, pp. 67, 64.

31. Three recently published books chronicle the end of traditional agriculture in the South, although only the first of them deals extensively with technological change. Gilbert C. Fite, *Cotton Fields No More: Southern Agriculture, 1865–1980* (Lexington, Ky., 1984); Pete Daniel, *Breaking the Land: The Transformation of Cotton, Tobacco, and Rice Culture since 1880* (Urbana, 1985); and Jack Temple Kirby, *Rural Worlds Lost: The American South, 1920–1960* (Baton Rouge, 1987).

32. The most complete account of the century-long effort to perfect a mechanical cotton picker is found in James H. Street, *The New Revolution in the Cotton Economy: Mechanization and Its Consequences* (Chapel Hill, 1957), but the comprehensive history of cotton mechanization is yet to be written.

33. For the former view, see Warren Whatley, "Southern Agrarian Labor Contracts as Impediments to Cotton Mechanization," *Journal of Economic History* 48 (March 1987): 45–70; and Moses S. Musoke, "Mechanizing Cotton Production in the American South: The Tractor, 1915–1960," *Explorations in Economic History* 18 (1981): 347–75. For the latter, see Jay R. Mandle, *The Roots of Black Poverty: The Southern Plantation after the Civil War* (Durham, 1978); and Jonathan M. Wiener, "Class Structure and Economic Development in the American South, 1865–1955," *American Historical Review* 84 (October 1979): 970–92.

34. Musoke, "Mechanizing Cotton Production," p. 352; Robert C. Williams, *Fordson, Farmall, and Poppin' Johnny: A History of the Farm Tractor and Its Impact on America* (Urbana, 1987), pp. 61–62.

35. The compound 2,4-dichlorophenoxyacetic acid was synthesized in 1941 by plant physiologists working at the University of Chicago and at the USDA research facility at Beltsville, Maryland. Their work was incorporated into the army's biological and chemical warfare program. Gale E. Peterson, "The Discovery and Development of 2,4-D," *Agricultural History* 41 (July 1967): 243–53.

36. Wayne Rasmussen, "Advances in American Agriculture: The Mechanical Tomato Harvester as a Case Study," *Technology and Culture* 9 (October 1968): 531–43.

37. Pete Daniel, *Breaking the Land*; Nan Woodruff, "The Disintegration of Sharecropping and Tenancy in the Mississippi Delta, 1930–1965," paper presented to Seminar in Southern History, University of California-Irvine, 1988; Robert C. McMath, Jr., "World War II and the Rural South: Death Knell for Traditional Community Life?," paper presented at the annual meeting of the Southern Historical Association, 1982.

38. Fite, *Cotton Fields No More*, p. 159.

39. For further discussion of this point, see Wright, "The Economic Revolution in the American South," p. 169.

40. Quoted in Bruce Joseph Schulman, *From Cotton Belt to Sunbelt: Federal Policy and Southern Economic Development, 1933–1980* (New York, in press), mss. p. 222.

41. The southern buildup of federally supported research and development in electronics, aerospace, and biotechnology attracted considerable attention from journalists during the 1980s, but is only beginning to receive scholarly attention. See especially, Schulman's chapter on this subject, entitled "Missiles and Magnolias," in *From Cotton Belt to Sunbelt*.

42. The term *high technology* resists easy definition. In part, the difficulty has to do with the appropriate unit of analysis. Is it an industry or a job? Would we say that a job assembling computer boards is high tech but one monitoring an electronically controlled knitting machine is not? The easiest way out (i.e., the approach most commonly taken by social scientists) is to use the industry as the unit of analysis. The standard definition of the U.S. Department of Labor would include drugs and medicine; office, computing, and accounting equipment; electrical and electronic equipment; aircraft and missiles; and instruments and related products. Glenna Colclough and Charles Tolbert, "High Technology, Work, and Inequality in Southern Labor Markets," unpublished manuscript, 1987, in possession of Robert C. McMath, Jr.

43. "Debate Grows over Adoption of a National Industrial Policy," New York *Times*, July 19, 1983; James Botkin, Dan Dimancescu, and Ray Stata, *Global Stakes: The Future of High Technology in America* (Cambridge, 1982), pp. 154–55; and Barry Bluestone and Bennett Harrison, *The Deindustrialization of America* (New York, 1982).

44. That was in Ronald Reagan's *first* term. For a brief review of Reagan's policies in support of electronics and computing in the second by a Democratic advocate of industrial policy, see Robert B. Reich, "Behold! We Have an Industrial Policy," New York *Times*, May 22, 1988, p. E29.

45. *Technology, Innovation, and Regional Economic Development* (Washington, 1984); and Richard P. Barke, "Technology and the States: A Continuing Experiment," unpublished manuscript, 1988, in possession of Robert C. McMath, Jr.

46. Quoted in Dale Whittington, ed., *High Hopes for High Tech: Microelectronics in North Carolina* (Chapel Hill, 1985), p. 19.

47. "Remarks of Governor George Busbee, Advanced Technology Strategy Conference, Peachtree Plaza Hotel, Henry Grady Room," October 15, 1982, in Advanced Technology Development Center File, Georgia Institute of Technology Archives, Atlanta.

48. Frederick E. Terman, "The Newly Emerging Community of Technological Scholars," reprinted in *Readings in Technology and American Life*, ed. Carroll W. Pursell, Jr. (New York, 1969), pp, 431–32. One component of Terman's plan, the Stanford Research Institute, was initially committed to regional economic development and was first known as the "Research Center of the West."

49. Robert C. McMath, Jr., et al., *Engineering the New South: Georgia Tech, 1885–1985* (Athens, 1985), chapter 1.

50. *Technology, Innovation, and Regional Economic Development.* Background Paper: Census of State Government Initiatives for High-Technology Industrial Development (Washington, 1983), passim, quote from p. 16.

51. William W. Falk and Thomas A. Lyson, *High Tech, Low Tech, No Tech: Recent Industrial and Occupational Change in the South* (Albany, 1988), pp. 45, 98–99. By their estimate, between 1977 and 1981, four hundred thousand new high-tech jobs were created, accounting for 9 percent of the South's private-sector employment; 80 percent of the jobs were in metropolitan areas. This finding is generally confirmed, but with a wider range of estimates for the percentage of the work force in high technology, by Colclough and Tolbert, "High Technology, Work, and Inequality in Southern Labor Markets."

52. Cobb, *The Selling of the South*, chapter 7.

53. Thomas C. Hayes, "Triangle Park: North Carolina's High-Tech Payoff," New York *Times*, April 26, 1987, p. 12F, cited in Barke, "Technology and the States," p. 33.

54. Paul Luebke, Stephen Peters, and John Wilson, "The Political Economy of Microelectronics in North Carolina" in *High Hopes for High Tech*, ed. Whittington, pp. 311–14; Marc Miller, "The Low Down on High Tech," *Southern Exposure* 14 (1986): 35–39.

55. Committee on National Strategy for Biotechnology in Agriculture, Board on Agriculture, National Research Council, *Agricultural Biotechnology: Strategies for National Competitiveness* (Washington, 1987), p. 17.

56. Jim Hightower, "Biotech Firms' Motives: Best Crop or More Cash?," Atlanta *Constitution*, January 5, 1989, p. A19.

4

The Weight of the Past versus the Promise of the Future: Southern Race Relations in Historical Perspective

HOWARD N. RABINOWITZ

More has been written about race relations than any other topic in southern history. This is as it should be given the centrality of race in the history of the South. Thus it is no small task to assess the prospects for southern race relations in the future, based on the history of the region's race relations to this point. I have therefore chosen to paint my picture with broad strokes and, to make my task a bit easier, I will basically use only two colors, that is, I will limit myself primarily to black-white relations, although I think we too often ignore other ethnic groups in our study of southern history and society.[1]

When I told some laypersons that I had been asked to prepare this chapter, they immediately wanted to know what I, in fact, thought of black-white relations in the South. My response, of course, was: compared to what? Any assessment of southern race relations in the future, or for that matter in the present, must place the subject within the proper comparative context.

There are many possibilities for comparison—Mikhail Gorbachev and Ronald Reagan once engaged in such an exercise when they contrasted human rights in Russia and the United States—but I want to simplify things by dealing with the two basic themes in southern history as identified by most southern historians: continuity and distinctiveness viewed within an American context.[2] That is, I want to survey briefly the history of southern black-white relations with an eye on the ways in which such relations have or have not resembled those of the United States in general and the degree to which southern black-white relations have or have not changed over time.

In doing so, I will divide American race relations somewhat arbitrarily into six periods, although allowing for considerable overlap: (1) 1619 to 1787; (2) 1787 to 1865; (3) 1865 to 1900; (4) 1900 to 1954; (5) 1954 to the present; and (6) the future. Despite the title of this volume, it is the past that will receive most of my attention. For without an understanding of that past, or what I have termed "the weight of the past," we cannot assess reasonably the prospects for what I have termed "the promise of the future." What is most striking about this comparison between North and South and between different eras of southern race relations is that after decades of troubling continuity in the failure of its race relations, the South now shows signs of breaking new ground and providing the nation's most favorable environment for positive racial change.

The arrival in Virginia in 1619 of twenty blacks purchased from a Dutch sea captain would, of course, seem to mark the beginning of black-white relations in the South, and for that matter in what was to become the United States. As the historian Winthrop Jordan has argued, however, the English colonists brought with them certain ideas about color and religion which predisposed them to consider blacks to be inferior and threatening. Other historians have argued that the badge of slavery tainted blacks rather than blackness itself leading to enslavement, yet all agree that the process of defining blacks as slaves was more complex and drawn out than once assumed.

Nevertheless, for our purposes it is clear that by the end of the seventeenth century slavery was a well-entrenched institution in both the North and the South. First through custom, then through law, most blacks found their terms of service extended to life and that status passed on to their children. Yet, if present in all of England's mainland colonies, slavery had already begun to give a special character to those in the South. In part this was reflected in the differences in the legal status of slaves in the colonial North and South. Northern colonies, for example, normally recognized slave marriages as binding and the right of slave parents to their children.[3]

There were, however, differences in race relations within the South based on factors such as demography, geography, staple agriculture, and the nature of the slave trade. As the historian Ira Berlin has noted, the character of African-American society and the relationship between blacks and whites emerged differently in the Chesapeake region and in the rural and urban areas of the Low Country. Yet in all parts of the South, after an initial period of greater autonomy or individual opportunity during the pioneering days of settlement, the firmer drawing of racial lines—marked by the legalization of slavery in the 1660s in Virginia and Maryland and the spread of the rice culture in South Carolina and Georgia during the early eighteenth century—restricted the rights of most blacks. This occurred even though such restrictions in the Chesapeake accompanied a decline in the slave trade while the 1770s brought a sharp increase in dependence on importation further south.[4] And as slavery flourished, so too did an ideology of freedom for whites. Indeed, the two were interrelated, for as the historian Edmund Morgan put it, "by lumping Indians, mulattoes, and Negroes in a single pariah class, Virginians had paved the way for a similar lumping of small and large planters in a single master class. . . . Racism became an essential, if unacknowledged, ingredient of the republican ideology that enabled Virginians to lead the nation."[5]

Thus on the eve of the Revolution slavery had strengthened its grip on the South, and the rights of blacks to their own property or labor had been greatly circumscribed. Yet northern blacks had undergone a similar transformation. Slaves became an increasingly important part of the northern colonial economy, replacing white indentured servants as a prime choice for menial labor. The greater demand for black labor led to the direct importation of slaves and to the emergence of a less acculturated black population. There was already, however, a major difference between the North and the South that was to have significant implications for the future character of race relations in the two regions. Although blacks comprised an indispensable part of the urban artisan class in Charles Town, more than 82 percent of southern blacks lived in rural areas, raising wheat or tobacco in the Chesapeake or rice further south. In the North, following an early period in which most blacks worked on small farms, there was a pronounced shift to the urban areas so that by the Revolution approximately 70 percent of northern blacks were urban.[6]

The Revolutionary Era helped sharpen the differences between the status of southern blacks and those elsewhere. White southerners were becoming more sensitive about what would soon be their "peculiar institution." This was evident in the striking of Thomas Jefferson's condemnation of the slave trade from the Declaration of Independence, an indictment that Newport, Rhode Island, slave traders admittedly objected to as well. Southerners were further incensed by British efforts to encourage rebellion or desertion by their slaves. And, of course, slavery became a major issue at the Constitutional Convention as delegates, especially from South Carolina and Georgia, sought to hold onto the foreign slave trade for as long as possible and debates over the counting of slaves for purposes of representation and taxation helped forge the South's definition of itself as a section.[7]

The years between the Convention and the end of the Civil War witnessed the continued efforts of white southerners to expand and defend the institution of slavery. In the process, the system lost much of its remaining flexibility, becoming ever more rigid, particularly in response to the prodding of northern abolitionists and perceived or actual threats of black rebellion such as those associated with Denmark Vesey and Nat Turner.[8] And as southern states passed law after law aimed at tightening their hold over slaves, free Negroes as well began to lose much of their freedom. Just as white southern concern over the need to draw the color line had resulted in the substitution of racial barriers for class barriers in the colonial period, now racial barriers threatened to overwhelm completely the distinction among blacks between free and slave status. Early forms of racial segregation, restrictions on property ownership and marriage rights, and the loss of the vote in the last of the southern states (Tennessee in 1834 and North Carolina in 1835) pushed free Negroes closer to the non-citizen status of the enslaved mass of blacks. Arkansas went so far as to pass legislation in 1858 expelling its free Negroes; only 144, mostly elderly, free Negroes remained in 1860. No other state took such a drastic step, but the variety of measures took its toll. Free Negroes in 1860 constituted only 6.2 percent of the South's total black population, down from a peak of 8.5 percent in 1810.[9]

On the surface, it would seem that race relations in the South during these years was indeed distinctive. As the southern states moved to buttress slavery, northern states between 1777 and 1817 whether for ideological, religious, economic, or some other reason, abolished the institution where it had existed. In the new states to be carved out of the Northwest Territory, slavery was prohibited. And in the years between 1790 and 1820, northern blacks, now even more concentrated in the region's cities, often enjoyed the right to vote, formed their own churches and voluntary associations, had homes scattered throughout the community, and availed themselves of new economic opportunities that sometimes, as in the case of Philadelphia sail-maker James Forten, made them the employers of whites.

Yet after 1820 and especially 1830, northern blacks lost ground, in part as a result of the influx of European immigrants who competed with them for jobs and housing. Either through de facto or less often de jure action, segregation was enforced in schools, public accommodations, housing, churches, and most other areas of northern life. Even about Massachusetts, the hotbed of abolition, Frederick Douglass in 1846 could write:

> There was in Boston . . . a menagerie I had long desired to see. . . . I was met and told by the doorkeeper, in a harsh and contemptuous tone, *"We don't allow niggers in here."* . . . Soon after my arrival in New Bedford from the South, I had a strong desire to attend the Lyceum, but was told, *"They don't allow niggers in here!"* On arriving in Boston from an antislavery tour, hungry and tired, I went into an eating house near my friend

Mr. Campbell's, to get some refreshments. I was met by a lad in a white apron, *"We don't allow niggers in here."* . . . On attempting to take a seat in the Omnibus [Weymouth], I was told by the driver, (and I never shall forget his fiendish hate) *"I don't allow niggers in here!"*

As their Federalist friends lost power, blacks in Rhode Island, New York, and elsewhere either lost the franchise or had access to it sharply restricted at the same time that universal white manhood suffrage was implemented. Many blacks lost even more in the series of race riots aimed at them and their white allies in Philadelphia, Providence, Boston, Cincinnati, and numerous other northern cities during the 1830s and 1840s.[10]

The point is that white northerners could and did oppose slavery on economic, political, social, or constitutional grounds while not embracing racial equality. Indeed, those same states in the Midwest which had slavery barred by the Northwest Ordinance were far more anti-black than their eastern counterparts, some going so far legislatively as to bar Negroes altogether. And although the American Colonization Society drew most of its support from such Upper South whites as James Madison and Henry Clay, its membership also included northerners such as Daniel Webster and William Seward. One advocate of colonization, Abraham Lincoln, told a political rally in 1858, "I am not, nor ever have been in favor of bringing about in any way the social and political equality of the white and black races— . . . I am not nor ever have been in favor of making voters or jurors of negroes, nor of qualifying them to hold office, nor to intermarry with white people."[11]

By the end of the Civil War then it would seem that the South was distinctive in terms of its support for slavery, but that it shared with much of the rest of the country a belief in Negro inferiority and desire to keep blacks in their place that denied even free blacks the basic rights other Americans enjoyed. And following an initial period of relative openness and flexibility in race relations during the early colonial period, the region had exhibited a remarkable continuity in seeking to fix more firmly the second-class status of its blacks, be they slave or free.

The years between 1865 and 1900 were different. On the one hand, they witnessed the region's sharpest break with its past to that point; on the other, during no period prior to the 1950s were the trends in race relations in the North and South more dissimilar. The primary agents of transformation were northern whites, who either came South or controlled the federal government, and southern blacks themselves.

Following a brief interlude of Presidential Reconstruction between 1865 and 1867 when southern whites were pretty much left to handle their own reconstruction and responded by seeking to minimize the effects of emancipation through black codes, economic intimidation, and violence, the northern victors imposed a more stringent Congressional Reconstruction on the defeated South. Although never as long or restrictive as white southerners claimed or blacks and most of their white allies hoped, this Reconstruction forced basic changes in southern race relations. Thanks to the Thirteenth, Fourteenth, and Fifteenth amendments and various civil rights acts, slavery was abolished, blacks were made citizens with equal rights before the law, and racial discrimination in voting was prohibited. And between 1868 and 1877 the national Republican party with varying degrees of commitment and success sought to use the powers of the federal government to protect the rights of blacks, while at the state level Republican governments, at least in Louisiana, Florida, and South Carolina, held power for as long as nine years.[12]

Yet without the blacks themselves little would have changed in the South. Even before the beginning of political reconstruction southern blacks had begun the region's social and economic transformation. The former slaves refused to accept their old status. They objected to laboring in gangs, removed their wives and children from the fields, and deserted the old slave quarters. Historians still debate the origins of the sharecropping system, but at the very least it represented a compromise between white expectations and black demands.[13] Other blacks exercised their new freedom of mobility to seek better opportunities further west or in the region's cities. And with enfranchisement after 1867, blacks formed the backbone of the Republican party. They voted, held office, and in general made white southerners wonder what had happened to their world. Blacks, especially those in cities, demanded access to schools, public conveyances, welfare institutions, and public accommodations. They won that right under Congressional Reconstruction, although usually, together with their white allies, accepted the promise of separate but equal treatment. Segregation thus became the rule in most areas of southern racial life, but ironically that was seen as, and indeed was, an improvement for blacks, for what it replaced was not integration but exclusion.[14]

White southerners objected that white northerners were forcing racial changes on them that the North itself would not accept. They had a point. Before the ratification of the Fifteenth Amendment in 1870, blacks could not vote in most northern states, and indeed several states, including New York, Wisconsin, and Connecticut, had voted down Negro suffrage after the war; most states still had anti-miscegenation laws and segregated schools and public accommodations; and there was widespread discrimination against blacks in housing and employment.[15] In fact, I would argue that in 1868 prospects generally speaking were better for blacks in the South than in the North.

The situation soon changed. With the return of the former Confederates to power in the South during the 1870s, the triumph of the Democrats in Congress, and the withering of northern determination to protect the rights of blacks in the South, conditions for southern blacks deteriorated.[16] The change was never as rapid nor drastic as once believed, but by the 1890s southern states had initiated a successful systematic program of disfranchisement and de jure segregation, blacks had been largely confined to menial jobs in the cities and to sharecropping in the countryside, white politicians spewed forth a vile political rhetoric of racial inferiority and hate, and white mobs increasingly sought to intimidate blacks and entertain themselves through hideous lynchings.[17]

But as things worsened for blacks in the South, they improved in the North, again reinforcing the distinctiveness of southern race relations. With the Republican and Democratic parties evenly matched in many northern states, the black vote became pivotal following ratification of the Fifteenth Amendment, particularly in presidential elections. Whether out of a sense of political necessity or concern for fairness, white politicians responded positively to black demands for better treatment. After the United States Supreme Court declared the Civil Rights Act of 1875 unconstitutional in 1883, northern states passed their own legislation. Segregated schools and public accommodations persisted in many places but were eradicated elsewhere, and in any case were now against the law. Anti-miscegenation statutes were stricken from the books as they were being reinstituted in the South, and the industrializing North provided better economic opportunities for blacks and perhaps less segregated housing.[18]

By the turn of the century, then, Reconstruction had brought southern blacks, in the historian Eric Foner's words, "nothing but freedom."[19] But that was worth much and in the rush to declare Reconstruction a failure we should not forget that it did confirm the death of slavery as well as lay the constitutional foundation for a more successful attack on southern racial mores in the mid-twentieth century. In the short run, however, Reconstruction legislation had a more longlasting effect in the North. Between 1860 and 1900, most notably after 1880, southern blacks who moved north usually enjoyed greater opportunities than those who remained behind. The last twenty years of the century witnessed in the North a decline in the extent of legally enforced segregation and discrimination, a greater role for blacks in politics, and perhaps an improvement in black prospects for economic success. After a more promising beginning, the social, political, and economic trends for blacks in the South ran in the opposite direction.

Nevertheless, as late as 1900, 90 percent of the nation's blacks remained in the South, more than 80 percent of them trapped in its rural areas,[20] the least dynamic sector of a region which, as a whole, lagged far behind the rest of the country economically and was most hostile to black aspirations. The sharecropping system, which might have been a good temporary solution to postwar agricultural dislocation, had become institutionalized, with the mass of blacks and about one-third of the whites mired in its grip. In other areas as well, despite claims of spokesmen such as Henry Grady and Richard Hathaway Edmonds for the existence of a "New South," the detrimental continuity of southern race relations was evident—remaining states, including the new one of Oklahoma (a kind of a southern fellow traveler) disfranchised their blacks, extended segregation laws throughout southern life, permitted the perpetuation of racial violence, made education even more separate and unequal, and elected to office race-baiting politicians like Tom Watson, James Vardaman, and Theodore Bilbo.[21]

World War I seemed to bring encouraging prospects for change. At a time when southern agriculture was threatened by flooding and the boll weevil, northern industry sought workers to replace those lost to the armed services or the suspension of foreign immigration. Despite the often-ingenious efforts of southern whites to stop them, southern blacks, especially from the Deep South's rural areas, headed north in the so-called Great Migration. The combination of economic hardship, violence in the South, and opportunities in the North led the black-owned Chicago *Defender* to ask "Do you wonder at the thousands leaving the land where every foot of ground marks a tragedy, leaving the graves of their fathers and all that is dear, to seek their fortunes in the North?" As one migrant to Chicago wrote to her sister-in-law: "I can get a nice place for you to stop until you can look around and see what you want. I am quite busy. I work in Swifts Packing Co. in the sausage department. My daughter and I work for the same company. We get $1.50 a day and we pack so many sausages we don't have much time to play but it is a matter of a dollar with me and I feel that God made the path and I am walking therein. Tell your husband work is plentiful here and he wont have to loaf if he want to work." Another person writing from Akron, Ohio, reported simply, "I am making good." Meanwhile, economic conditions improved somewhat for those who remained behind as labor grew scarce, even if little else changed.[22]

Unfortunately, race relations in the two sections once again renewed their parallel development to the detriment of all blacks. What changed this time was the situation for blacks in the North after 1900, and especially after the Great Migration. If the passage of a state segregation law in Louisiana in 1877 symbolized the shift in direction in the South, then Kansas's decision in 1903 to reverse thirty years of progress in school relations by enforcing segregation symbolized the North's retreat from social progress.[23] Republican hegemony during the Fourth Party System (1894–1932) eliminated the incentive to woo northern Negro voters, and the growing number of black migrants alarmed whites at the same time that a massive influx of foreigners provided formidable competitors for jobs and housing. Those blacks who went North thus initially found greater economic opportunity, but once the war was over they encountered the wrath of returning white veterans. Whites had already resorted to violence against blacks in the New York City race riot of 1900, but far more frightening and bloody were the Great Migration-induced riots in East St. Louis in 1917, Chicago in 1919, and elsewhere.[24] Although there were occasional riots in the South during these years as in New Orleans (1900), Atlanta (1906), and Houston (1917),[25] the most serious ones were in the North, reflecting the extent to which white southerners had succeeded in keeping blacks "in their place" compared to the continued relative openness of northern society.

The riots were only the most visible manifestation of the assault on black rights. De facto segregation once again became the norm in all areas of northern life, schools became more separate and unequal, blacks lost factory jobs and service positions as waiters, barbers, and caterers to white immigrants, and large-scale black ghettoes emerged not merely in response to the voluntary growth of black community life, but to white-orchestrated discrimination. Whether in New York's Harlem, Philadelphia's Seventh Ward, Chicago's South Side, or Baltimore's Druid Hill Avenue, the reality was depressingly similar. By 1920 in Chicago, for example, 35 percent of the city's blacks lived in census tracts that were more than 75 percent black; only 7.4 percent lived in neighborhoods less than 5 percent black, a sharp reduction from 32.7 percent in 1910.[26]

Black migration slowed in the 1920s, but the persistent decline of the cotton economy, the lure of jobs in the North, and hopes for greater personal dignity kept the movement going until the depression brought it to a halt. Southern blacks continued to leave the rural areas, but the more likely destination was the region's own cities rather than those in the North. Between 1930 and 1940 the percentage of black urban dwellers in the South increased from 31.7 percent to 36.5 percent while the northern black urban population merely went from 88.1 percent to 89.1 percent.[27]

Movement off the farms was often fostered by New Deal agricultural policies which rewarded white land-owners rather than black tenants. There were other ways in which the New Deal perpetuated racial discrimination—Civil Conservation Corps camps and public housing were segregated, greenbelt towns excluded blacks altogether, the National Recovery Administration allowed a wage differential for the South, and so on, but through its relatively color-blind relief policies and the publicized activities of enlightened key figures such as Eleanor Roosevelt and Harold Ickes, the New Deal brought northern blacks into the Democratic party and paved the way for the great changes that would follow.[28]

Nevertheless, as important as they were in preparing the way for future advances, neither the New Deal nor World War II (which was fought by a segregated armed forces) basically altered the pattern of race relations during the years between 1900 and 1954. A nascent protest movement in the North sought to end segregation, spearheaded in the courts by the NAACP and in the streets by the new Congress of Racial Equality, while those southern blacks and white liberals pushing for change initially sought truly equal separate treatment or an end to the vestiges of exclusion. Although in 1932 a communist-led interracial group defied the law requiring segregated seating at the Norfolk City Auditorium, more typical were demonstrations in the 1930s aimed at more equitable segregated treatment at Raleigh's War Memorial Auditorium, Richmond's Mosque Theater, and a "sit-down strike" at Alexandria, Virginia's whites-only public library.[29] But despite court suits, marches, sit-ins, bus and school boycotts, "don't-buy-where-you-can't-work" campaigns, and rent strikes that produced occasional victories, prospects for most blacks in the northern urban ghettoes seemed little different from those facing their largely rural southern counterparts. Symptomatic were the race riots in Harlem, Detroit, and Mobile during World War II, although in the South blacks were still more likely to be victims than to share the tendency of northern blacks to initiate their own riots out of frustration over their treatment.[30]

Yet a new era was approaching. Spurred on by black organizations like the NAACP and leaders such as Bayard Rustin, northern blacks effectively challenged the racial barriers against blacks in politics, education, employment, and public accommodations. Following less visible courtroom triumphs, and benefiting from a cold-war environment in which domestic racial discrimination had become an embarrassment abroad, the *Brown v. Board of Education* decision in 1954 ushered in our fifth period, the one in which we still live despite the momentous developments in the mid to late 1960s. And ironically, this period was to

resemble in many ways the years between 1867 and 1877 in that southern race relations came to be distinctive in a positive sense, for, although
met with sickening violence, the civil rights struggle seemed to bring
greater benefits to southern blacks than to their northern counterparts.

As eighty years before, the central elements of this "New Reconstruction," as C. Vann Woodward once termed it, were the federal
government and southern blacks. Yet thanks to the New Deal and the
continued migrations north, northern blacks, who formed a critical
voting bloc, also played a major role in forcing racial change in the
South. In the face of considerable white resistance, remarkable gains
were made by the forces of change that combined grass-roots black
protest with white liberal (some of it southern) and northern black
pressure on the federal government. In a relatively brief time, they
brought an end to legally enforced segregation (despite, as in the case
of the Montgomery bus boycott, an initial inclination to settle for the
more traditional aim of truly equal separate treatment), abolished the
poll tax and removed other barriers against black voting, and opened
new economic opportunities for a southern black population that was
by 1960 for the first time in history more than 50 percent urban.[31]

In retrospect, the process of change proved easier to accomplish
than most people had anticipated. That was because the primary aim
was to remove artificial bars to racial equality before the law. And contrary to widespread belief, but as the psychologist Thomas Pettigrew
correctly predicted in 1961, attitudes did not have to be first altered
in order to force changed behavior.[32]

The contrast with the North was again instructive; as circumstances
improved in the South, they seemed to worsen in the North. One week
after Lyndon Johnson signed the Voting Rights Act of 1965, the Watts
Riot ushered in a period of long hot summers during which it became
clear that the solution to racial inequality in this country required more
than the eradication of legalized segregation and the protection of the
ballot. More troubling were the serious economic imbalances and examples of de facto segregation that could not be altered through legislation or marches—be they in Selma or Cicero.[33] Court challenges to
or direct action against unjust southern laws could work because of a
growing consensus among whites, even in the South, that such barriers
were unfair; there was no such consensus regarding positive steps that
included busing, affirmative action, and scattered-site public housing to
make up for years of less formal discrimination in the North in the
areas of education, jobs, and housing.

The past thirty-five years, then, have brought marked progress in
southern race relations to the point where, to many, the South seems

to be, as its whites had so long falsely claimed it to be, the best place for blacks. Migration patterns suggest the recency of this development. Although the 1960s was the first decade in a hundred years during which more individuals moved into the South than out of it, it was not until the 1970s that more *blacks* moved from the North to the South than in the traditional reverse direction.[34] And no wonder. Darenda Mason, a black employment agency supervisor who had left Charlotte, North Carolina, for New Jersey in 1968, was amazed "at how much difference fifteen years has made." Explaining her reasons for returning South, she cited "changes in housing and employment opportunities, professional association, and civic and political leadership."[35]

Outside of Charlotte, the story is the same. Thanks to the Voting Rights Act of 1965, increased turnout among black registered voters, and an abatement of the racially charged political atmosphere of the 1950s and 1960s, there are now more elected black officials in the South than in any other region. Although the South contains just over 50 percent of the nation's black population, it had 62 percent of all elected black officeholders in 1987, well ahead of the North Central states with their 19.2 percent. Led by Mississippi's 548 officials in 1987, four of the five states with the most black officeholders are in the South, as are the next three highest. While concentrated on the local level, these officials include three congressmen, most notably Mike Espy of Mississippi, elected in 1986 and reelected in 1988 following two narrow defeats in the same district by another black, Robert Clark, a veteran state legislator.[36]

Most striking, however, was the election in 1989 of Lieutenant-Governor L. Douglas Wilder as governor of Virginia. The fifty-eight-year-old grandson of slaves, who began his political career as a young militant state senator from Richmond, thus became not only the South's, but also the nation's first elected black governor. To have received the Democratic nomination in the first place was remarkable enough, but to win in a state more than 80 percent white personified the changes at work in this region. As Wilder remarked during the campaign, "This is a far, far different state than it was when I got into politics 20 years ago. After all, I'm now the Lieutenant Governor. A lot of people have moved into the State. There's been a lot of economic and social change, particularly up around Washington and down around Norfolk." Arguing that he was "as Virginian as any Virginian," Wilder maintained that "This race will not be decided on race. Virginia has moved away from that." A less personally involved political scientist, Larry Sabato, agreed: "any effort by his opponent to make it an outright black-white race will backfire because the state has just grown and changed so much in recent years."[37]

To a certain extent such predictions proved too rosy. Despite pre-election polls which showed him well ahead of his Republican opponent, Wilder won by less than ten thousand votes and ran well behind other members of the statewide Democratic ticket. And some polling data suggest that race was more of a factor than anyone chose to admit. Yet several issues (especially abortion) were of greater concern than race to most voters, and, most tellingly, Wilder received an estimated 39 percent of the white vote, roughly the same percentage garnered by the previous two Democratic gubernatorial candidates. By contrast, on the same day, after a campaign involving many of the same issues but in which race was more central, David Dinkins was selected the first black mayor of New York City while attracting less than 30 percent of the white vote.[38]

The South seems less resistant to change in other respects as well. Schools in all sections remain heavily segregated, but since the early 1970s, southern schools have become more integrated than northern ones, in part because of the artificially forced nature of much of the original segregation and the success of busing and other court-ordered measures.[39] Residential segregation among blacks, although still high even when compared to other minorities, is generally less than in the North. Most recently, two sociologists, Douglas S. Massey and Nancy A. Denton, identified "a significant core of 10 large metropolitan areas within which blacks are very highly segregated on at least four dimensions of residential segregation." Containing 29 percent of all blacks in the United States, the cities were Baltimore (the only one even remotely southern), Chicago, Cleveland, Detroit, Milwaukee, Philadelphia, Gary, Los Angeles, New York, and St. Louis. The concentration and isolation of these black residents is so severe that Massey and Denton had to coin the term *hypersegregation* to describe it.[40]

Economic prospects for southern blacks compared to blacks elsewhere have improved thanks to the decline of northern industry, especially in the cities of the Northeast and Midwest, and the end of the South's separate labor market that had kept wages low and limited occupational choices. The latter point is especially important, for it reflects the transformation of southern agriculture since the 1940s. On the one hand, agriculture became more mechanized and on the other, its overall importance to the southern economy, while still great, declined. The effect was to lessen the region's historic dependence on a fixed labor supply for its plantation-style agriculture, a source of continuity that had long clashed with the free-labor ideology, if not always practice, of the rest of the country. With greater options for their labor, southern blacks were more likely to pursue both geographic and economic mobility, and to do so with less opposition from whites.[41]

While many migrants continued to look to the North and West, an increasing number cast their lot with the South's booming cities. For at least some, it must have been a wise choice. One study using 1980 census statistics ranked the nation's forty-eight metropolitan areas with a hundred thousand or more black residents in each of nine categories reflecting opportunities for black advancement in income and home-ownership and concluded that many of the most promising communities were in the South. Following Long Island among the five best economic communities for blacks were Miami, Columbia, Richmond, and Newport News-Hampton. The bottom five were Newark, Milwaukee, Chicago, Cleveland, and Buffalo.[42]

Perhaps most of all in accounting for the growing attractiveness of the South, blacks seem more comfortable there, whether because of the climate, slower pace of life, or because of southern whites themselves, whom most blacks view, at the least, as less hypocritical than northern whites. Too many blacks have encountered or heard about incidents such as that in California, where a department store manager wrote in a memo to her employees, "If any black person returns any sheet sets, refuse a cash voucher or exchange or credit for any reason."[43] As Taylor Wilson, a black electrician from Chicago whose father left Mississippi earlier in the century, said, "I'm moving South for the same reasons my father came here from Mississippi. He was looking for a better way of life."[44]

The South, then, still provides a distinctive environment for blacks, and its race relations are different. Yet now it is distinctive because despite its considerable failures, it seems better; and also, unlike in the past, the region seems to be truly departing from its troubling continuity dedicated to the maintenance of white supremacy. Even those blacks unwilling to place the South ahead of the North recognize the force of change in both sections. As William Cunningham, a Gadsden, Alabama, city councilman and rubber plant worker put it, "I do a lot of traveling, but I think it's just as bad up there [in the North]. I think people have a distorted view of the South."[45]

At this point I need to make my position explicit, lest it be misunderstood. I am not presenting a brief for the South. Nor do I wish to be thought Pollyannaish. There is still need for much improvement in the region's race relations, as the election of a Klan leader in Louisiana, the sending of letter bombs, or the march of racists in suburban Atlanta reminds us. And one could argue that the present-day South looks good only in relation to its own sorrowful past and the more severe problems in the North. But there is no denying that the break with the past is real and quite remarkable. Referring to what was, let us not forget, very recent systematic racial oppression, a black student at Selma High School told a reporter in 1985: "Try as you can, you can't believe that white people once treated black people that way. It seems like something that happened long, long ago."[46]

But what does the future hold? After all, as the journalist Harry Ashmore pointed out in 1958, the traditional elements of southern race relations seen as defining a distinctive South are in the past—disfranchisement, de jure segregation, the sharecropping system, and one-party rule.[47] Yet departure from the past while meaning an end to continuity does not necessarily mean an end to a distinctive pattern of southern race relations. In part this is due to the persistence of one aspect of historical southern continuity and distinctiveness. The South remains the region within the nation in which blacks are most concentrated. Although it is no longer the home for 90 percent of the nation's blacks as it was for most of our history and as late as 1900, it still contains more than 52 percent of the nation's blacks, who comprise 20 percent of the region's population.[48]

And thanks to the recent revolution in southern economic, political, and social life and a relatively homogeneous and paternalistically inclined white leadership, together with the new unattractiveness of the Northeast and Midwest, a majority of blacks will continue to remain in the South in the future, although they will be increasingly urban as in the North. If current trends continue, as they should, their numbers will be augmented by new or returning black migrants from other sections who seek a compatible place to work and raise families.

The presence of large numbers of blacks and the continued acceptance of them, as well as changing racial attitudes by whites, will bring additional blacks into political office, although growing Hispanic influence will present problems in Texas and Florida, the least "southern" of the former Confederate States. (That influence, often in contradictory ways, perhaps accounts for the relative, although still limited, success Republicans have had in attracting black voters, evidently largely middle class, in those states.)[49] There will be more councilmembers, state legislators, mayors, and governors to join Douglas Wilder—and U.S. senators as well. In the short run, however, a good deal will depend on the presence of high-visibility issues such as abortion which, as in Wilder's victory, are likely to undercut the effectiveness of racist appeals. And, of course, even more than is generally the case with southern white politicians, victorious black candidates will, again like Wilder, have to project a nonthreatening, moderate-to-conservative, "let's bring us together" image.

Political power will also contribute to greater economic power as blacks will benefit along with whites as the region continues to move forward economically; perhaps even lowly Mississippi (fiftieth in per capita income) will join the Sunbelt boom. Predictions about income are always risky, especially given the diversified nature of the southern economy and the region's growing ties to a global economy, but if recent trends are any guide, black economic status will continue to improve in absolute and relative terms, both within the region and compared to residents of other parts of the country. In 1939, for example, median income for black men was 67 percent of the white median income in both the Northeast and Midwest, 56 percent in the West, and only 43 percent in the South; the figures for women were 67 percent, 60 percent, 60 percent, and 31 percent. By 1984, southern blacks had sharply closed the income gap in all respects. While the median income for black men in the South was still only 56 percent that of whites, this represented the greatest improvement for any region, left the South ahead of the Midwest, and constituted the only instance in which the gap between whites and blacks had not worsened in the years since 1969. And the black male median income of $8,800 was for the first time greater than that of midwestern counterparts and was much closer to blacks and whites in other sections than it had normally been over the previous forty-five years. Southern black women did even better, so that by 1984, their median income was 84 percent that of southern whites, although this still trailed the other three sections including the West, where the black median income was actually slightly higher than the white one. In short, as the sociologists Reynolds Farley and Walter Allen argue, "Blacks in the South have always had smaller incomes than those in other regions, but the regional disparity has decreased." Equally encouraging for the future are 1979 figures which indicate that southern blacks were less plagued by unemployment than blacks in other sections. And of those who were employed in 1982, 10 percent held higher-status white-collar employment (banking, commerce, education, law, and medicine) compared to less than 3 percent as late as 1975.[50]

Increased per capita income will continue the present trend toward decreased forced residential segregation although there will always be blacks who, like members of other successful ethnic groups, prefer to live among "their own kind." Indexes of residential segregation will thus remain high despite years of progress reflected in declines in Atlanta from 94 in 1960, to 92 in 1970, to 86 in 1980; from 92 in 1960 and 1970 to 85 in 1980 in Memphis; and from 95 to 91 to 79 in

Richmond. During the same period, Chicago went from 89 to 92, Philadelphia from 87 to 88, and Cleveland remained at 91.[51] And more southern blacks will, like their counterparts elsewhere, move into often heavily, but not exclusively, black suburbs on the fringes of the region's major cities. As southerners increase their commitment to public education, the environment for learning will improve and the less segregated southern metropolitan areas and growing economic parity of the races will widen still further the gap between northern and southern prospects for meaningful desegregation.

Yet the future will also bring some of the problems that have long troubled the North. Some of these will involve changes in the rural areas, but for the first time in the region's history, the nature of southern race relations will depend most on what happens within the region's cities. Open housing legislation, altered attitudes, and economic realities will lead to similar kinds of residential succession struggles, unlike the past when space for black housing was often found on unwanted, undeveloped land; the influx of northerners, Asians, Hispanics, and others will create new sources of competition in a more multicultural and less biracial society; economic opportunities that cannot possibly keep pace with rising expectations will probably lead, as they did in the North in the 1960s, to urban race riots such as most recently in Miami, by those being left behind; the success of some blacks will widen the gap, with the lower or underclass trapped in blighted urban neighborhoods or the decaying countryside, and although forced segregation will be a thing of the past, it will not necessarily be replaced by integration.

The latter point is worth emphasizing because many well-meaning whites are already beginning to despair about the lack of integration now that artificial barriers to social interaction have been removed, especially in the schools. For example, David Fleischaker of Louisville, Kentucky, a white liberal who worked hard to bring the races together in local schools, created a highly charged debate by writing a column in a national magazine and appearing on Oprah Winfrey's television show to ask why, despite busing, his youngest children had no black friends and little contact with blacks in schools. "Segregation and integration look like tweedledum and tweedledee," he wrote. "Even the lunchroom looks like a segregated restaurant."

Hazel Lane, who had attended the largely black Duvalle Junior High School in western Louisville in the late 1950s, had a different reaction. She knew that meaningful change had occurred. Faced with second-hand books, old typewriters, and less rigorous classes, she made sure her children would have it better when fifteen years later she became a plaintiff in the lawsuit that led to busing and the merger of the city and county school systems. "What I wanted initially was that the schools would be equal," she said, and she believes that she succeeded. Three of her children were bused to high school and graduated with what she felt was a good education. Her son was one of the first black students from the South to visit the Soviet Union in an exchange program and, besides, "his very, very best friend was a white boy." She did not understand why Fleischaker was questioning the effectiveness of the city's busing program.[52]

Having white friends, of course, depends as much upon housing patterns, socioeconomic factors, common interests, and family attitudes. Mrs. Lane pointed correctly to the fact that "Social integration begins at home."[53] Yet it should not be forgotten that integration, while a hope for some, was not the primary goal of the civil rights movement; rather it was equal opportunity and freedom of choice. Blacks demanded to have access to the kinds of opportunities open to all other Americans. Such freedom of choice might indeed lead to a continuation of separate Negro churches, voluntary associations, colleges, neighborhoods, or even separate lunchroom tables at school. When truly voluntary, such separation, unlike so much of that in the past, would not represent a failure of American democracy, but rather confirmation that America is a pluralistic society in which one should not be prevented by artificial barriers from choosing where or with whom to work, play, and live. Ironically, given the region's tragic history, for the foreseeable future the prospects for such a reality seem most promising in the American South.

NOTES

Revisions for this chapter were completed while I was a Fellow at the Center for Advanced Study in the Behavioral Sciences. I am grateful for financial support provided by the Center, the National Endowment for the Humanities Grant #RA-20037–88, and The Andrew W. Mellon Foundation. I also want to thank the participants in the Center's seminar series, audiences at the Berkeley, San Diego, and Santa Barbara campuses of the University of California, and Michael Les Benedict, Peter Kolchin, August Meier, and Arthur Mann for their comments about earlier versions of this chapter.

1. For the experiences of other groups see, for example, James H. Merrell, "Some Thoughts on Colonial Historians and American Indians," *William and Mary Quarterly*, 3d ser., 46 (January 1989): 94–119; Ira Berlin and Herbert G. Gutman, "Natives and Immigrants, Free Men and Slaves: Urban Workingmen in the Antebellum South," *American Historical Review* 88 (December 1983): 1175–200; Lucy M. Cohen, *Chinese in the Post Civil War South: A People without a History* (Baton Rouge, 1984); Randall M. Miller and George E. Pozzetta, eds.,

Shades of the Sunbelt: Essays on Ethnicity, Race, and the Urban South (Westport, 1988).

2. For an extended discussion of the limits and possibilities of this approach that focuses on the pre-twentieth century, see Carl N. Degler, *Place over Time: The Continuity of Southern Distinctiveness* (Baton Rouge, 1977).

3. Winthrop D. Jordan, *White over Black: American Attitudes Toward the Negro 1550–1812* (Chapel Hill, 1968), chapters 1 and 2, passim. See also, Oscar Handlin and Mary F. Handlin, "Origins of the Southern Labor System," *William and Mary Quarterly*, 3d ser., 7 (April 1950): 199–222; Carl N. Degler, "Slavery and the Genesis of American Race Prejudice," *Comparative Studies in Society and History* 2 (October 1959): 49–66; Edmund S. Morgan, *American Slavery American Freedom: The Ordeal of Colonial Virginia* (New York, 1975); William M. Wiecek, "The Statutory Law of Slavery and Race in the Thirteen Mainland Colonies of British-America," *William and Mary Quarterly*, 3d ser., 34 (April 1977): 258–80.

4. Ira Berlin, "Time, Space, and the Evolution of Afro-American Society in British Mainland North America," *American Historical Review* 85 (February 1980): 44–78. See also, Allan Kulikoff, *Tobacco and Slaves: The Development of Southern Cultures in the Chesapeake, 1680–1800* (Chapel Hill, 1986).

5. Morgan, *American Slavery*, p. 386.

6. Berlin, "Time, Space, and Evolution of Afro-American Society," pp. 45–54, passim.

7. Carl L. Becker, *The Declaration of Independence: A Study in the History of Political Ideas* (New York, 1942), pp. 212–21; Paul Finkelman, "Slavery and the Constitutional Convention: Making a Covenant with Death," in *Beyond Confederation: Origins of the Constitution and American National Identity*, ed. Richard Beeman, Stephen Botein, and Edward C. Carter, II (Chapel Hill, 1987), pp. 188–225; Drew R. McCoy, "James Madison and Visions of American Nationality in the Confederation Period: A Regional Perspective," in *Beyond Confederation*, ed. Beeman, Botein, and Carter, pp. 226–58.

8. Richard C. Wade, "The Vesey Plot: A Reconsideration," *Journal of Southern History* 30 (May 1964): 143–61; Stephen B. Oates, *The Fires of Jubilee: Nat Turner's Fierce Rebellion* (New York, 1975).

9. Ira Berlin, *Slaves without Masters: The Free Negro in the Antebellum South* (New York, 1974); John Hope Franklin, *The Free Negro in North Carolina 1790–1860* (Chapel Hill, 1943).

10. Leon Litwack, *North of Slavery: The Negro in the Free States 1790–1860* (Chicago, 1961); Leonard P. Curry, *The Free Black in Urban America, 1800–1850: The Shadow of the Dream* (Chicago, 1981); Gary B. Nash, *Forging Freedom: The Formation of Philadelphia's Black Community, 1720–1840* (Cambridge, 1988); Shane White, " 'We Dwell in Safety and Pursue Our Honest Callings': Free Blacks in New York City, 1783–1810," *Journal of American History* 75 (September 1988): 445–70; Douglass quoted in August Meier and Elliott Rudwick, *From Plantation to Ghetto*, 3d ed. (New York, 1976), p. 96.

11. Litwack, *North of Slavery*, pp. 20–24, 66–74, Lincoln quoted, p. 276.

12. For the traditional assessment of Reconstruction, see William A. Dunning, *Reconstruction, Political and Economic 1865–1877* (New York, 1907) and Claude G. Bowers, *The Tragic Era: The Revolution after Lincoln* (Cambridge, 1929); for more recent (and accurate assessments), see John Hope Franklin, *Reconstruction after the Civil War* (Chicago, 1961) and Eric Foner, *Reconstruction: America's Unfinished Revolution 1863–1877* (New York, 1988).

13. Peter Kolchin, *First Freedom: The Responses of Alabama's Blacks to Emancipation and Reconstruction* (Westport, 1972); Roger L. Ransom and Richard Sutch, *One Kind of Freedom: The Economic Consequences of Emancipation* (New York, 1977); Harold D. Woodman, "Sequel to Slavery: The New History Views the Postbellum South," *Journal of Southern History* 43 (November 1977): 523–54.

14. Howard N. Rabinowitz, *Race Relations in the Urban South, 1865–1890* (New York, 1978); Howard N. Rabinowitz, "More Than the Woodward Thesis: Assessing *The Strange Career of Jim Crow*," *Journal of American History* 75 (December 1988): 842–56.

15. Foner, *Reconstruction*, pp. 223–24.

16. William Gillette, *Retreat from Reconstruction 1869–1879* (Baton Rouge, 1979).

17. Rabinowitz, *Race Relations in the Urban South*; J. Morgan Kousser, *The Shaping of Southern Politics: Suffrage Restriction and the Establishment of the One-Party South, 1880–1910* (New Haven, 1974); Joel Williamson, *The Crucible of Race: Black-White Relations in the American South since Emancipation* (New York, 1984); C. Vann Woodward, *Origins of the New South, 1877–1913* (Baton Rouge, 1951).

18. These generalizations about the nature of northern black life are based on a wide variety of studies including, David M. Katzman, *Before the Ghetto: Black Detroit in the Nineteenth Century* (Urbana, 1973); Kenneth L. Kusmer, *A Ghetto Takes Shape: Black Cleveland, 1870–1930* (Urbana, 1976); Elizabeth Hafkin Pleck, *Black Migration and Poverty: Boston, 1865–1900* (New York, 1979); W. E. B. DuBois, *The Philadelphia Negro: A Social Study* (Philadelphia, 1899); David A. Gerber, *Black Ohio and the Color Line, 1860–1915* (Urbana, 1976); Lawrence Grossman, *The Democratic Party and the Negro: Northern and National Politics, 1868–92* (Urbana, 1976).

19. Eric Foner, *Nothing but Freedom: Emancipation and Its Legacy* (Baton Rouge, 1983).

20. Bureau of the Census, *Negro Population, 1790–1915* (Washington, 1918), pp. 90–91.

21. Woodward, *Origins of the New South*; Kousser, *Shaping of Southern Politics*; Williamson, *Crucible of Race*, part 2; Paul M. Gaston, *The New South Creed: A Study in Southern Mythmaking* (New York, 1970); Louis R. Harlan, *Separate and Unequal: Public School Campaigns and Racism in the Southern Seaboard States, 1901–1915* (Chapel Hill, 1958).

22. *Defender* quoted in Alan H. Spear, *Black Chicago: The Making of a Negro Ghetto 1890–1920* (Chicago, 1967), p. 135; migrants quoted in "Additional Letters of Negro Migrants of 1916–1918" [collected under the direction of

119

Emmett J. Scott], *Journal of Negro History* 4 (October 1919): 457, 465; see also, Florette Henri, *Black Migration: Movement North, 1900–1920: The Road from Myth to Man* (New York, 1975); Peter Gottlieb, *Making Their Own Way: Southern Blacks' Migration to Pittsburgh, 1916–30* (Urbana, 1987); James R. Grossman, *Land of Hope: Chicago, Black Southerners, and the Great Migration* (Chicago, 1989).

23. J. Morgan Kousser, "Before *Plessy*, Before *Brown*: The Development of the Law of Racial Integration in Louisiana and Kansas," California Institute of Technology Social Science Working Paper 681, October 1988.

24. See, for example, Gilbert Osofsky, *Harlem: The Making of a Ghetto: Negro New York, 1890–1930* (New York, 1966), pp. 46–52; Elliott M. Rudwick, *Race Riot at East St. Louis, July 2, 1917* (Carbondale, 1964); William M. Tuttle, Jr., *Race Riot: Chicago in the Red Summer of 1919* (New York, 1970).

25. William Ivy Hair, *Carnival of Fury: Robert Charles and the New Orleans Race Riot of 1900* (Baton Rouge, 1976); Ray Stannard Baker, *Following the Color Line* (New York, 1908); Arthur I. Waskow, *From Race Riot to Sit-In: 1919 and the 1960s* (New York, 1967).

26. Spear, *Black Chicago*, p. 142. For the causes and effects of growing discrimination on northern blacks see Kusmer, *A Ghetto Takes Shape*; Gerber, *Black Ohio*; Gottlieb, *Making Their Own Way*; Henri, *Black Migration*; Osofsky, *Harlem*; Spear, *Black Chicago*; Thomas Lee Philpott, *The Slum and the Ghetto: Neighborhood Deterioration and Middle-Class Reform, Chicago, 1880–1930* (New York, 1978).

27. U. S. Bureau of the Census, *Historical Statistics of the United States: Colonial Times to 1970*, part 1 (Washington, 1970), p. 22.

28. See, for example, Harvard Sitkoff, *A New Deal for Blacks: The Emergence of Civil Rights as a National Issue: The Depression Decade* (New York, 1978); Nancy J. Weiss, *Farewell to the Party of Lincoln: Black Politics in the Age of FDR* (Princeton, 1983).

29. August Meier and Elliott Rudwick, "The Origins of Nonviolent Direct Action in Afro-American Protest: A Note on Historical Discontinuities" in *Along the Color Line: Explorations in the Black Experience*, ed. August Meier and Elliott Rudwick (Urbana, 1976), pp. 307–44, especially p. 341.

30. Dominic J. Capeci, Jr., *The Harlem Riot of 1943* (Philadelphia, 1977); Robert Shogan and Tom Craig, *The Detroit Race Riot [1943]: A Study in Violence* (New York, 1976); James A. Burran, "Urban Racial Violence in the South during World War II," paper presented at the Citadel Conference on the "New South," Charleston, April 20–22, 1978.

31. For the best introduction to these momentous times, see C. Vann Woodward, *The Strange Career of Jim Crow*, 3d rev. ed. (New York, 1974), chapters 4–5, but for the problems involved in substituting "Second" for "New" Reconstruction, see Rabinowitz, "More than the Woodward Thesis," pp. 851-53. For an especially good discussion of the conflicting approaches to the civil rights movement, see Charles W. Eagles, ed., *The Civil Rights Movement in America* (Jackson, 1986). For the slow journey of southern white liberals from a separate but equal to an integrationist orientation, see Morton Sosna, *In Search of the Silent South: Southern Liberals and the Race Issue* (New York, 1977) and John T.

Kneebone, *Southern Liberal Journalists and the Issue of Race, 1920–1944* (Chapel Hill, 1985). The nation's black population as a whole had surpassed the 50 percent urban figure in 1950, Bureau of the Census, *Historical Statistics*, p. 22, and Reynolds Farley, "The Urbanization of Negroes in the United States," *Journal of Social History* 1 (Spring 1968): 241–58. For the initial aim of truly equal separate treatment in Montgomery, see Martin Luther King, Jr., *Stride Toward Freedom: The Montgomery Story* (New York, 1958), pp. 63–64.

32. Thomas Pettigrew, "Social Psychology and Desegregation Research," *American Psychologist* 16 (March 1961): 105–12.

33. William Julius Wilson, *The Declining Significance of Race: Blacks and Changing American Institutions*, 2d ed. (Chicago, 1980); Woodward, *Strange Career*, chapter 6.

34. Marcus E. Jones, *Black Migration in the United States with Emphasis on Selected Central Cities* (Saratoga, Calif., 1980), pp. 97–98.

35. Quoted in David R. Goldfield, *Promised Land: The South since 1945* (Arlington Heights, 1987), p. 216.

36. "South Leads in Black Officeholders," *Southern Changes* 9 (December 1987): 25; Bill Minor, "Congressman Espy from Mississippi," *Southern Changes* 8 (December 1986): 1–3; for the changed political environment in the South, see Alexander P. Lamis, *The Two-Party South*, exp. ed. (New York, 1988).

37. New York *Times*, April 16, 1989, sec. 1, p. 22.

38. *Time*, November 20, 1989, pp. 54–57; New York *Times*, November 8, 1989, pp. 1, 14-16. For the centrality of race in the New York City mayoral campaign, see Joe Klein, "The Real Thing," *New York Magazine*, November 13, 1989, pp. 16, 19–20.

39. Gary Orfield et al., *School Segregation in the 1980s: Trends in the United States and Metropolitan Areas* (Washington, 1987); Sar A. Levitan, William B. Johnston, and Robert Taggart, *Still a Dream: The Changing Status of Blacks since 1960* (Cambridge, 1975), pp. 279–83; New York *Times*, January 16, 1972, sec. 1, p. 60.

40. Douglas S. Massey and Nancy A. Denton, "Hypersegregation in U.S. Metropolitan Areas: Black and Hispanic Segregation Along Five Dimensions," *Demography* 26 (August 1989): 373–91. See also, Douglas S. Massey and Nancy A. Denton, "Trends in the Residential Segregation of Blacks, Hispanics, and Asians: 1970–1980," *American Sociological Review* 52 (December 1987): 802–25; Reynolds Farley and Walter R. Allen, *The Color Line and the Quality of Life in America* (New York, 1987), pp. 141, 143, 145.

41. On economic problems in the Northeast and Midwest, see William Julius Wilson, *The Truly Disadvantaged: The Inner City, the Underclass, and Public Policy* (Chicago, 1987); on the integration of the South into the national labor market see, Gavin Wright, *Old South, New South: Revolutions in the Southern Economy since the Civil War* (New York, 1986), chapters 6–8; for the emergence of Atlanta's black middle class, perhaps the region's most visible and successful, see Peter Ross Range, "Capital of Black-Is-Bountiful," *New York Times Magazine*, April 7, 1974, pp. 28–29, 68–78.

42. William O'Hare, "The Best Metros for Blacks," *American Demographics* 8 (July 1986): 26–33.

43. "Business Outlook," Albuquerque *Journal*, July 11, 1988, p. 29.

44. Quoted in Goldfield, *Promised Land*, p. 216.

45. Quoted in *Wall Street Journal*, February 25, 1988, p. 15.

46. Quoted in Wright, *Old South, New South*, p. 269.

47. Harry Ashmore, *An Epitaph for Dixie* (New York, 1958).

48. Bureau of the Census, U.S. Department of Commerce, *Statistical Abstract of the United States, 1988, Negro Population* (Washington, 1987), p. 24.

49. Lamis, *The Two-Party South*, p. 296.

50. Farley and Allen, *The Color Line*, pp. 300–303, 238–39, quote, 301; Goldfield, *Promised Land*, p. 216.

51. Farley and Allen, *The Color Line*, pp. 140-45; Massey and Denton, "Trends in Residential Segregation." Compare the more recent advances in southern residential desegregation with the pessimistic findings based on trends down to 1960 in Karl E. Taeuber and Alma F. Taeuber, *Negroes in Cities: Residential Segregation and Neighborhood Change* (New York, 1969).

52. Louisville *Courier Journal*, August 5, 1988, metropolitan section, pp. 1 and 6.

53. Ibid., p. 1.

5

The View from Atlanta:
Southern Women and the Future

MARGARET RIPLEY WOLFE

The time is evening, February 10, 1988; the place, Atlanta; the setting, the Robert W. Woodruff Arts Center. Delegates have just toured the High Museum of Art, a modern Le Corbusier-like structure, designed by Richard Meier and gathered at the Atlanta College of Art for a reception. The entrance hall is packed, and the noise level rises. Bits of conversation waft through the din of voices: "I first met Bella [Abzug] in Nairobi"; "I've been a feminist all my life"; "I knew them all—Steinem, Friedan. . . ."; "I'm from a little no-name place in Georgia. My mother was widowed. She was a strong woman."

Two understated limousines arrive with a retinue of Secret Service men and motorcycle police. Two well-coiffed and elegantly dressed women emerge and make their way through the pressing crowd. They are native-born southern white women, former First Ladies Lady Bird Johnson and Rosalynn Carter, hostesses for a national—yes, even international—gathering. Sponsored by the Carter Center at Emory University, Georgia State University, and the Jimmy Carter Library, the symposium Women and the Constitution: A Bicentennial Perspective is officially under way. Literally and figuratively, it has been a long road from the first women's rights convention in 1848 at Seneca Falls, an isolated rural village in upstate New York, to Atlanta, the pulsating, self-proclaimed capital of the New South.

Atlanta is the site of Spelman College, the nation's first college for black women, which opened in 1881, and southern belles, those mobile bouquets of pastel ruffles, have been known to parade the streets of this clay-hill city during Fourth of July celebrations. "The typical Atlantan," according to a visitor's guide, is a female in a metropolitan area where women account for 52 percent of the 2.4 million population. She is twenty-nine years old, earns $19,118 a year, is married, and has one child. Chances are one in three that she was born outside Georgia. If she is not a southern native, she nonetheless is mortally in danger of being co-opted into the regional culture. Can this be the city where

123

General Sherman, "an able man . . . a kind of careless man about fire" created the inferno from which Prissy, Miss Melanie, and Miss Scarlett fled?[1]

Change is something of a universal constant, and to say that the status and role of women has changed in the South since the Civil War is a gross understatement, the dimensions of which can be gauged in part by the publication in 1982 of a handbook for pregnant miners.[2] One might be encouraged to exaggerate possibilities for the future and speculate about southern women astronauts reaching for the stars; Rhea Seddon of Murfreesboro, Tennessee, has been a crew member on a space-shuttle mission.[3] A black woman, Nikki Giovanni, from Knoxville has volunteered that she would like to be the first poet in space. "There should be a black woman in space and if it couldn't be a black woman, it should be a woman from Appalachia," she added. "We need some-body in space who would recognize life if they saw it."[4] One might even marvel about the possibilities of producing the children of Dixie by artificial insemination and in vitro fertilization, but southern ladies gen-erally prefer more conventional methods. There is a thing called history, however, more specifically southern history, where the reality of change is rivaled only by the reality of continuity.

In the novel *Waterland* by Graham Swift, "a curly-haired boy called Price" who is a student of the narrator, Tom Crick, "a teacher-baiter, a lesson spoiler," jolts his teacher with the observation that "the only important thing about history . . . is that it's got to the point where it's probably about to end."[5] This work is predicated on the assumption that history is not "probably about to end." It may be that those who ignore the lessons of history are doomed to repeat them. It may also be that those who attempt to predict the future are merely doomed. The historian's training provides little if any direction for this quest. Indeed, neophytes have been admonished to avoid the present tense, pen their prose in past tense, and forget the future perfect. To probe the future is a quantum leap into the unknown and a license to cross disciplinary boundaries and even to seek truth in unlikely places.

Fortunately, some intellectual perspective on the future has already been established and provides some source of comfort for a historian whose only road maps for the future are the navigational charts of the past. Willis W. Harman in *An Incomplete Guide to the Future* offers six underlying principles governing societies and social systems: (1) conti-nuity, (2) self-consistency, (3) similarities, (4) cause-effect relationships, (5) holistic trending, and (6) goal seeking. He also adds a word of cau-tion: "It is particularly difficult to overcome the bias that results from being immersed in a particular culture—from living in a particular area of the globe at a particular time in history. One is a product of his culture."[6] Robert L. Heilbroner in *The Future as History* observes that "an attitude of optimism, for all its emphasis on personal striving and accomplishment . . . rests on a judgement about our historic capacities. At bottom, *a philosophy of optimism is an historic attitude toward the future.*"[7] Furthermore, the future is a reflection or mirror of the past predicated on a judgment call about the inevitability of progress. Heilbroner argues that a waning of confidence has occurred, that American optimism has reached an impasse, and that the possible has limitations.[8] Feminists routinely insist, joined by women who abhor the label, as have Annie Cheatham and Mary Clare Powell in *This Way Daybreak Comes* that "if we are going to have a future world different from the one we have now—i.e., a world safe to live in—women are the best hope for getting us there."[9] Nonetheless, the so-called experts are sometimes pessimistic about the future and what it holds for Americans.[10]

The dawning of the twenty-first century appears to be a boon to futurists, troublesome for mystics, and inspirational to a wide assortment of groups and individuals. The American Association of University Women Educational Foundation conducted a conference in Washington, D.C., during June 1988 entitled "Preparing for the 21st Century: Who Will Shape Society's Agenda?" A report of the ad hoc Committee on the Future of the American Historical Association has noted, "We have seen the future and it needs work."[11] Obviously, the occult and fantastic are on the rise when a May 1988 Associated Press story could be headlined, "Summit: The Gipper Visits the 'Evil Empire.' "[12] According to White House chief of staff Donald T. Regan, Nancy Reagan relied upon and was influenced by astrology, thereby giving new meaning to the Reagan administration's "star wars" agenda.[13] For the record, Nancy Reagan's mother, Edith Luckett Davis, was a southern-born woman whose own mother had retreated to Petersburg, Virginia, from the nation's capital for the birth of her children, because she refused, as she put it, to bring a "damned Yankee" into the world. Nancy Davis Reagan herself spent much of her childhood in Bethesda, Maryland.[14] The new age movement with its emphasis on the magical powers of crystals has set people to digging for quartz, both legally and illegally, in the Quachita National Forest of west central Arkansas.[15] Veins of earthy wisdom, however, lie virtually untapped at Jimmy Carter's (no relation to the former president, apparently) emporium, gateway to Myrtle Beach, near Florence, South Carolina, where one plaque reads, "A woman should know how to look like a girl, act like a lady, think like a man, and work like a dog."[16]

Much of the American experience has been undergirded with "ritual optimism" according to Peter Schrag in *The End of the American Future*, and historian Henry F. May in *The End of American Innocence* identifies "inveterate optimism" as "a permanent flaw in American nineteenth-century thought."[17] Phrases like *mission, destiny,* and the *pursuit of happiness* reverberate through the masculine realm, whereas *responsibility, duty,* and *service* characterize the feminine past. Women have often been subject to diminished expectations. Janet Zollinger Geile in *Women and the Future: Changing Sex Roles in Modern America* observes that presently "women are disproportionately found in peripheral positions that society has undervalued; men, on the other hand, are more frequently found in core positions that draw attention and command greater social rewards." She perceives "the future challenge to society as one of learning how to engage in both affirmative action and institutional change."[18]

If the past is a guide, women should approach the future with caution. In a cleverly turned phrase, Tish Sommers, a self-described free-lance agitator on matters pertaining to women and aging, calls tomorrow "a woman's issue."[19] Some women have had to believe in the future because their present has been unpalatable. It has not been unusual for southern women to trust in the Rock of Ages, wrap themselves in piety, and wait for their rewards in eternity.[20] Many others have comforted themselves with the notion that their sacrifices have been justified because "the children, after all, [carry] the hopes of the family into the future."[21] Nevertheless, the dominant southern culture, masculine and feminine, has drawn and continues to draw heavily on the past. Indeed, on a more personal level, it is all too easy to find contemporary middle-aged women who sustain themselves with the warm nostalgia of cheerleading squads, homecoming parades, and "sweet sixteen" parties. Since at least the late nineteenth century, however, and perhaps earlier, a vanguard of southern women—a small minority—have subscribed to a notion of progress in which human beings take a hand and make "a conscious effort to reach a better world" which can "be glimpsed, or at least imagined, in the future."[22]

In Atlanta during February 1988, that vanguard was in full array—the foot soldiers of the civil rights and recent women's movements, the lawyers and professors, political partisans, clubwomen, and even survivors of "Ladies for Lyndon" and "The Peanut Brigade." Former President Jimmy Carter appeared before the delegates assembled in the Grand Ballroom of the Hilton Hotel with a crowd-pleasing self-introduction as "the son of Lillian, the husband of Rosalynn, the father of Amy, and the grandfather of Sarah and Maggie." Michigan Lieutenant Governor Martha W. Griffiths, a former congresswoman, reminded the audience that this nation was *not* born in Philadelphia but in wigwams, log cabins, and places of every description across America "out of the agony of women." United States Supreme Court Associate Justice Sandra Day O'Connor noted that from her office, she views a red-brick building, the home of the mother of the Equal Rights Amendment, Alice Paul, and the headquarters of the National Woman's party. Coretta Scott King prophesied that women "might just save this nation from its pending appointment with Armageddon." Erma Bombeck added levity when she observed that the only thing that females have to fear from unisex restrooms is having to clean them. Judy Carter, daughter-in-law of the First Family from Plains, explained that she had toiled for ratification of the ERA so when her grandchildren asked what she had done in the movement that she would not have to say, "I gave at the office." Delegates signed petitions for reintroduction of the ERA in the United States Congress and volunteered their time and money. In the closing moments, Lady Bird Johnson pronounced the symposium "a feast of the mind and spirit."[23]

The Women and the Constitution Symposium was a heady, exhilarating experience, a giant feminist pep rally. It occurred in the South, it was hosted by southern-born wives of presidents, and southern women were in attendance. It would be simple-minded, however, to overrate this event because the chasm that separates the overwhelming majority of southern women and the delegates to this event is staggering. Economics alone would have prevented the majority of southern women from even attending such a meeting. This observation is not intended to discredit that event, merely to put it in perspective. To their credit, the organizers, through a few scholarships, made an effort to promote diversity. Still, it is likely that the women who did not or could not attend need feminist reforms more than those in attendance and that the elitist sisterhood is more often than not out of touch with the sisters.

In the quest for equal rights, southern women have possessed a triple handicap: (1) the stigma sometimes associated with being southern, that is, the full weight of southern history, mythology, and legends; (2) the limitations of being female and the enduring, constraining images of the belle and the lady; and (3) the hamstrings of race applicable directly to the experience of black women and somewhat less directly but just as relevantly to white females. Gender, of course, is a common denominator, but gender does not transcend race, class, point of view, and a host of other factors. Soft-pedaling race and class may be good internal strategy within the feminist movement, but this approach is poor historical methodology in an external context.[24] Regional manifestations of feminism that are different from the New England model also occur.[25]

127

For example, southern women subscribe without hesitation to concepts of *equality* and *partnership* with men more often than not. At the same time, they recoil from the label *feminist* or the word *feminism* and disdain the old symbolic gestures of bra burning and male baiting.

Nontraditional assignments do not lend themselves well to conventional methodology. The analysis herein is both academic and empirical as well as impressionistic. Many who study and write women's history are searching for themselves. Even if unaware of the quest for self, they probably reflect themselves anyway. Taking a stand does not necessarily preclude or negate good scholarship. Furthermore, women's studies is grounded in political activism and can hardly escape praxis—putting theory into action. I believe in human rights—I also believe that women are human and I admit to being a born-again feminist.[26] Furthermore, as a wife for almost a quarter of a century and the mother of a teenage daughter, I agree with the historian Carl N. Degler's thesis that the family has been a barrier to American women's aspirations for individual autonomy and self-fulfillment.[27] In his exasperating book *The Failure of Feminism*, Nicholas Davidson declares that every feminist he has known has two predictable elements in her life story, an unusually strained relationship with her father and having been a tomboy as a girl.[28] The author confesses to the latter but emphatically refutes the first.

Being emotionally mature enough to find humor in life and still being physically able to laugh are great advantages of middle-age and effective antidotes for poisonous, dark hours of the soul. Even with life experiences that span a wide spectrum of the female life-cycle and being not so very far from that stage that Erma Bombeck terms "between estrogen and death," I cannot, indeed dare not, speak for all southern feminist historians, much less all southern females. It is relatively safe to say, however, given the historical record, that southern women can glimpse the future with cautious optimism.

Despite the quintessential symbol of the southern lady that hovers over women below the Mason-Dixon line, the daughters of Dixie are remarkably diverse,[29] a historical truism likely to persist, even intensify, in the future. As the purveyor of culture and tradition, the southern lady has been expected to possess the traits of "modesty, chastity, meekness, godliness, and compassion."[30] Grady McWhiney's study of the Celtic connections of the South, however, calls attention to "the uninhibited conduct of the plain folk," both men and women. Observers declared that feminine modesty was rare, that southerners swapped their wives like cattle, and that licentiousness, fornication, and adultery were common.[31] The sociosexual subjugation of black women by white masters is a matter of historical record.[32]

128

Typecasting of southern women is a treacherous business for a historian. The most cursory examination of the nameless and faceless undermines favored assumptions. Consider, for example, the matrilocal residence pattern of southern Native Americans; males lived in the household of their wives' lineage, and property belonged to the wives' families.[33] Remember the seventeenth-century indentured white women of the Chesapeake, outnumbered by men three to one and certain to find husbands if they wanted them.[34] Note the deprivation of the women of the Carolina backcountry of the 1760s, without eating utensils and undergarments.[35] Do not forget the "soiled sisters," those women of pleasure, to be found in such cities as Nashville, Richmond, and New Orleans.[36] Observe the toil of poor white girls who became human cogs in the southern textile industry.[37]

Attach names to these diverse faces. Sit with Virginian Nancy Langhorne Astor, the first woman in the British House of Commons, or pose with her sister, Irene, the model for her husband Charles Dana Gibson's "Gibson girl."[38] Go back to Grabtown, South Carolina, where Lucy Johnson was born on December 24, 1922; movie-goers knew her as Ava Gardner.[39] Take a cruise on the *Monkey Business* with 1988 Democratic presidential hopeful Gary Hart and South Carolina Phi Beta Kappa Donna Rice.[40] Take the oath of office with Governor-elect Martha Layne Collins of Kentucky.[41] Look at the studio filled with beautiful prizes," as the camera zooms in on the heaving bosom of "Wheel of Fortune's" Vanna White from North Myrtle Beach.[42] Prowl the streets of New Orleans with televangelist Jimmy Swaggart and stop off at the Travel Inn Motel for an afternoon with Debra Murphee.[43] Cross enemy lines in a transsexual disguise with Pauline Cushman, a southern actress, who toasted Confederates at Wood's Theatre in Louisville and went south as a federal agent.[44] Travel from Packard, Kentucky, to the bright lights of Broadway with Patricia Neal and then to Hollywood for a blighted, abortion-scarred romance with Gary Cooper.[45] Sit on death row in North Carolina with Velma Barfield in 1984.[46] Stand with Margaret Bowen when she leads a walkout in 1929 at German-owned rayon plants in Elizabethton, Tennessee.[47] Live with Eula Hall, the founding mother of the Mud Creek Clinic in eastern Kentucky, who subscribes to the battle cry of Mother Jones, "Pray for the dead and fight like hell for the living," and who declares that "you never know when you're going to have to get a bunch of women and take to the hills" to fight the strip miners.[48] Do not forget Rosa Louise Parks in Montgomery, or other noble black women like Harriet Tubman, Septima Poinsette Clark, Fannie Lou Hamer, and Bernice Robinson.[49]

The present is the busy intersection of the past and the future. Three of Harman's six principles for future research are continuity, self-consistency, and similarities among social systems. Generally, he observes, social systems exhibit continuity and change smoothly, although such events as the French Revolution and the American Civil War present some exceptions. Furthermore, societies tend to be internally consistent, the various segments interacting with rather than contradicting each other. Finally, although individuals within societies may differ, social systems possess certain anthropological similarities.[50]

Even with the remarkable diversity of personalities and the varieties of experiences to be found among southern women, a common thread binds them. They are, after all, products of their respective times and places and peculiar regional culture. Much of the tenor of their history and the region's has derived from slavery and the rural life-styles of the South, a legacy that has carried over into the twentieth century. Three-fourths of the families of the antebellum South owned no slaves, and the majority of slaveowners possessed fewer than twenty chattels. Nonetheless, the minority at the top of the heap determined, to a considerable extent, the nature of southern culture. Plantation mistresses constituted an intricate component of the productive and reproductive units of slave society, those island communities in the great expanse of the southern landscape. Isolation and economic bondage made home, as these women knew it, dramatically different from their northern counterparts. Male heads of the plantation households dominated extended families of wives, children, and slaves and exercised a paternalism more far-reaching than that north of the Mason-Dixon line.[51] The degree of that paternalism and the pattern that it established intensified the subordination of women, making it all the more difficult for southern women to extricate themselves from positions of inferiority.

Yet, in some respects, southern women have not been unlike their northern sisters; they share the commonality of a life-cycle that encompasses the reproductive years from menarche to menopause, and they are all Americans. "Contrary to what some have implied," Degler remarked in his 1986 presidential address before the Southern Historical Association, "American history is not simply a northern product that for some reason has failed to transform the South. Neither region identifies the nation; both are its creators simply because each has been different." American history "is something more than simply a scrappy dialogue between North and South," it is "the *interaction* of North and South—a Hegelian synthesis that has emerged from the dialectic of a southern thesis and a northern antithesis."[52]

At this juncture, a review of the plot-line of southern women's history is in order. The players have been a subgroup within a societal continuum that has yielded to and sometimes shaped the external forces of a larger historical drama. It is safe to acknowledge that the great majority of southern women have succumbed to the status quo; some, perhaps many, have lent it support and worked to reinforce it. A few have resented it, and even fewer have railed against it. If southern women—blacks, whites, and Native Americans—enjoyed any flexibility in status from the colonial era through the early national period, that flexibility diminished as the nation and the region matured. Burdened by arduous labor and seemingly incessant childbearing and cut off from extensive social contacts and outside influences, the antebellum southern women had few opportunities to challenge the paternalistic order that had so firmly entrenched itself.

The coming of the Civil War displaced individuals as well as traditional roles, and, temporarily at least, disrupted male dominion over everyday life. Anne Firor Scott has persuasively addressed the impact of the Civil War and Reconstruction on southern women. "The challenge of war," she writes, "called women almost at once into new kinds and new degrees of activities. . . . southern women were changing to meet the changed time," all of which "would become increasingly apparent as the century wore on." The "new southern woman," who might have joined a ladies' club or temperance society or crusaded for suffrage, was not unlike the "new American woman" of the late-nineteenth and early-twentieth centuries. More so than ever before, a few southern women found themselves in step with the American feminist vanguard. If, however, "functionally the patriarchy was dead, though many ideas associated with it lived on for years," as Scott maintains, southern men managed to recoup their temporary losses in public affairs.[53] Nonetheless, southern female activists developed public roles for women.

Coming to terms with activist women in the South—indigenous and nonindigenous, black and white—requires more attention to the subtleties of reform and the nuances of women's life and work than to the grand historical schemes of war, diplomacy, and politics; but Joan W. Scott identifies an implicit irony in historical arguments. "The subject of war, diplomacy, and high politics frequently comes up," she observes, "when traditional political historians question the utility of gender in their work." She argues further that "power relations among nations and the status of colonial subjects have been made comprehensible (and thus legitimate) in terms of relations between male and female," that is, "the need to defend otherwise vulnerable women and children" and "the duty of sons to serve their leaders or their [father the] king, and of associations between masculinity and national strength." Scott adds that "gender is one of the recurrent references by which political power has been conceived, legitimated, and criticized. It refers to but also establishes the meaning of the male/female opposition."[54]

Beginning in the late-nineteenth century, scattered groups of southern women constituting a definite minority of females in the region launched serious efforts to reform southern public culture. These collective efforts, which in large part have involved the struggles of southern women to extricate themselves from the constraints of privatism, continued into the twentieth century.[55] The private-public dichotomy has been overworked in women's historiography, but, as Linda K. Kerber notes, "The metaphor remains resonant because it retains some superficial vitality":

> For all our vaunted modernity, for all that men's "spheres" and women's "spheres" now overlap, vast areas of our experience and our consciousness do not overlap. The boundaries may be fuzzier, but our private spaces and our public spaces are still in many important senses gendered. The reconstruction of gender relations, and of the spaces that men and women may claim, is one of the most compelling contemporary social tasks. It is related to major social questions: the feminization of poverty, equal access to education and the professions, relations of power and abuses of power in the public sector and in the family. On a wider stage, the reconstruction of gender relations is related to major issues of power, for we live in a world in which authority has traditionally validated itself by its distance from the feminine and from what is understood to be effeminate.[56]

In the late-nineteenth-century South, whatever mitigating private influences may have been at work to cope with human misery, gross inequities and callousness characterized the public arena. In this milieu, southern female activists developed public roles for women. The first generation from the 1890s to the 1920s derived their strength from church groups, women's clubs, and such progressive efforts as prohibition, suffrage, and social welfare. The second generation were post-suffragettes, who from the 1920s to the 1950s concentrated on anti-lynching, labor education and organizing, and limited racial integration. The third generation of the post-1950s was at least partially a product of the civil rights movement. The lowly status accorded women by their male counterparts in New Left organizations also spurred them toward militant feminism. While there are some nebulous ties between the two earlier generations, the third emerged quite ignorant of the other two, only to discover them later as a result of feminist research and women's studies programs concomitant to a phase of the recent women's movement.

Describing and analyzing the lives of southern women historically is a "report from the trenches" in a field of research that is relatively new. When the recent wave of "organized feminism was born," according to John Demos, "it expressed an anguished cry from the depths of oppression. The plot-line of women's history ever since has been a stop-and-go effort to escape those depths—or, stated in less extreme terms, to push back the limits of constraints."[57] Sharon McKern, author of *Redneck Mothers, Good Ol' Girls and Other Southern Belles*, has observed that southerners from their earliest years have been taught two separate histories—one learned "in school, in the company of other children" and the other, "after supper, in the company of fireflies and chiggers, on the veranda." Family tales revolved around ancestors, especially "strong *female* forebears," who had done nothing more remarkable than survive.[58] Storytelling is a way of outwitting reality, according to Graham Swift.[59] Maybe that explains McKern's remembrances, for much of the recorded history of the South has provided scant attention to and little understanding of the southern woman. That written history itself has been shaped by cultural prejudices and biases, and it remains to be seen what impact the serious study of women's history may have on the future of the South.

Feminist scholars who cultivate the fertile field of southern women's history have amassed a considerable body of useful literature. Landmark studies include Julia Cherry Spruill's *Women's Life and Work in the Southern Colonies* (1938), A. Elizabeth Taylor's articles on the suffrage crusade in several southern states, and her book, *The Woman Suffrage Movement in Tennessee* (1957). Scott's *The Southern Lady: From Pedestal to Politics, 1830–1930* appeared in 1970 and heralded a new era in the study of southern women's history. Timely and seminal, it signified the developing interest in southern women as historical figures and inspired graduate students as well as established scholars to undertake major projects.

Biography has proved to be a useful historical vehicle, especially for an emerging specialty. Gerda Lerner's pioneering *The Grimké Sisters of South Carolina: Rebels Against Slavery* appeared in 1967. During the 1970s, such scholars as Paul E. Fuller and Jacquelyn Dowd Hall continued this approach with fine studies of Laura Clay and Jessie Daniel Ames respectively.[60] Detailing the lives of activists and the upper classes has always held an attraction for historians,[61] but specialists in southern women's studies have moved beyond biographical and elitist strategies, among them, Suzanne Lebsock, Julia Kirk Blackwelder, and Jacqueline Jones.[62] The prize-winning *Like a Family: The Making of a Southern Cotton Mill World* by Hall and others is in keeping with the move away from

133

elitism. Nonetheless, scholars surely know more of planter-class women already studied by Catherine Clinton and their relations with the black female slaves because of Elizabeth Fox-Genovese's *Within the Plantation Household: Black and White Women of the Old South*. As Jean Harvey Baker has observed, women's history has transcended the imposition of "male-centered paradigms . . . to investigate concerns . . . that emerge from the female experience," from what Lerner has termed "contributory history" to an aggregate approach.[63] Lerner opined in 1988 that "trying to pin the field of women's studies down at this juncture would be like trying to describe the Renaissance—10 years after it began."[64]

The First Southern Conference on Women's History convened in Spartanburg, South Carolina, at Converse College during June 1988 under the auspices of the Southern Association for Women Historians and a second was to be held in 1991 at the University of North Carolina at Chapel Hill. If the 1988 gathering was an indication, scholarship in southern women's history is in good hands; it is vital, innovative, and exciting; its future looks more promising than ever. The status of southern women and their prospects for the future, however, must of necessity receive mixed reviews—as indeed must those of American women collectively. Complete equality of opportunity, or even the possibility of complete equality of opportunity for women, has not existed in American society to date. This is not a national culture where feminine influence has been at parity with masculine power.[65]

Along with sharing the national feminine experience, southern women are also heiresses to thousands of years of human experience. If Riane Eisler's *The Chalice and the Blade: Our History, Our Future* is to be believed, there may indeed have been "a time when women and men lived in harmony with each other and nature—before a male god decreed that women henceforth be subservient to men."[66] As Gerda Lerner recognizes in *The Creation of Patriarchy*, "Women are essential and central to creating society; they are and always have been actors and agents in history." "History-making," however, "is a historical creation. . . . Until the most recent past," she writes, "these historians have been men, and what they have recorded is what men have done and experienced and found significant."[67]

A significant gap exists between pontificators and practitioners—the exhorters and the real honest-to-God people—between southern feminist historians specifically and southern women generally. Scholars measure out their lives in footnotes and come and go speaking of *patriarchy* and *post-structuralism*. Hall once observed that feminist scholars tell their stories to save their lives, for imagined readers, and for those who fear their power.[68] The future of southern women will probably not be decided in academic halls but more likely in political arenas, in workplaces, in boardrooms, in bedrooms, over kitchen tables, and within the confines of families. Nonetheless, academics have a role to play. Education at every level is a vital component of political change and citizenship. Each generation has its own challenges and its own obligations: positive ideas need to be nurtured. Therefore, the crusade for women's rights is an ongoing concern for those who believe in the expansion of democracy.

Achieving equality for women in American society is a political objective; women's studies and women's history have political overtones, and educators have a duty to encourage female students, just as they do male students. For most of the history of this country and, indeed, throughout most of the history of the human race, the talent of the majority of people has been stymied because of class, racial, and sexual bigotry. Contemporary society can ill afford the loss, misuse, or mishandling of that talent.

The first generation of southern female activists used the technique that the historian Paula Baker describes as "domestic politics." "During the Nineteenth Century," she writes, "women expanded their ascribed sphere into community service and care of dependents, areas not fully within men's or women's politics." The second generation, however, shied away from "adopting formerly male values and behavior" as did the "new [American] woman" of the 1920s.[69] From the 1920s to the 1950s, southern feminists embraced a somewhat different strategy than the first generation, and one more at odds with the masculine power structure on racial and economic issues. Radical feminists of the strident third generation moved so far to the left of traditional male politics in the South that they could hardly expect success in the regional legislative sanctums.

American women have had difficulties in defining and realizing collective political objectives, and feminist attempts to score victories on traditional male political turf have been plagued by failure. Using the Nineteenth Amendment and the proposed Equal Rights Amendment as indicators of political achievement reveals that the first generation of southern feminists, by the most optimistic assessment, obtained mixed results; the third generation failed miserably. Only Texas, Tennessee, Kentucky, and Arkansas ratified the Nineteenth Amendment.[70] The poor showing was in part tied to weaknesses of feminism in the South, but it also reflected the staggering obstacles that women confronted in public life. Nine of the fifteen state legislatures that refused to ratify the Equal Rights Amendment were in former Confederate states.[71]

The historical record suggests that legal rights for women have been determined by male interests. Southern men seem unlikely to endorse any agenda purely out of concern for the feelings, thoughts, or opinions of women themselves. Lebsock's findings in her study of property rights for women during the era of Radical Reconstruction, for example, indicate that homestead exemptions and married women's property laws received support because they protected families from economic disaster, provided debtor relief, and reflected the interests of the males who wrote and enacted the legislation. She concludes that "the reforms enacted by the radicals continued an established southern tradition of legislation, a tradition of progressive expansion of the property rights of married women for utterly nonfeminist purposes."[72]

It is comforting but perhaps erroneous to assume that the interests of women would inevitably be better served if more females held elected office. Studies of women who have served in southern state legislatures, conducted principally by Joanne V. Hawks and Mary Carolyn Ellis, have produced fundamental and highly significant findings. The thirty-two southern women legislators in ten southern states during the postsuffrage decade fell into the category of "cultural traditionalists" and "short-term legislators." At the end of the 1920s, according to Hawks and Ellis, "Neither Armageddon nor the millennium had occurred. Legislative chambers still stood, and proceedings droned on as they always had."[73]

The same scholars have investigated Florida's women legislators from 1928 to 1986 and concluded that "the women in . . . legislative roles illustrated in microcosm the diversity among all the legislative women," adding: "They differed markedly in focus and style, ranging from ultraconservative to liberal. Many insisted that there was no such thing as a woman's voice or vote in the legislature. Some of the women consciously avoided informal women's agenda meetings, because they felt that too close an identification with women's issues was detrimental to their ability to function effectively. Nevertheless, many women and men acknowledge that the presence of women has changed the way the legislature functions and the issues that are considered."[74]

A similar study revealed that during recent years, when women in state legislatures have generally increased elsewhere, a decrease has occurred in Mississippi. Those who had served there between 1924 and 1981 were short-termers, "sometimes because voters rejected their re-election bids, sometimes because, for whatever reason, they decided not to continue in office. Those who became embroiled in controversy found their legislative careers short-lived." Finally, "Many of the women were hard-working, conscientious public servants; few were innovators or supporters of unpopular issues. Few made notable lasting achievements."[75]

In South Carolina, Ellis and Hawks note that women who served before the mid-1960s "juggled roles." "They had the ambition to be political figures, but both our society and their own nonassertiveness were factors mitigating against any real success." Carolyn Frederick, a pivotal figure first elected in 1966, while maintaining graciousness and charm, "hammered away at issues, often took controversial stands, spoke publicly and forthrightly about the topics of the day, and, in so doing, served as a model for future female legislators." Frederick "proved that the dominant culture's ideal of femininity could be successfully combined with a healthy dose of assertiveness and open ambition." A woman's caucus still had not materialized by 1984, but the female legislators dared speak out on women's issues and other matters. According to Ellis and Hawks, "A new sense of confidence was pervasive; women no longer took a back seat or walked on the proverbial egg shells. Rather they acquired a degree of power, and they were not afraid to use it."[76]

The mere presence of female legislators does not guarantee significant attention to women's issues. Building grass-roots support is a serious problem across the nation and probably an even greater one in the South. A study conducted in 1967 and another one twenty years later found women to be less active in traditional politics than men. Data collected for both surveys by the National Opinion Research Center at the University of Chicago showed women participating at about 84 percent the rate of men in 1967 and 85 percent in 1987. No significant gains had been registered, although women seemed to be better educated and were working outside the home in greater numbers. In an analysis of data collected from more than 1,800 adults, Thomas M. Guterbock of the University of Virginia counted such activities as making campaign contributions, contacting public officials, and attempting to solve community problems as involvement. Guterbock found men to be more active in partisan politics than women, whereas the sexes registered about equal interest in community matters.[77]

There is some indication that women enter politics—that is, demonstrate strong party commitment and seek appointive and elective office—later in life than men.[78] This pattern may well be tied to the female life-cycle, especially the childbearing and childrearing years. Furthermore, this may also explain in part the level of traditional political activity gauged by the 1967 and 1987 surveys. According to a study conducted by an insurance firm, the Travelers Company, the average American woman can expect to spend seventeen years raising children and eighteen years caring for an elderly parent or parent-in-law.[79] The care of the elderly may dog them into their own old age, and some mothers hardly have time to think about "empty nests" before the "boomerang kids" are back. With the enormous demands on their time posed by personal responsibilities as well as employment-related tasks, it is hardly surprising that women are left with little energy to devote to "back-slapping deals" in those venerable "smoke-filled rooms." They predictably focus on concrete issues of the here and now in their own communities.

The presence of women in high-visibility positions is encouraging and desirable, but public female profiles alone provide no more of a panacea for discrimination than the random sprinkling of women law-makers in state legislatures. Women do not automatically think alike or vote alike, although it can be argued that, to some extent, women and men view the world somewhat differently. Women, however, are not necessarily any more noble in positions of authority than men. Fur-thermore, some of the high-visibility positions are cameo roles, not part of the long political apprenticeship to senior-level elected or appointed positions that shape policy. It is heartening, of course, that Texas's elected treasurer, Ann Richards, gave the keynote address at the 1988 Democratic convention in Atlanta.

Billed by *Southern Magazine* as "the mouth that roared," Richards has not been all talk. According to Dave McNeely, political editor of the Austin *American-Statesman*, "she took the Texas treasury from quill-pen backwardness into the computer age." Hiring practices, not just upgrading machinery, also received her attention. Minority represen-tation on her staff exceeded that to be found in the Texas population at large. Richards established a first-name relationship with her em-ployees, and she was not afraid to send flowers and write warm notes. Known for her dart-like socially conscious lines, she once observed that she was not a radical and certainly no bra-burner, declaring, "I couldn't dare burn it; I wasn't about to burn anything that was a source of support." Nonetheless, she took women's issues seriously. According to McNeely, Richards noted that "over the past 70 years, women have come from being denied the right to vote along with aliens and the insane to the point that they were expected to provide 10 million more votes than men in the 1988 election." Richards has opined that as more females seek elected positions and an increasing number of women exercise the franchise, they will place such topics as childcare, pay eq-uity, prenatal and postnatal care, and similar issues of concern to women and families in the forefront.[80]

Encouraging signs are also to be found in the Upper South. In Virginia's November 1989 elections, Lieutenant Governor L. Douglas Wilder, already the first black to be elected to a statewide political post in the South since Reconstruction, became the first black governor in the entire nation. Four years earlier in the same state, Mary Sue Terry took the attorney general's race and became the first female to be elected to statewide office in the Old Dominion.[81] Taking advantage of the state constitution that allows the chief executive to fill vacancies when the state legislature is not in session, Governor Gerald L. Baliles, in November 1988, named Elizabeth B. Lacy to the Virginia supreme court, the first woman to sit on the bench of the state's highest court.[82]

In *The Life and Death of the Solid South*, the historian Dewey W. Grantham perceives an evolving political activism of southern women: "Although southern women took the lead in organizing a regional suffrage movement early in the century, played a vital role in many reform campaigns, and gradually found new opportunities for public service, they were not prominently involved in electoral politics, seeing that as a male sphere. But that has changed, and they have become more active, not only as voters, but also as party workers, candidates, and officeholders, particularly in local and municipal politics."[83]

On the national front, in December 1988, President-elect George Herbert Walker Bush chose a prominent southern woman, Elizabeth Dole, a North Carolina native and a Harvard-educated attorney, to be his secretary of labor. She previously served as Ronald Reagan's secretary of transportation.[84] Notwithstanding her many attributes, Dole has been in the company of an administration hardly noted for enlightened views on women's issues. The status of women in southern society has been governed by a cultural continuity and self-consistency, analogous to Harman's principles for futures research. Produced by the nature of southern females as well as males, these forces have been subject to the ameliorating influence of rising social consciousness. Given the peculiarities of Dixie, southern women are still not immune to the social, political, and economic nuances of the larger American context. The South and other regions of the country may differ in degree on public stances, but they share many of the undulating national trends.

Furthermore, such issues as reproductive freedom transcend regional boundaries. Presidential candidate Bush promised "a gentler, kinder America," but as he prepared to assume the nation's highest office, the United States Supreme Court—bearing the heavy stamp of Ronald Reagan—agreed to hear a case arising from a Missouri law that restricted abortions and declared that human life begins at conception. During the Reagan administration, opposition to abortion became a kind of litmus test for his Supreme Court nominees, and Bush did not separate himself from the Reagan position. In 1973, in the cases of *Roe v. Wade* and *Doe v. Bolton*, the tribunal had ruled on the constitutionality of a woman's right to have an abortion, under certain conditions, during the first six months of pregnancy. In 1986, after thirteen years of repeated attempts to narrow or overturn the *Roe* decision, the Supreme Court reaffirmed women's right to reproductive freedom in *Thornburgh v. American College of Obstetricians and Gynecologists.*[85]

Following the November 1988 presidential election, not until the outcome of the fall campaign was known, the United States Department of Justice took the unusual step of asking the Supreme Court to review the *Roe v. Wade* decision and intervened in a Missouri case that the Court had not at that time agreed to hear. With a conservative William H. Rehnquist now at the helm, joined by Reagan appointees Sandra Day O'Connor, Antonin Scalia, and Anthony Kennedy, Associate Justice Harry Blackmun, author of the *Roe* decision, warned publicly that it might not stand through the Court term.[86] In July 1989, the United States Supreme Court undermined *Roe v. Wade* with its decision in *Webster v. Reproductive Health Services.* State legislators, overwhelmingly male and perhaps even more susceptible to pressure from vocal minorities than the United States Congress, have returned to cutting deals over women's bodies.

Issues of special contemporary interest to women and those likely to remain so in the future cannot be isolated from the context of times. Harman's remaining three principles of futures research—cause-effect relationships, holistic trending, and goal seeking—require closer scrutiny. Given the female physiology and anatomy, reproductive rights are and will likely continue to be fundamental to women's rights. If the mature female cannot have governance over her own body, she can hardly influence her own future, much less society's. Furthermore, women are more likely to make gains or garner more attention for their agenda in reformist eras. In American history, women seemingly fare better during liberal swings in the political pendulum even if conservatism is just below the surface and sexism still is not hidden. The eight years from 1981 to 1989 witnessed the so-called Reagan Revolution, predicated on the social values of grade-B movies, contriving a return to a world that probably never existed except in Ronald Reagan's mind. Nonetheless, this eclectic rightist vision was reminiscent of the late-nineteenth-century politics and society of the Gilded Age, the economic philosophy of the 1920s, and the foreign policy of the 1950s.

Certainly, women are more likely to garner support on key issues and score successes if men perceive those issues to be of interest to themselves. Sound feminist political strategy suggests linkage. Unfortunately, history demonstrates that when such linkage occurs, the women's issues are soon subordinated to a nobler, more important goal; and women are expected to wait their turn and sacrifice achieving their own rights to the more pressing expedient of the times. The abolitionist crusade and the civil rights movement provide useful examples.

During the first half of the nineteenth century, the American women's movement emerged from the same social context that spawned abolitionism. Nonetheless, those women who dared look to their own rights were admonished even by their own male counterparts to remember that it was the black *man's* hour. The 1848 women's rights convention at Seneca Falls gave rise to certain goals. Achieving suffrage soon gained ascendancy during the coming decades; realization occurred during the Progressive Era when Americans gave serious attention to pressing social problems. Small gains hardly eliminated the second-class citizenship of blacks or women, and eventually a new full-blown protest effort forced the country to face the painful reality. As historian William H. Chafe makes clear, "No protest movement occurs in a vacuum . . . and it is unlikely that feminism could have gained the energy it did during the 1960s had not Americans been preoccupied with the demand to eliminate prejudice and discrimination . . . the civil rights revolution dramatized the immorality of discriminating against any group of people on the basis of physical characteristics. It provided a model of moral indignation and tactical action which women quickly adopted as their own."[87]

In this context, the South became a crucible for the development of an important wing of women's liberation, for, not unlike their abolitionist sisters of the preceding century, New Left women, products of the civil rights movement, recognized their own oppression. The drama of protest that unfolded in the South also included scores of women who were not southern. Mary King and Sandra Cason were two of the native daughters. Speaking at the Atlanta symposium in February 1988, King, a "dressed-for-success" radical who dared describe Sandra Cason (at one time married to Tom Hayden) as "a beautiful blonde from Texas," and who herself might aptly be called a gorgeous brunette, remembered their evolving consciousness. While working with the Student Nonviolent Coordinating Committee during the 1960s, afraid to speak openly about women's rights, they anonymously drafted a paper on the subject. A black woman, Ruby Doris Smith Robinson, presented the paper during a SNCC retreat at Waveland, Mississippi, in November

1964. Stokely Carmichael's reported rebuttal that "the only position for women in SNCC is prone" galvanized some females. King explained more than two decades later that "in the brooding silence of those times on that issue, we were afraid of ridicule. Imagine! We who had been forced to reckon with our own deaths before going to work for SNCC were afraid of ridicule."[88]

With women's rights enjoying a subordinate but nonetheless symbiotic relationship with the civil rights movement and riding the crest of a somewhat liberal wave of the times, females realized some important gains. Indeed, a significant portion of the protective legislation that "expands" opportunities for women rather than "restricts"—as, in fact, did some of the legal stances of the Progressive Era—dates from the 1960s; the Suffrage Amendment and, to a lesser extent, the Fourteenth Amendment, which is unreliable on gender-related issues, are notable exceptions. The Equal Pay Act of 1963 and Civil Rights Act of 1964 provide examples of "expansive" protections. As amended, the Equal Pay Act of 1963 prohibits those firms with more than twenty employees engaged in interstate commerce from paying men and women differently if they work for the same company and perform jobs requiring equal skill and responsibility in similar working conditions. Title VII of the Civil Rights Act of 1964 prohibits sex discrimination by private and public employers with fifteen or more workers. Representative Howard W. Smith of Virginia initiated the addition of the word *sex*, believing it would make the bill seem ridiculous and divide liberals, thereby preventing passage of the legislation. Representative Martha Griffiths of Michigan, the leading feminist in the House, considered it a serious matter and realized that Smith probably carried a hundred votes with him. Smith and his followers had their day; the uproar that ensued went down as "Ladies Day in the House."[89]

A few women ever since have been "laughing" all the way to the Equal Employment Opportunity Commission (EEOC) or to the federal courts as individual and class actions dealing with sex discrimination have been filed. Other "expansive" milestones are Executive Order 11246, as amended in 1967, from the Johnson administration and Executive order 11478 from the Nixon administration. These require that equal employment opportunity be provided by both the federal government and firms that contract with the federal government. In tandem with Title VII of the Civil Rights Act of 1964, they provide the legal basis for "affirmative action," the idea that discrimination can be eliminated when employers take positive steps to identify and change policies and practices and alter institutional barriers that cause or perpetuate inequality. Nondiscrimination is more than merely halting ongoing discriminatory practices.[90]

Other beneficial measures include the Women's Educational Equity Act (WEEA) of 1974 and Title IX of the Education Amendments of 1972, as well as the Civil Rights Restoration Act of 1988 (passed over President Reagan's veto) and the earlier Equal Credit Opportunity Act. Although the House of Representatives approved the Federal Equitable Pay Practices Act for the third time during September 1988, a similar bill slated for action in the Senate was withdrawn by its sponsors when support was deemed insufficient for passage.[91]

Harman, referring to holistic trending as a concept for futures research, observes that "in their process of evolving and changing, social systems behave like integrated organic wholes. They have to be perceived in their entirety; thus there is no substitute for human observation and judgment about the future state of the system."[92] The National Organization for Women has charged that "throughout the Reagan administration, conservative policy makers have sought to repeal or reverse the few existing legal guarantees which exist for women in employment, education, family law, and job benefits. . . . Under federal 'deregulation' schemes, proposed changes include[d] repealing affirmative action regulations, easing enforcement procedures for equal employment laws, and eliminating equal education laws."[93] Holistic trending suggests that if liberal eras can prove beneficial to women, conservative swings can provide setbacks. Ratification of the Equal Rights Amendment to the United States Constitution might afford some relief from the shifting political moods that weigh heavily on statutory law and policy implementation.

Feminists as well as other women must guard against responding over-optimistically to such watersheds or milestones as the opportunities that came for southern women after their men were defeated in the Civil War, with the advent of suffrage, during the civil rights movement, or with the convening of the Atlanta symposium. In some respects, American society has experienced more progress in race relations than in sex equity. Most public figures, for example, dare not make the denigrating remarks about blacks that some seem to consider almost perfunctory about females. Most of the southern males serving in the United States Senate were not about to risk being called racists by openly supporting Ronald Reagan's nomination of Robert Bork to the United States Supreme Court; being sexists poses far less risk to their political fortunes.

During much of the South's history, black women and white have lived and worked in rural households dominated by men. A male guise of self-righteous chivalry denied them or blinded them to the possibilities of autonomy. Southern men revere their mothers and pamper their daughters, but they are and have been, in many instances, less charitable and less adept in dealing humanely or equitably with their wives, their sisters, and the women of their own generation. Nonetheless, southern women like being female; they love men; they need intimacy; and they have a formidable capacity for tolerating the opposite sex. As country-music outlaws Willie Nelson and Waylon Jennings sing, "She's a good-hearted woman in love with a good-timin' man; she loves him in spite of his wicked ways that she don't understand."

Southern women, indeed many southern feminists, have never renounced their femininity. Radical feminists are hard to find in the South; the great majority of females have no truck with lesbianism; they do not bare their breasts or go out in public without their cosmetic masks. Furthermore, they do not subscribe to the notion of an all-encompassing cross-cultural and historical patriarchal plot to subjugate women. If, in fact, such a plot has existed, many southern women have been all-too-willing accomplices. All those things that have been regarded as radical feminist rites of passage have never been embraced warmly south of the Mason-Dixon line. Southern women also have sense enough to know that males and females are different, and that females, incubators and nurturers of the species, do require some special consideration. At the same time, as human beings, they deserve equity before the law.

The millennium for women has not yet arrived globally, nationally, or regionally; indeed, it may never arrive. Futures research and the perennial optimism of the human spirit require goal seeking. Mary King, in February 1988, listed certain "genuine civil rights issues . . . at the core of any concern for women both today and tomorrow": equal pay, stereotyping, lack of constitutional guarantees, problems of self-perception, too few women in elected positions, and poverty.[94] Most activists could agree with these and also add their own shopping lists. Harman maintains that "societies have goals . . . not necessarily declared ones" and "seek destinies they have never explicitly proclaimed," and believes that "social change is not aimless."[95] The last twenty to twenty-five years, he claims, "have witnessed a growing challenge to the legitimacy of the present social system of the industrial world." That challenge targets the economic, political, technological, industrial, and scientific aspects of the prevailing order. For a social system and its power base to possess legitimacy, that social system must be "duly constituted," should conform to "adequate guiding moral principles," and be effective "in achieving agreed upon goals." Harman identifies the people of

144

underdeveloped nations, the aged, the young, consumers, and women as those cut off from the prevailing order.[96]

Yet many would argue—and on some counts correctly—that women have overcome tremendous barriers and made enormous strides, and therefore are well on their way to being politically and economically empowered. Nicholas Davidson and Sylvia Ann Hewlett, a historical writer and an economist, respectively, would probably disagree. Although Davidson's book is a scathing attack on feminism according to his own narrow definition, some passages are models of rationality. He writes, for example, that "feminism has been a force for progress and a force for alienation. It has given positive direction to women's lives and created personal anguish. It has given some women greater pride in themselves and created unspeakable difficulties in their relations with men." His objectivity deteriorates quickly when he adds that "women's rights are too important to be left to women."[97] Davidson's concern rests with men and the family and with keeping women in their place. He is correct in his realization that the empowerment of women poses a threat to the patriarchal and traditional family.

Hewlett deserves more serious consideration, for she, as a professional woman, a wife, and a mother, speaks with the voice of experience. She has discovered what many women of her generation, North and South, have encountered as they have struggled to give birth to children and care for them while engaged in professions, careers, or other types of work that take them out of the home. In her words, "the rigid standards of the 1950s' 'cult of motherhood' are impossible to combine with the equally rigid standards of our fiercely competitive workplaces."[98] The sad fact is that many couples cannot provide a decent standard of living for children without a second income, and all the forces of society seem arrayed to make working mothers' lives more difficult. The Economic Policy Council family policy panel which Hewlett initiated compiled a tentative list of suggestions including (1) pay equity, (2) maternity and parental leave, (3) maternal and child health coverage provided by the federal government, (4) flexible work schedules, (5) preschool and early childhood education, and (6) childcare with private sector initiatives.[99]

To Hewlett's dismay, she gradually realized that her own panel members did not respond warmly to these issues. The men were "molded by the fifties and believed that children should be looked after by their mothers"; childcare, from their perspective, was "not an appropriate sphere for government action." Career women who served on the panel did not want to concede that "working women might need special benefits" because "they had absorbed the feminist message of the 1970s, which was that if women wanted equal opportunities, they should behave like men." The panel members who were trade unionists, meanwhile, "had risen to power fighting for a family wage for family men; they had not yet adjusted to the labor market realities of the 1980s."[100]

Such issues as care for the young and elderly are fundamental to society, and others like pay equity will probably not go away. A June 1988 fact sheet compiled by the National Organization for Women declared that "the inadequate supply of affordable quality child care in America has reached crisis proportions." The statistics are eye-openers. Nationally, one in five children lives with a single parent, and half of all children born in 1988 will probably spend a significant portion of their childhoods with one parent. In two-thirds of all married couples with children both mother and father work. Seventy percent of mothers with school-age children are in the paid labor force, and 57 percent of those with children under three years of age. Most of them work because of economic necessity. A quarter of these women have husbands making less than $10,000 annually; half are wives of males bringing home less than $20,000.[101]

Given the divorce rate, the instability of family life in America, and the feminization of poverty, women must be concerned with wage discrimination. Frances C. Hutner, a labor economist, calls equal pay for comparable worth "the working woman's issue of the Eighties." "As more and more women support themselves and their families and look forward with concern to what they are going to live on in their old age, they see sex-based wage discrimination as a serious problem. Growing numbers of the poor are women—young and old—and the children of women who are heads of households."[102] The most vulnerable group in the battle with poverty is the single female-headed households with children. Twenty-seven percent of white single-parent households live below the poverty line, approximately $11,200 for a family of four in 1986; 50.5 percent of those are headed by black women, and 53 percent headed by Hispanic females.[103] Furthermore, millions of older women deal daily with lives of poverty from which death seems to provide the only escape.

Women can ill afford to ignore the issues, and they must insist individually and collectively that they be addressed. However trite, it is true; the personal is political—for southern women, too. Demographics suggest that the underpinnings of patriarchy in Dixie are not quite as secure as they once were, but the news is ambiguous. The statistical southern woman is a member of a multiracial sisterhood. Certain trends raise interesting possibilities. In every southern state, females outnumber males. Except in Kentucky and West Virginia, approximately one-half or more of females live in urban areas. Using high-school education as a standard, more women than men from eighteen to twenty-four have diplomas in every southern state, also in every southern state females comprise 49 percent or more of students enrolled in southern colleges and universities. The highest percentage of women with children under six years of age and who work outside the home, 52 percent or more, are clustered in the Deep South, but many are below the poverty level. The feminization of poverty is particularly apparent in Kentucky and the Deep South, although it is juxtaposed with amazing individual success stories. Florida, Louisiana, and West Virginia are the only southern states in which fewer than 44 percent of married women work outside the home; elsewhere, the 50 percent range is the norm. The percentage of practicing professionals who are women is also in the range of 50 percent in the South.[104] At the same time, women bear a disproportionate share of housework and care-giving for the elderly and the young; they work in both national and regional social settings that are hostile—at best inattentive—to the needs of women and the conditions of their lives.[105]

In the public arena, women face discrimination; privately, some of them have to deal with personal abuse like date rape, wife battering, and attacks on their children. The South has had a long-standing appointment with violence, and there is no particular reason to assume that the region experiences less domestic turmoil than the rest of the country. According to a television documentary aired in 1988, one American woman is physically abused by her husband or boyfriend every fifteen seconds.[106] Some experts claim that date rapes generally go unreported because women either blame themselves or do not equate sexual acts forced on them by acquaintances with the crime of rape.[107] The appearance of "safe houses" for battered women and their children across the region suggests that some good ol' boys are not unlike abusers elsewhere. There is no way to ascertain how many children, both male and female, have been victimized,[108] but enough incest cases get on the court dockets to demonstrate that child abuse occurs in the South.

Sexual harassment is also inordinately common. By definition, it is explicit derogatory statements or sexually discriminatory remarks in the workplace "that are offensive or objectionable to the recipient, or which causes her discomfort or humiliation that interferes with job performance."[109] Still, women endure and generally have longer life expectancies than men. With the graying of America, the numbers grow, and so does political potential. With the exception of Florida, the Deep South, however, has had the lowest life expectancy for females in the country, according to a recent study. Infant mortality is higher in the Deep South than elsewhere.[110] Contemporary women still have the option of exercising some control over their reproductive lives, but considerable ignorance exists. Whether by choice, medical incompetence, or a raging virus, the South has the highest rate of hysterectomies in the country; the same is true of tubal sterilizations. Tennessee, Mississippi, Alabama, and Georgia have had the highest number of reported cases of syphilis and gonorrhea among females in the lower forty-eight states.[111] This raises questions about the human papilloma virus (HIV) or condyloma, which causes venereal warts, and whether it is inordinately common to the South. At least five of the fifty-two known strains of condyloma have been associated with cervical cancer.[112] Southern women, especially blacks and other minorities, will also face the horror of the AIDS epidemic in the coming years. Nationally, women are the fastest growing group of people with AIDS, 26 percent of all newly diagnosed cases. The disease seems to target women of color; 63 percent of male sufferers are white, but 72 percent of the females are either black or Hispanic.[113]

Men and women constitute the human race, but males and females are different. Hormones impact on history, and emotion frequently triumphs over rationality.[114] If American women are fed up with specific men, as Shere Hite has claimed, southern women are not fed up with men in general.[115] Several southeastern states have marriage and divorce rates that exceed the national average, suggesting that southerners "were quick to marry but just as quick to divorce"—and nervy enough to try again.[116] A prominent black woman from Texas, Barbara Jordan, gives great odds for the future—a future she sees as "men and women working together—in our common humanity—trying to assure at every turn that we live in peace and freedom with civility, and order."[117]

Generations come and go, reforms ebb and flow, but ideas endure; they are virtually indestructible. Expanding democracy is a noble, highly moral pursuit. Still, the South is the region that fought women's suffrage and blocked the Equal Rights Amendment. Southern women generally have not rushed to join the National Organization for Women; those polled, however, seemed to have been opposed to Robert Bork's nomination to the United States Supreme Court.[118] Females, like males, look for quick fixes, although there is no quick fix to patriarchy.[119]

Much of southern history has been sexually polarized. Long-standing assumptions about woman's place relegated her to a private world where she was afforded a modicum of authority, saddled with duty, and undergirded with an assumption of significance. When she entered the public arena as a male accessory or to support a masculine cause, she did so at the pleasure of the dominant power structure. If she dared find an alternate route into southern public society, she challenged the prevailing order and risked censure. Gradually, for complex and far-ranging reasons, this rigid arrangement, bound in ribbons of sentiment and honor, has been eroded, and opportunities for women have materialized in the South. The future may witness a continuing expansion of choices for women; although it cannot be taken for granted, the range of female experience may become even more varied. Margaret Atwood's chilling novel *The Handmaid's Tale* is a bit extreme, but it is a reminder that doors that have been opened can be closed again. Barring future cataclysmic societal changes, the lines of a favorite Baptist preacher used by Martin Luther King, Jr., might be applicable to the prospects of southern women: "We ain't what we want to be. We ain't what we gonna be. But, thank God, we ain't what we was."

Below the Mason-Dixon line, high priests and priestesses of the past still stand ready to invoke the deities of Dixie's pantheon and to summon the mythical southern lady to suppress recalcitrants. The last word has not been said or written about woman's place and role, and the end of southern women's history is not in sight. The threat to reproductive freedom that developed during the 1980s has seemingly reinvigorated the once-languishing women's movement on several fronts and also stirred a younger generation of females who had complacently accepted the hard-won gains of the past. This issue alone promises to make the future a dramatic theater.

Furthermore, given present trends in the nation and region, women, motivated principally by economic necessity, but also by the need for self-fulfillment, will in all likelihood be found in ever-increasing numbers in the workplace as the South enters the twenty-first century. Pay equity, opportunities for advancement, medical benefits, childcare, and retirement policies are certain to weigh heavily and possibly may create political activism. Educated, employable females in urban environments can be more independent than the economically dependent and isolated farm and plantation women of yesteryear, overwhelmed by physical labor and numerous pregnancies. Then, too, women participants in the public arena sometimes discover that they are allowed to run the race but not permitted to win. Hard, cold reality may well be the most potent ingredient in consciousness raising.

Equality of opportunity for women is an idea whose time has come, but implementation requires steadfastness to duty and purpose. Gains have to be safeguarded with eternal vigilance. To paraphrase Alice Paul,[120] southern women need to live so as to not be scarred with the shame of a cowardly and trivial past, but they also need to remember the words recorded at Seneca Falls: "In entering upon this great work before us, we anticipate no small amount of misconception, misrepresentation, and ridicule; but we shall use every instrumentality within our power to effect our object."[121] Amid the swirling mists of racism, classism, and sexism in southern history, the feminine foot soldiers of the future in the company of masculine support troops march slowly and with determination to the soft cadence of equality, equality, equality.

NOTES

1. *A Visitors Guide to the City of Atlanta*, 1987–88 ed. (n.p., 1988), pp. 7, 13. Henry W. Grady's "New South" address, New York City, 1886, quoted on p. 5. I was a delegate from Tennessee to the Women and the Constitution symposium.

2. Kingsport *Times-News*, September 23, 1982 (a Tennessee newspaper). *Pregnant and Mining: A Handbook for Pregnant Miners* was released by the Coal Employment Project, an advocacy group for women miners.

3. Peter Stoler, " 'The Patient Was Already Dead': *Discovery's* Crew Makes a Valiant Attempt to Fix a Satellite," *Time*, April 29, 1985, pp. 66–67.

4. Quoted in Kingsport *Times-News*, October 18, 1985.

5. Graham Swift, *Waterland* (New York, 1983), pp. 5 and 6. The character, Price, might have sympathized with Francis Fukuyama's views: "What we may be witnessing is not just the end of the cold war, or the passing of a particular period of postwar history, but the end of history as such: that is, the end point of mankind's ideological evolution and the universalization of Western liberal democracy as the final form of human government." See Francis Fukuyama, "The End of History," *The National Interest* (Summer 1989): 3–18.

6. Willis W. Harman, *An Incomplete Guide to the Future* (San Francisco, 1976), pp. 10–15.

7. Robert L. Heilbroner, *The Future as History* (New York, 1968), p. 17, emphasis in original.

8. Heilbroner, *The Future as History*, pp. 18–40, 49–58, 181–209.

9. Annie Cheatham and Mary Clare Powell, *This Way Daybreak Comes: Women's Values and the Future* (Philadelphia, 1986), p. xix.

10. Hoyt Gimlin, ed., *The American Future* (Washington, 1976), p. 9, passim.

11. American Historical Association, *Perspectives*, September 26, 1988, pp. 1–2.

12. Kingsport *Times-News*, May 29, 1988.

13. Barrett Seamn, "Good Heavens!," *Time*, May 16, 1988, pp. 24–25; Donald T. Regan, *For the Record* (New York, 1988).

14. Nancy Reagan, "Happy Mother's Day, Mother," *Family Weekly*, May 13, 1984, pp. 4, 13.

15. Beth Arnold Graves, "Crystal Clearing: The Environment and the New Age Collide," *Southern Magazine* (June 1988): 14.

16. From the author's personal notes.

17. Peter Schrag, *The End of the American Future* (New York, 1973), p. 40; Henry F. May, *The End of American Innocence: A Study of the First Years of Our Own Time, 1912–1917* (New York, 1959, repr. Chicago, 1964), p. 397.

18. Janet Zollinger Giele, *Women and the Future: Changing Sex Roles in Modern America* (New York, 1978), p. x.

19. Tish Sommers, "Tomorrow Is a Woman's Issue," in *The Technological Woman: Interfacing with Tomorrow*, ed. Jan Zimmerman (New York, 1983), pp. 273–78, 295.

20. See Anne Firor Scott, "Women, Religion and Social Change in the South, 1830–1930" in *Religion and the Solid South*, ed. Samuel S. Hill, Jr., et al. (Nashville, 1972), pp. 92–121; see also John Patrick McDowell, III, "A Social Gospel in the South: The Woman's Home Mission Movement in the Methodist Episcopal Church, South, 1886–1939," Ph.D. diss., Duke University, 1979, and *The Social Gospel in the South: The Woman's Home Mission Movement in the Methodist Episcopal Church, 1886–1939* (Baton Rouge, 1982); and Jean E. Friedman, *The Enclosed Garden: Women and Community in the Evangelical South, 1830–1900* (Chapel Hill, 1985).

21. John Demos, *Past, Present, and Personal: The Family and the Life Course in American History* (New York, 1986), p. 33.

22. The quoted phrases represent a definition of progress set forth in May, *The End of American Innocence*, p. 21.

23. From the author's notes on the Women and the Constitution: A Bicentennial Perspective Symposium, February 10–12, 1988, Atlanta.

24. Margaret Ripley Wolfe, "Feminizing Dixie: Toward a Public Role for Women in the American South," in *Research in Social Policy: Historical and Contemporary Perspectives*, ed. John H. Stanfield, II, vol. 1 (Greenwich, 1987), pp. 186–90; see also, Joan Kelly, *Women, History and Theory: The Essays of Joan Kelly* (Chicago, 1984), pp. 51-64; Kelly acknowledges a "doubled vision" of gender and class. For a more sophisticated approach on matters of gender and race, see Elizabeth Fox-Genovese, *Within the Plantation Household: Black and White Women of the Old South* (Chapel Hill, 1988).

25. For some thoughts on geography and gender based on the British experience, see Women and Geography Study Group of the Institute of British Geographers, *Geography and Gender: An Introduction to Feminist Geography* (London, 1984).

26. Nancy F. Cott defines feminism as (1) belief in sex equality, (2) the presumption that women's condition is socially constructed, and (3) the supposition that women represent not only a biological but also a social grouping, see *The Grounding of Modern Feminism* (New Haven, 1987), pp. 4–5.

27. Carl N. Degler, *At Odds: Women and the Family in America from the Revolution to the Present* (New York, 1980).

28. Nicholas Davidson, *The Failure of Feminism* (Buffalo, 1988), pp. 310–11.

29. One might add that southern women are also amazingly resilient. According to the Associated Press, Carrie White, a 114-year-old Florida woman with a taste for Red Man chewing tobacco, was to be certified by the *Guinness*

Book of World Records as the world's oldest living person; she had been institutionalized since 1909; reported in Kingsport *Times-News*, November 17, 1988.

30. Arthur Schlesinger, *Learning How to Behave: A Historical Study of American Etiquette Books* (New York, 1946, repr. New York, 1968), pp. 6–7.

31. Grady McWhiney, *Cracker Culture: Celtic Ways in the Old South* (Tuscaloosa, 1988), pp. 171–92, particularly p. 177; see also, Jean Markale, *Women of the Celts*, trans. A. Mygind, C. Hauch, and P. Henry (Rochester, Vt., 1986), pp. 9–40.

32. An excellent source is Herbert G. Gutman, *The Black Family in Slavery and Freedom, 1750–1925* (New York, 1976); see also, Catherine Clinton, "Caught in the Web of the Big House," in *The Web of Southern Social Relations: Women, Family, and Education*, ed. Walter J. Fraser, Jr., et al. (Athens, 1985), pp. 19–35.

33. Theda Perdue, "Southern Indians and the Cult of True Womanhood," pp. 35–51 in *The Web of Southern Social Relations*; see also, Jon A. Schlenker, "An Historical Analysis of the Family Life of the Choctaw Indians," *Southern Quarterly* 13 (July 1975): 323–34.

34. Lorena S. Walsh, "The Experiences and Status of Women in the Chesapeake, 1750–1775," pp. 1–18 in *The Web of Southern Social Relations*. More specifically, see Lois Green Carr and Lorena S. Walsh, "From Indentured Servant to Planter's Wife: White Women in Seventeenth-Century Maryland," in *The Underside of American History: To 1877*, 5th ed., vol. 1, ed. Thomas R. Frazier (San Diego, 1987), pp. 33–55.

35. The Reverend Charles Woodmason, quoted in Shirley Abbott, *Womenfolks: Growing Up Down South* (New York, 1983), p. 41.

36. Jeffrey Simpson, comp., *The Way Life Was: A Photographic Treasury from the American Past* (New York, 1975), pp. 98–102; James A. Ramage, *Rebel Raider: The Life of General John Hunt Morgan* (Lexington, Ky., 1986), p. 80; and David Kaser, "Nashville's Women of Pleasure in 1860," *Tennessee Historical Quarterly* 23 (December 1964): 379–82. Simpson offers photographs from the New Orleans Storyville district, and Ramage provides comments on wartime Richmond.

37. This opinion is based on my research in the Southern Summer School Papers contained in the American Labor Education Service Records, Labor-Management Documentation Center, Martin P. Catherwood Library, Cornell University, Ithaca, N.Y., and National Board Young Women's Christian Association Records, the Sophia Smith Collection, Smith College, Northampton, Mass. See also, James A. Hodges, "Challenge to the New South: The Great Textile Strike in Elizabethton, Tennessee, 1929," *Tennessee Historical Quarterly* 23 (December 1964): 343–57; Jacquelyn Dowd Hall, "Disorderly Women: Gender and Labor Militancy in the Appalachian South," *Journal of American History* 73 (September 1986): 354–82; and Jacquelyn Dowd Hall et al., *Like a Family: The Making of a Southern Cotton Mill World* (Chapel Hill, 1987).

38. Elizabeth Langhorne, "Nancy Langhorne Astor: A Virginian in England," *Virginia Cavalcade* 23 (Winter 1974): 38–47.

39. "Southern Portrait: Ava Gardner," *Southern Style* (November-December 1987): 32.

40. Michelle Green, "Chronicle of a Ruinous Affair," *Parade Magazine,* June 15, 1987, pp. 105–8; Walter Shapiro, "Fall from Grace," *Time,* May 18, 1987, pp. 16–20.

41. Kay Orr and Helen Boosalis, "Current Profile," *U.S. News and World Report,* May 26, 1986, p. 8.

42. Harry F. Waters with Michael A. Lerner, "What a Deal!" *Newsweek,* February 9, 1987, pp. 62–68; Diane White, "Vanna Can Be a Tough Cookie," [Kingsport, Tennessee] *Times-News TV,* June 6–12, 1987, p. 3.

43. Richard N. Ostling, "Now It's Jimmy's Turn," *Time,* March 7, 1988, pp. 46–48.

44. "Unconventional Warfare" exhibit, Tennessee State Museum, Nashville.

45. James Brady, "In Step With: Patricia Neal," *Parade Magazine,* June 12, 1988, p. 16.

46. Anne Gibson and Timothy Fast, *The Women's Atlas of the United States* (New York, 1986), p. 194.

47. Hodges, "Challenge to the New South"; Hall, "Disorderly Women."

48. From my notes on Eula Hall's speech, March 7, 1987, Kentucky Women's History Conference, Midway College, Midway.

49. Wolfe, "Feminizing Dixie," pp. 200–203.

50. Harman, *An Incomplete Guide to the Future,* pp. 11–13.

51. C. Vann Woodward, "Slaves and Mistresses" [review of Elizabeth Fox-Genovese, *Within the Plantation Household: Black and White Women of the Old South*], *The New York Review of Books,* December 8, 1988, pp. 3–4.

52. Carl N. Degler, "Thesis, Antithesis, Synthesis: The South, the North, and the Nation," *Journal of Southern History* 53 (February 1987): 18.

53. Anne Firor Scott, *The Southern Lady: From Pedestal to Politics, 1830–1930* (Chicago, 1970), pp. 81, 102, 106–84.

54. Joan W. Scott, "Gender: A Useful Category of Historical Analysis," *American Historical Review* 91 (December 1986): 1073.

55. Wolfe, "Feminizing Dixie," pp. 179–211.

56. Linda K. Kerber, "Separate Spheres, Female Worlds, Women's Place: The Rhetoric of Women's History," *Journal of American History* 75 (June 1988): 39.

57. Demos, *Past, Present, and Personal,* pp. 4, 11.

58. Sharon McKern, *Redneck Mothers, Good Ol' Girls and Other Southern Belles: A Celebration of the Women of Dixie* (New York, 1979), p. xii.

59. Swift, *Waterland,* p. 15.

60. Paul E. Fuller, *Laura Clay and the Woman's Rights Movement* (Lexington, Ky., 1975); and Jacquelyn Dowd Hall, *Revolt against Chivalry: Jessie Daniel Ames and the Women's Campaign against Lynching* (New York, 1979).

61. Sara Evans has provided some valuable insights into the lives of privileged post-World War II youth—both black and white—caught up in the swirling social changes in the South, see, *Personal Politics: The Roots of Women's Liberation in the Civil Rights Movement and the New Left* (New York, 1979). Catherine Clinton's *The Plantation Mistress: Woman's World in the Old South* (New York, 1982) reveals that in reality elite females have not necessarily been privileged in their positions.

62. Suzanne Lebsock, *The Free Women of Petersburg: Status and Culture in a Southern Town, 1784–1860* (New York, 1984); Julia Kirk Blackwelder, *Women of the Depression: Caste and Culture in San Antonio, 1929–1939* (College Station, 1984); and Jacqueline Jones, *Labor of Love, Labor of Sorrow* (New York, 1985).

63. Jean Harvey Baker [review of Anne Firor Scott, *Making the Invisible Woman Visible*], *Journal of Southern History* 51 (February 1985): 132–33.

64. Karen J. Winkler, "Women's Studies after Two Decades: Debate over Politics, New Directions for Research," *The Chronicle of Higher Education*, September 28, 1988, p. A6.

65. For a candid assessment of the status of contemporary feminism, see Germaine Greer, "Women's Glib," *Vanity Fair* (June 1988): 32, 37, 38, 40.

66. Riane Eisler, *The Chalice and the Blade: Our History, Our Future* (San Francisco, 1987), p. xv; see also, Eva C. Keuls, *The Reign of the Phallus: Sexual Politics in Ancient Athens* (New York, 1985), pp. 1–15.

67. Gerda Lerner, *The Creation of Patriarchy* (New York, 1986), pp. 4, 5.

68. From my notes on Jacquelyn Dowd Hall's paper, "Partial Truths," June 10, 1988, First Southern Conference on Women's History, Converse College, Spartanburg, S.C.

69. Paula Baker, "The Domestication of Politics: Women and the American Political Society, 1780–1920," *American Historical Review* 89 (June 1984): 625, 644.

70. Scott, *The Southern Lady*, p. 184.

71. Washington *Post*, October 7, 1978; "Countdown on the ERA," *Time*, June 14, 1982, p. 25; Edith Mayo and Jerry Frye, "ERA: Postmortem of a Failure in Political Communication," Organization of American Historians *Newsletter* (August 1983): 21–24; and "Women March on Houston: Feminists and Their Foes Square Off Around the Big National Meeting," *Time*, November 28, 1977, pp. 12–14; see also, Mary Frances Berry, *Why ERA Failed: Politics, Women's Rights, and the Amending Process of the Constitution* (Bloomington, Ind., 1986, repr. 1988).

72. Suzanne D. Lebsock, "Radical Reconstruction and the Property Rights of Southern Women," *Journal of Southern History* 43 (May 1977): 197.

73. Joanne V. Hawks and Mary Carolyn Ellis, "Heirs of the Southern Progressive Tradition: Women in Southern Legislatures in the 1920s" in *Southern Women*, ed. Carolyn Matheny Dillman (New York, 1988), pp. 81, 82, 87, 88–89.

74. Joanne V. Hawks and Mary Carolyn Ellis, "Creating a Different Pattern: Florida's Women Legislators, 1928–1986," *Florida Historical Quarterly* 65 (July 1987): 83.

75. Joanne V. Hawks, M. Carolyn Ellis, and J. Byron Morris, "Women in the Mississippi Legislature (1924–1981)," *Journal of Mississippi History* 53 (November 1981): 293.

76. M. Carolyn Ellis and Joanne V. Hawks, "Ladies in the Gentlemen's Club: South Carolina Women Legislators, 1928–1984," *Proceedings of the South Carolina Historical Association* (1986): 28–29.

77. E. K. C., "Women Less Active in Politics than Men Are, Study Finds," *The Chronicle of Higher Education*, November 23, 1988, p. A5.

78. Hawks and Ellis, "Creating a Different Pattern," 76. For a national perspective on the political participation of women, see Susan J. Carroll, *Women as Candidates in American Politics* (Bloomington, 1985; repr., 1987).

79. *Hope Healthletter* (October 1988): 7.

80. Dave McNeely, "Leave 'Em Laughing," *Southern Magazine* (January 1989), 22 and 24–25.

81. Howard Fineman, "The New Black Politics," *Newsweek*, November 20, 1989, pp. 52–53; Frank Cormier and Margot Cormier, "Elections," in *The 1986 World Book Year Book [Events of 1985]* (Chicago, 1986), p. 305.

82. Associated Press report in Kingsport *Times-News*, November 23, 1988.

83. Dewey W. Grantham, *The Life and Death of the Solid South: A Political History* (Lexington, Ky., 1988), p. 196.

84. Associated Press story by Joan Mover, "Elizabeth Dole Tapped for Secretary of Labor," Kingsport *Times-News*, December 25, 1988.

85. Ira Glasser, "Reagan's Legacy: Supreme Court Threatens to Turn Back the Clock on Civil Rights," *Civil Liberties* (Spring-Summer 1988): 1, 6; "High Court Asked to Review *Roe v. Wade*, *National Times* (October-November-December 1988): 1, 3; and "Facts on Reproductive Rights," NOW [National Organization for Women] Legal Defense and Education Fund, June 1988.

86. "Facts on Reproductive Rights." On July 20, 1990, George Bush learned that Justice William J. Brennan was retiring from the U.S. Supreme Court, giving him the opportunity to nominate a replacement; his choice, David Souter. See Richard Lacayo, "A Blank Slate," *Time*, August 6, 1990, pp. 16–18; and Margaret Carlson, "An Eighteenth Century Man," ibid., pp. 19–22.

87. William H. Chafe, *The American Woman: Her Changing Social, Economic, and Political Role, 1920–1970* (London, 1972, repr. 1974), 232, 233. See also Nancy Woloch, *Women and the American Experience* (New York, 1984), pp. 113–50, 167–99.

88. From the author's notes and the published proceedings of Women and the Constitution: A Bicentennial Perspective (Atlanta, 1988), pp. 27–31; see also Mary King, *Freedom Song: A Personal Story of the 1960s Civil Rights Movement* (New York, 1987). Also useful are Evans, "Personal Politics," pp. 45–53, 83–89, 217; Jo Freeman, *The Politics of Women's Liberation: A Case Study of an Emerging Social Movement and Its Relation to the Policy Process* (New York, 1975), pp. 44–70; and Abbott, *Womenfolks*, pp. 197–208.

89. Freeman, *The Politics of Women's Liberation*, pp. 53–54.

90. "Facts on Affirmative Action," NOW Legal Defense and Education Fund, June 1988; *National Times* (October-November-December 1988).

91. Ibid.; "Facts on Legal Rights for Women," NOW Legal Defense and Education Fund, June 1988.

92. Harman, *An Incomplete Guide to the Future*, p. 14.

93. "Facts on Equal Rights Amendment," NOW Legal Defense and Education Fund, June 1988.

94. Mary King's comments are in *Women and the Constitution*, p. 30.

95. Harman, *An Incomplete Guide to the Future*, p. 14.

96. Ibid., pp. 116, 117.

97. Davidson, *The Failure of Feminism*, p. 1.

98. Sylvia Ann Hewlett, *A Lesser Life: The Myth of Women's Liberation* (New York, 1986), pp. 15–16.

99. Ibid., pp. 377–79. The Economic Policy Council that Hewlett has directed since 1981 is, according to her book, "a powerful private-sector think tank made up of business leaders, labor leaders, economists, educators, and policy analysts" (p. 16).

100. Ibid., p. 381.

101. "Facts on Child Care," NOW Legal Defense and Education Fund, June 1988. Other useful sources are Alfred J. Kahn and Sheila B. Kamerman, *Child Care: Facing the Hard Choices* (Dover, Mass., 1987); and Ralph E. Smith, *Women in the Labor Force in 1990* (Washington, 1979).

102. Frances C. Hutner, *Equal Pay for Equal Work: The Working Woman's Issue of the Eighties* (New York, 1986), p. vii.

103. "Facts on Women and Poverty," NOW Legal Defense and Education Fund, June 1988.

104. Gibson and Fast, *The Women's Atlas*, pp. 14, 26, 32, 35, 58–60, 61, 70, 78.

105. *Hope Healthletter* (October 1988):7.

106. "My Husband Is Going to Kill Me," "Frontline," PBS television, June 28, 1988.

107. Notes on conference at Towson, Md., in the Kingsport *Times-News*, January 13, 1989. For a detailed study of rape and one of the most significant books of the women's liberation era, see Susan Brownmiller, *Against Our Will: Men, Women, and Rape* (New York, 1975).

108. David Hechler, *The Battle and the Backlash: The Child Sexual Abuse War* (Lexington, Mass., 1988) provides a treatment of the subject of child abuse.

109. "Facts on Sexual Harassment," NOW Legal Defense and Education Fund, June 1988.

110. Gibson and Fast, *The Women's Atlas*, pp. 138, 164.

111. Ibid., pp. 168, 172; 10.5 hysterectomies per thousand women aged fifteen to forty-four; 16.1 tubal sterilizations per thousand women aged fifteen to forty-four; and 60–79 cases per ten thousand.

112. Sheila Anne Feeney, "Warts Latest STD Problem," for the New York *Daily News*, reported in Kingsport *Times-News*, December 29, 1988.

113. "Facts on Women and AIDS," NOW Legal Defense and Education Fund, June 1988.

114. Trying to unlock human minds of the past is perennially challenging to historians; articles on this subject include Ellen K. Coughlin, "With the Assistance of Social Scientists and Psychologists, Historians Explore the Human Mind in Centuries Past," *The Chronicle of Higher Education*, May 25, 1988, pp. A4, A14; see also, American Historical Association, *Perspectives* (May-June 1988): 16–19.

115. Claudia Wallis, "Back off, Buddy: A New Hite Report Stirs up a Furor over Sex and Love in the 80s," *Time*, October 12, 1987, pp. 68–73; "Footnotes," *The Chronicle of Higher Education*, December 9, 1987, p. A4.

116. Gibson and Fast, *The Women's Atlas*, p. 115; Kingsport *Times-News*, September 29, 1986; the article, based on a UPI story, quotes Richard Cline of the National Center for Health Statistics and cites the center's *Monthly Vital Statistics Report*.

117. *Women and the Constitution*, p. 8.

118. Kingsport *Times-News*, October 2, 1987; of the women polled in the South, 24 percent favored the nomination, 54 percent said they opposed Bork, and apparently 22 percent were undecided. The telephone survey was conducted by the Roper organization for the Atlanta *Journal-Constitution*.

119. Georgia Witkin, "Beware of Quick Fixes," *Parade Magazine*, May 15, 1988, pp. 12–13.

120. From a quote on a National Organization for Women postcard.

121. From "A Woman's Declaration of Independence, 1848," at the National Women's Hall of Fame, Seneca Falls, N.Y.

6

Many Souths and Broadening Scale: A Changing Southern Literature

DORIS BETTS

The Old Local-Universal Debate

In April of 1935 at the Conference on Literature and Reading in the South and Southwest sponsored by Louisiana State University, Allen Tate complained that "in the South we have the writer whose society is in one place and whose public is in another," to which Ford Madox Ford snapped, "That is true of every writer."[1] No doubt when a reviewer of Bobbie Ann Mason's fiction noted that she is a southern writer who depicts the kind of southern characters who would never read her stories, Ford rolled over in his grave, muttering, "Characters such as the Pequod's crew and Defoe's Moll Flanders and Steinbeck's Okies? Southern writers like Thomas Hardy, Bret Harte, Jack London, William Kennedy?"

But the chorus of professional southerners would simply raise its unified voice. Nobody points with greater perverse pride to the South's distinctiveness more than native southerners; and no one else views with louder, also sometimes perverse, alarm Dixie's famous intellectual backwardness, nor takes deeper offense when outsiders minimize or criticize either. H. L. Mencken's 1917 sneer at the "Sahara of the Bozart" only condensed into a catchy phrase what William Gilmore Simms, Henry Timrod, and other natives had said long before: how poorly the South has always supported its artists and intellectuals. And despite video images of "Boss Hogg" or films like *In the Heat of the Night*, the South has spawned its share of intellectuals as far back as William Byrd (1674–1744), who owned 3,600 books although he may have had few well-read neighbors to discuss them with. There are also painful southern stories of disguise and suppression of intellect, especially among blacks. Richard Wright as a boy in Memphis is said to have borrowed a library card from a white friend so he could check out books—the friend sent along an explanatory note: "Dear Madam: Will you please let this nigger boy have some books by H. L. Mencken."[2]

Not only the South but also America at large has been criticized as anti-intellectual; see Henry James's catalog of what constitutes a "culture," how these qualities were absent in America, and why he thus left and went to England. At least that part of America below the Mason-Dixon line has had excuses, claiming that war and occupation helped stunt its cultural growth and that national ostracism later stifled or ignored it. "Antisouthernism is the anti-Americanism of the North," said historian C. Vann Woodward.[3] Left to itself after Reconstruction, and left defensive, the South has alternated habitual nonsupport of its own serious literature with unpredictable bursts of loyalty to amateur county poets. One contributing factor to a history of apathy is that serious southern writers, by portraying violence and racial injustice, have sometimes won the wider audience Tate referred to, largely outside those former Confederate states already carrying a mass inferiority complex. And one example of a burst of undiscriminating provincial pride might be the leatherbound, seventeen-volume *Library of Southern Literature*, completed in 1923 and still displayed although largely unread in many regional libraries. Its more than six thousand pages were selected by the editors to do "ample justice" to 278 writers whose work is more amply "southern" than "literary."

Such alternating southern apathy with undiscriminating localism may also be symptomatic of the audience void Allen Tate cited, since the South has historically lagged behind the rest of America in both the wealth and community self-confidence that Michael O'Brien considers necessary if any "self-conscious intellectual class" is to thrive—as it thrived in Emerson's Boston or Matthew Arnold's Oxford.[4] There has been a slow and uneven increase in O'Brien's requirement of regional wealth over the last twenty-five years, during which yesterday's downtown South has been exploding into today's metropolitan Atlanta, Dallas, and Charlotte. Ted Spivey, in *Revival*, has traced the influence of this urban South on a past generation of writers: Ransom, Tate, Faulkner, Wolfe, Aiken, Williams, Ellison, O'Connor, and Percy.

But O'Brien's second requirement of community self-confidence has been harder to document. The South has felt like a second-class American region for good cause. Even today, these glittering new business centers studded like rhinestones on the Sunbelt remain embedded in states with few good newspapers and little serious book criticism although slightly increased book sales; a South that still spends 20 percent less per public school student than the national average, with only 68 percent of its ninth-graders due to graduate from high school; a South whose seniors score lower on college boards than those from most other states; a South where one in four of all adults never went beyond eighth grade (for black southern adults the ratio is three out of eight).[5] Greater wealth is not accumulated by functional illiterates, and certainly a strong literary culture grows more vigorously if some of its sophisticated audience is composed, as Allen Tate desired, of friends and neighbors.

Despite weak public education and historically weak or inconsistent support of art, there are surprising signs that the Sunbelt is hungry for more than economic enlightenment. During the recent decades of economic growth, mayors and committees from many southern cities and towns have rushed forward, sometimes with shoestring money and sometimes to compete for grants, sometimes with hopes more elevated than their accompanying taste, to establish a multitude of county arts councils, local museums, poets-in-the-schools programs, friends-of-libraries, humanities extension courses, college creative writing majors, little theaters, elderhostels, historical associations, writers-in-residence, arts and crafts classes in community colleges and senior citizen centers, writers' clubs, and arts newsletters. Shirley Ann Grau has commented on the vitality of the statewide Louisiana Writers' Guild, which has parallels in many southeastern states. While anecdotal evidence is suspect, I do marvel at changes personally observed in two decades: how adult groups from Sanford, North Carolina (brick capital of the world) now fly regularly to London for the Shakespeare plays; the audience drives in from as far away as Asheville and Hatteras when Eudora Welty speaks in Chapel Hill; nine women artists from my state exhibit their paintings in Washington, D.C., in 1989 before making the southern tour (although nothing in their art seemed particularly female *or* southern); and Louis Rubin's small North Carolina press, Algonquin, places first novels not just on the best-seller list but on page one of the *New York Times Book Review* and among the Pulitzers.

Similar evidence, much of it anecdotal from various southern communities, causes academic specialists in southern literature to argue enthusiastically for an ongoing vitality among area writers and readers. They point to a revival of southern crafts (*Foxfire*) and folklore as well. Furthermore, they believe the national mainstream audience for things southern has increased, now that the civil rights struggle has cooled and the region is no longer assumed to be populated largely by off-duty Klansmen. They also credit a wider specifically southern audience, enlarged by the immigration which new business and industry brought, for arts and humanities public programs across the region. Southern chauvinists have their opponents, such as Richard Kostelanetz, who believes these enthusiasms run in cycles, largely fueled by special interest groups. Kostelanetz observes that nearly all the "prominent critics and novelists of the fifties and sixties were either Southerners or Jews or regular contributors to *The New Yorker*," and his book attacks the "collective dominance" and artificial trends that groups (or essays like this) invent and cultivate.[6] Just as Hugh Kenner has said that one may "declare a kingdom in order to proclaim himself king," Kostelanetz and others charge that present scholars of southern literature, aided by their graduate students now strategically tenured in various universities, have a vested interest in maintaining a kingdom that actually fell forty years ago. How likely is it, they ask, that the category of "Southern Literature" will be seriously questioned, much less repudiated, by—for instance— the Society for the Study of Southern Literature (founded 1968), the Institute for Southern Studies (University of South Carolina), the Center for the Study of Southern Culture (University of Mississippi), or magazines entitled *Southern Literary Journal, Southern Studies, Southern Review*, and *Southern Quarterly*?

Other literary critics, instead of attacking the regional category, merely ignore it. Frederick Karl resists grouping writers regionally in his *American Fictions 1940–1980*, believing that certain political or beat or minimal fictions, certain female or surreal or pastoral writers, only speak their American themes in a southern drawl; that is, as Hawthorne and Melville struggled against contradiction, Walker Percy's struggle is set in a warmer climate. William Styron is sometimes cited as one writer for whom the South often serves as setting for stories that could easily be relocated, a writer whose existentialist characters decide like Percy's (although with more bombast) that it is better to live than to die, but whose presence in the South has not modified their essence very much. Karl, who believes that all American writers are still learning lessons from Joyce, Kafka, Proust, and other modernists, implies that since Faulkner the South's writers (perhaps being slower learners) are especially overdue in applying those modernist lessons to their vision of one particular area of America.

This old argument about whether or not modern southern literature is really distinctive continues to flourish. In June 1989, I sat on a panel sponsored by the National Endowment for the Arts with a sociologist who specializes in things southern, John Shelton Reed of the University of North Carolina-Chapel Hill, and a North Carolina poet and teacher, Michael McFee. Our audience was composed of several hundred public arts leaders who had come to Durham from across the southeast. We had been told to discuss those resources in the contemporary South that feed into art—not mere local color, mind you, but regional Art, perhaps Art along the lines of Thomas Mann's comment about Chekhov, "He wrote the universe into Russia." As our panel's definitions and distinctions grew murky, and then murkier, we finally asked the audience itself to share its own regional experience, to declare what in their opinion made the arts in the South different from arts elsewhere in the country. Many who hurried to the microphones had moved South from the West or Northeast; most were persuaded, some passionately, that life and thus art were markedly different at the latitude where they had become its professional promoters, although all admitted that both art and life here had proved different from their stereotyped expectations.

As we talked back and forth, new definitions seemed required of this latest "new" South and its characteristics in poetry and fiction. Quotations from both audience and panelists were dated. We took note that Eudora Welty's famous essay "Place in Fiction" (which only calls "place" one of the lesser angels watching over fiction, not a major wing-beater like character, plot, or symbolic meaning) had after all been published thirty-three years before. Allen Tate had been born in 1899, John Crowe Ransom in 1888. Yes, things in the South had definitely changed, said various speakers; the South was rising one more time, announced some; others insisted that in the South the more things changed the more they stayed the same and that the philosophy of the Agrarians still applied.

For quite a while this audience representing public arts programs from all over the region talked back to the panel and asserted that southern art and its audiences were distinctive. (I took these notes: "your books focus on *people*." . . . "oral storytelling in that particular accent." . . . "context in the time-frame of the past, the generations." . . . "rhythms of speech and jazz and country music." . . . "people *feel* Southern, that they belong to a community. . . ." If there was any consensus, it was that contemporary artists handle old themes and the ways these have been usurped, but using mainstream techniques. Nobody specified which techniques.

I carried my notes home and held them alongside Walker Percy's list of southern literary characteristics in the self-interview he published in *Esquire* in 1977:

> I've heard about that, the storytelling tradition, sense of identity, tragic dimension, community, history, and so forth. But I was never quite sure what it meant. In fact, I'm not sure that the opposite is not the case. People don't read much in the South and don't take writers very seriously, which is probably as it should be. I've managed to live here for 30 years and am less well-known than the Budweiser distributor. The only famous person in this town is Isaih Robertson, linebacker for the Rams, and that is probably as it should be, too. There are advantages to living an obscure life and being thought an idler. If one lived in a place like France, where writers are honored, one might well end up like Sartre, a kind of literary political Pope, a savant, an academician, the very sort of person Sartre

made fun of in *Nausea*. On the other hand, if one is thought an idler and a bum, one is free to do what one pleases.

One day a fellow townsman asked me, "What do you do, Doc?" "Well, I write books." "I know that, Doc, but what do you really do?" "Nothing." He nodded. He was pleased, and I was pleased.[7]

Unlike Allen Tate, Percy never wanted to join a writers' colony on the Mississippi River's Left Bank; he rejoiced that Covington, Louisiana, had not become a slower-paced Greenwich Village. Although both he and Tate made the same diagnosis forty-four years apart—that the southern writer and the southern audience are disjointed—Tate found the prognosis of this continuing separation gloomy. That separation was Percy's postmodern bread and butter, because he felt the disjunction helped him write about living "at the end of modern times . . . the end of Christendom as we know it"; his novels ask whether his characters are more or less normal than the society around them.[8]

What Percy found gloomy—and I do, too—is the likelihood that in the busy postmodern South there will be no Lost Cove to escape to when his characters and mine need it, no place for Tom Moore to live on the bayou and run his trotline, that long before then writers and audiences alike will have embraced the status quo without malaise and be sharing very frank confessions about their lives and arts on the "Donahue Show." Frequently.

To test whether or not conformity is likely to submerge both southern writers and southern readers, let us first examine how ideas about the South and southern literature have changed during our own reading lifetimes.

Wanted: Southern Renascence—Dead or Alive

Before predicting any specific future for southern literature (which sounds like something the government would appoint a commission to do) let us begin with a view considered typically southern: looking at today's southern writers as inheritors of the older southern fiction most of them have read. Donald R. Noble applies this perspective when he assesses current writers and makes his own predictions in "The Future of Southern Writing."[9] After defining a card-carrying southern writer as "someone who has spent his childhood in the South and conceives of himself as southern even if he resides in Connecticut now," Noble then avoids another shopworn debate by saying straightaway that if the fabled Southern Renascence is narrowed to the region's literary output between 1925 and 1955 then, yes and ho hum, the Renascence has indeed ended. Because present and future southern writers continue to be measured against its primary figures, a simplified summary of the Southern Renascence follows.

Most critics emphasizing the distinctiveness of southern literature say those distinctions were rooted in the nineteenth-century South, with its tradition of oral storytelling as it functioned in an agrarian, family-centered, insular society, the storytelling nourished technically by language and plots from the King James version of the Bible and nourished thematically by the view of humanity and the moral values provided by Christianity. The short list of nineteenth-century writers is topped by Edgar Allan Poe and Mark Twain, followed at some distance by Thomas Nelson Page, William Gilmore Simms, George Washington Cable, Joel Chandler Harris, Thomas Dixon, Kate Chopin, Sidney Lanier, and others.

After losing the Civil War and enduring Reconstruction, the defeated South entered the twentieth century even more withdrawn from neighboring states, still feeding itself on overblown myths of the antebellum past—at least the white South did. Southern blacks had been freed from slavery into more subtle forms of poverty and oppression. Even World War I did not shake white southerners loose from their regional obsessions especially in Deep South plantation territory. Although William March is an obvious exception, most southern novelists preferred to create Confederate, not doughboy, heroes.

However, after 1918, when, according to Allen Tate, the South reentered the larger, more industrialized world, that change clashed with its long backward glance, and the conflict "gave us the Southern Renascence, a literature conscious of the past in the present." Donald Davidson has agreed with the nature and 1920s and 1930s' timing of this literary Renascence, comparing new southern perspectives after 1918 with the way similar sharp shifts of balance have caused clashes within other traditional societies, such as "Greece in the 5th Century, B.C., Rome of the late Republic, Italy in Dante's time, England in the 19th Century." The stimulus of the Scopes trial in Tennessee in 1925 helped produce *I'll Take My Stand*, a collection of essays described in Ransom's introduction as supporting "a Southern way of life against what might be called the American or prevailing way." The southern way was agrarian, fundamentalist, traditional; the American was centralized, urban, materialistic.[10]

That twilight of the old and at least philosophically unreconstructed southern culture being pushed aside by the new is called by Walter Sullivan the "gotterdammerung theory of Southern Literature."[11] Like marble monuments taking their own stand in that twilight, their faces turned for that backward glance deep into the southern past of paradoxical guilt, loss, and honor, loom the literary heroes: Faulkner on the tallest pedestal, then Wolfe, Glasgow, Tate, Ransom, Welty, Porter, Warren, and others—some marked as Fugitives and Agrarians, a few smaller statues labeled in parentheses (Women). Although Noble keeps these monumental figures and their long shadows in place while he extends the Renascence period as late as 1955, Sullivan thinks even Faulkner's best and most characteristic work was over long before, and that the Renascence ended with a bang when Robert Penn Warren published its "philosophical swan song," *All the King's Men*, in 1946, presenting materialistic New South mythologies which endorsed Willie Stark's achieving good ends by any means, and showing how Jack Burden's collaboration cost him even the potential love of the father who had never claimed him.

Afterward: 1960–80

Sullivan stated these views in the Lamar lectures at Mercer University, although previous Lamar lecturers like Louis Rubin and Lewis Simpson had argued that the Southern Renascence only entered a new phase during the 1950s, different but still vigorous, productive, recognizably southern, still distinctive.

Most of us remember the decade of the 1960s not as a sequence of pages we read but as rapid video images flashed on our faces in glaring strobe pulses: Martin Luther King leading protest marches, his Nobel prize, his murder; Watts riots; Kennedy's election, his popularity, his assassination, Jackie; the Civil Rights Act of 1964; Vietnam, the protests, the peace sign, Kent State, Woodstock, music; artificial heart, heart transplant; space flights, fire on Apollo I, the moon landing; *Soul on Ice*, George Wallace, James Meredith, church bombings; Oswald, Ruby, Bobby Kennedy, Chappaquiddick, the Manson family.

The emphasis seemed national, the South lost in the weather map and the six o'clock news. Truman Capote published two books during the 1960s, one about a southerner named Holly Golightly who was living in New York City, and one about the murder of a Kansas family. Carson McCullers died in 1967; her last novel, *Clock without Hands*, about Judge Fox Clane of Georgia, an octogenarian still hoping to redeem Confederate bonds and currency, seemed like a parody.

During the late 1960s, as he observed America's new sexual freedom as a feeding frenzy, Walter Sullivan was busy completing *Death by Melancholy*, which argued that the old behavioral restraints had been replaced by such unrestrained pursuit of physical satisfactions that these were symptoms of fatal moral sickness.

But the 1970s brought more than the decline of Victorian sexuality and the end of the Vietnam War, most school segregation, and organized youth protest. Gradually scenes also faded off the television screen showing southern whites siccing dogs or using electric cattle prods against southern blacks. Then in 1976 a southerner was elected to the White House. Although for fifty of the seventy-two years between Washington and Lincoln southerners had held the U.S. presidency, only the expatriate Woodrow Wilson had held the office between Andrew and Lyndon B. Johnson until Democratic Georgia governor Jimmy Carter defeated Gerald Ford.

Suddenly the national press and media became so fascinated by the South that stereotypes threatened to become institutionalized. All southerners, like their caricatures on the "Dukes of Hazzard," were quickly assigned down-home residence in imaginary rural counties where the Appalachians and the Bayou swamps were located right next door. During this kitsch outbreak, television also introduced "Roots" to provide a melodramatic mythology for black viewers and revived *Gone With the Wind* to reinstate a melodramatic mythology for southern white viewers. (As Roy Blount has said, "You got to put the kibble over where even the slow dogs can get some.")[12]

During this period, too, James Dickey reaffirmed that the South was the most "fertile literary region that has ever existed in this country."[13] And because President Carter, his wife, his faith-healing sister, his Peace Corps mother, and even his beer-drinking brother Billy were followers of a Bible Belt Christianity thought nearly extinct, reporters struggled through earnest if puzzled interviews with southern fundamentalists about what it really meant to be "born again," although nobody had a literary renascence in mind.

To the contrary, even during this 1970s' media blitz, some continued to argue that southern literature was declining or dead. Floyd Watkins, in *The Death of Art* not only castigated southern stereotypes but also said that since *Brown vs. Topeka Board of Education* in 1954, propaganda had replaced art in southern fiction. Both cliché and propaganda respond only to the marketplace, he said, not to the imagination.

A more scathing attack came from Richard Gilman, who reviewed Reynolds Price's novel *The Surface of Earth* for the *New York Times Book Review*. Calling it "extinct, a mastodon," a "relentless family saga" out of synch with American audiences who were now "self generated" readers who, because they had "obliterated pasts," were thus cured of Price's obsessions with history, generations, and memories, Gilman used the occasion to indict all southern writing. He found it local, florid, without

166

distinction; in fact, he said, there was no important regional literature being created anywhere in the United States.[14]

But even a partial list of southern writers publishing prose and poetry during the 1970s, some of it regional, some arguably not, at least suggests that the mastodon might have only been napping when Gilman called, that as new black and female writers began to appear, the species might be acquiring hybrid vigor.

During that decade, for instance: Pulitzer Prize-winner Shirley Ann Grau published three books; James Alan McPherson won the Pulitzer for *Elbow Room* in 1978; Alice Walker (Pulitzer 1982) published *Meridian* in 1976; and Anne Tyler, who would not receive her Pulitzer until 1989, published *Celestial Navigation*, set as usual in Baltimore. Eudora Welty's most successful novel with its themes of family history, *The Optimist's Daughter*, was published in 1972; she also leapt to Price's defense in a spirited letter to the New York *Times* disputing Gilman's review. In 1971, Ernest Gaines published *The Autobiography of Miss Jane Pittman*. Mary Lee Settle, known for her Beulah Quintet about the coal-mining region of West Virginia, won the National Book Award in 1978 with *Blood Tie*. The very southern protagonist of Walker Percy's *Lancelot* (1977) was compared to Quentin Compson; Percy himself said that suicide is easy, that Binx Bolling is a Quentin Compson who didn't commit suicide.[15]

And on the long list of southern writers publishing during the 1970s were David Madden, Gayl Jones, Lillian Smith, Berry Morgan, Sylvia Wilkinson, Alex Haley, Heather Ross Miller, Madison Jones, Gail Godwin, Ishmael Reed, Lee Smith, Elizabeth Spencer, James Still, Lisa Alther, William Goyen, Hollis Summers, Reynolds Price, George Garrett, Guy Owen, James Whitehead, William Price Fox, Peter Taylor, Borden Deal, Barry Hannah, Harry Crews, Cormac McCarthy, Sallie Bingham, Joan Williams, Beverly Lowry, Guy Davenport, Bobbie Ann Mason, Ellen Douglas, Lucille Clifton, Rita Mae Brown, Toni Cade Bambara, Robert Day, Nikki Giovanni, Wendell Berry, Julia Fields, William Styron, Albert Murray, Archie Ammons, John Barth, James Dickey, William Harmon, William Hoffman, Fred Chappell, Elizabeth Hardwick, William Humphrey, Ovid Williams Pierce, Calder Willingham, Dabney Stuart, Andre Dubus, and Maya Angelou.

Although any such listing always proves incomplete, and although categories prove inadequate or ill-defined or arguable, I will persist and lengthen this one. Literary work appeared during the 1980s not only from older writers (some of them named above) who continued to publish but also from southern newcomers: Josephine Humphreys, Ellen Gilchrist, Kaye Gibbons, Josephine Jacobsen, Beth Henley, Samm Art

Williams, Jill McCorkle, Marianne Gingher, Pat Conroy, Padgett Powell, Dave Smith, Emily Ellison, Ferrol Sams, Anne Siddons, Clyde Taylor, Tim McLaurin, Randall Kenan, Joe Ashby Porter, Mary Hood, Henry Taylor, James Seay, Jonathan Williams, Eve Shelnutt, Gerald Barrax, Robert Morgan, Charles Wright, Ellen Voigt, Coleman Barks, John Ehle, A. B. Spellman, James Applewhite, Van K. Brock, Charleen Whisnant, John Owen, John Oliver Killens, Breece Pancake, Betty Adcock, Richard Tillinghast, Allen Wier, Susan Ludvigson, Beverly Jarrett, Martha Lacy Hall, John Finlay, Louise Shivers, Linda Pastan, Marion Montgomery, Charles Rowell, James Whitehead, Miller Williams, Heather Ross Miller, Peggy Payne, Charles Edward Eaton, Max Steele, Elizabeth Sewell, Wilma Dykeman, Alice Adams, J. R. Salamanca, Mary Mebane, William Mills, Don Hendrie, Jr., R. T. Smith, Joy Williams, Janet Burroway, Lee Zacharias, Emily H. Wilson, R. H. W. Dillard, and Nancy Hale. Fuller listings by states, as well as a source to check disputed categories (natives? residents? expatriates? Florida? West Texas?) may be found in the annual *Directory of American Poets and Fiction Writers*, as well as *Southern Writers: A Biographical Dictionary*. These will include the names of too many writers to reproduce here.[16]

Since there are so many regional novelists, story writers, essayists, poets, and crossover journalists, it is no wonder that the Fellowship of Southern Writers was founded in the 1980s (and has been lightly mocked by Michael Skuube, Pulitzer book editor of the Raleigh *News and Observer*), nor that Washington *Post* critic Jonathan Yardley said on late-night radio in the summer of 1989 that the South kept on producing a disproportionate number of good American writers, that its sense of history might still be the reason. (Human narrative equals "his" story; lately it has been "her" story as well.)

Nor is it any wonder that Louis Rubin, at a 1985 conference on southern writing, commented, "They say there is no such thing as southern writing, that it's just a form of local chauvinism. But can you imagine a meeting like this being held on Rocky Mountain writing?"[17]

Southern Rivers, Woods, Streams, Swamps, Mountains

Rubin thus echoes the more caustic comment of Flannery O'Connor that "in the South there are more amateur authors than there are rivers and streams. It's not an activity that waits upon talent. . . . The woods are full of regional writers, and it is the great horror of every serious Southern writer that he will become one of them."[18]

If Sherman's army today might have to march to the sea knee deep in aspiring writers of varying talent, county poets, teens being lovesick in free verse, and graduates of college M.F.A. programs, the sheer numbers of such people do signify change in the South's literary consciousness since Allen Tate's day. For one thing, the serious writers have read all that the Southern Renascence produced, whereas O'Connor said that in college outside the South she only heard Poe and Joel Chandler Harris mentioned very much. The proportion of talent may be no larger in the 1980s, but the aspiring young have learned by osmosis what Anne Tyler learned in one Eureka gasp as she read about Welty's character Edna Earle, "who was so slow-witted she could sit all day just pondering how the tail of the C got through the loop of the L on the Coca-Cola sign. Why, I knew Edna Earle. You mean you could *write* about such people? I have always meant to send Eudora Welty a thank-you note, but I imagine she would find it a little strange."[19]

Young southern writers today also mature in a climate where, at least in their home states, scholarship about regional writers has become academically respectable. Some would say the "Southern Mafia" dates back to the Fugitives and Agrarians who grew up in the 1920s around Vanderbilt University. Literary criticism on southern writers now forms a sizable library by such scholars as Louis Rubin, Hugh Holman, Robert Jacobs, Walter Sullivan, Frederick Hoffman, George Core, Lewis Simpson, Thomas Daniel Young, Cleanth Brooks, Lewis Leary, Richard Beale Davis, and many others, and with at least eight major quarterlies plus dozens of campus magazines that feature southern writing and criticism, especially *Callaloo*, now at Southern University in Baton Rouge, which since 1976 has focused on black southern artists and writers.

So contemporary southern writers, their ranks swollen by black and feminist poets and fiction writers, emerge in a different literary tradition from that of their forebears, with scholarly attention, and write to a national but also a regional audience that by migration and self-improvement is, despite the South's backwardness, wider and better read than when Allen Tate complained.

Many of these writers are their own eloquent spokesmen on what the South is or is not, and what effect locale has had on their writing. One cautionary note before allowing them to "tell about the South": it is a fact of the literary life that if you come from the South and write books, you will be asked to issue pronouncements. Walker Percy is only one of many writers to complain, "I'm sick and tired of talking about the South and hearing about the South . . . if there's anything more boring, it is the answers southerners give. If I hear one more northerner ask about good ol' boys and one more southerner give an answer, I'm moving to Manaus, Brazil, to join the South Carolinians who emigrated after Appomattox and whose descendants now speak no English and have such names as Senhor Carlos Calhoun."[20]

Keeping Percy's fractiousness in mind, it will be useful to read with a whole boxful of salt anything southern writers themselves say about the South because they may be truthful, merely polite, bored, or actively fantasizing. Their responses rarely reveal the full context of how they were asked, or by whom. The best way to immunize oneself against too much gullibility will be to recall what Roy Blount, who is one of us, wrote in *What Men Don't Tell Women*.

> If a Northern visitor makes it clear to Southerners that he thinks it would be typical of them to rustle up a big, piping hot meal of hushpuppies and blackstrap, Southerners will do that, even if they were planning to have just a little salad that night.
>
> Then the visitor will ask how to eat hushpuppies and blackstrap. . . . The strictly accurate answer is that nobody in his or her right mind eats these two things together, in any way at all. But that isn't a sociable answer. So Southerners may say, "First you pour your plate full of the molasses, and then you crumble your hushpuppies up in it, and then you take the *back* of your spoon and. . . ." Southerners will say things like that just to see whether it is still true that Northerners will believe anything. About the South.[21]

Some of what Blount describes as southerners getting a "charge out of being typical" may be discerned in the following comments of other writers about being a southerner and a southern writer. But notice, too, those places where the Souths described do not coincide, but grind together like tectonic, unmatching geologic plates.

Berry Morgan, born on a plantation near Port Gibson, Mississippi, in 1919, "listened to the wisdom of the Negroes, a considerable wisdom that I still feel is my own by osmosis and love if not by heritage." Jump ahead to Reynolds Price, born twenty-four years later in eastern North Carolina, who says he was reared by two blacks who had been born slaves and who told him stories. He suspects that's how blacks survived slavery, by believing they were "moral tutors, the consciences of whites." I do not think that is quite what Alice Walker had in mind in "The Black Writer and the Southern Experience" when she retold her mother's stories that dealt solely with a community of black people, with little reference to vindictive whites living nearby. She mentions the rich heritage of having an "underprivileged" southern background, but uses the words of non-southerner Camus to call it "halfway between misery and the sun" where people know that "though all is not well under the sun, history is not everything."[22]

170

Alex Haley, who now owns a farm near Knoxville, says, "I don't know anything I treasure more as a writer than being a southerner." In speeches and interviews Rita Mae Brown has called the South "a good environment for writers" because it "allows itself eccentrics." Americans from other regions seem duller to her, too rational. "Art is intensely emotive and at least in the South you are allowed your emotions," she says.[23]

The farther away you get from Richmond gentility to ascend into the Virginia mountains and have a blessed descent into the lower classes, the more virtue characters will exhibit in Lee Smith's novels, noted for their rhythmic, concrete, earthy dialog. The loss of an authentic past in her *Oral History* and its replacement by a tawdry historical park that charges admission are themes both Allen Tate and Harriet Arnow would applaud. The old Agrarian theme of rural life close to Nature and the old fear that war and carpetbaggers had ruined the true South surface in Josephine Humphreys's work as anger against housing developments, interstates, and prettified museum towns with their costumed tour guides. She agrees with her teacher from Duke, Reynolds Price, that fiction is best set in a town of fewer than ten thousand souls, "a town from whose center open country can be reached by a fifteen-minute walk."[24]

Padgett Powell's remembered South is the one of Elvis Presley's early 45's and a father whose war tales, set not in Gettysburg but far away in the South Pacific, already seemed like movies. Powell, from South Carolina, sounds a lot like Barry Hannah from Mississippi, who grumbles at the standard southern questions. "You can't imagine how often I get asked about how Faulkner influenced me and why there's so many good Southern writers and all that shit." Although he is not interested in labels at all, and grew up listening to "The Green Hornet" and "The Shadow" and having bee-bee gun fights with Reds and Nazis in other people's yards and basements, Hannah also visited the Vicksburg battlefields, "had the Civil War in my blood and read the books about it," and remains proud to be a southerner.[25]

Conrad Aiken, a doctor's son, wrote of his house in Savannah in "Strange Moonlight," but it hardly seems the same city where Langston Hughes was once accosted by a local policeman for buying a newspaper in the whites-only waiting room in the railroad station. James Alan McPherson also remembers not grace and beauty, but grinding poverty in Savannah, living on welfare, wearing clothes from the Salvation Army, and going without lights or heat for years at a time. The joyous train rides he took to Augusta for Christmas holidays gave him a life-long love of trains. The defeat he saw was not that of the old Confederacy, but a personal loss carved into his father's face when the family visited him in the Reidsville prison where he underwent shock treatments. After three years at Catholic school, McPherson transferred to the "retarded" section of grade three at Florence Street School, surviving mentally by steady reading at the Colored Branch of the Carnegie Public Library. "During all my years in Savannah, I never had peace or comfort or any chance to rely on anyone else." He ends his memory of a southern childhood by saying that like all "permanent exiles, I have learned to be at home inside myself."[26]

So evidently did Robb Forman Dew, granddaughter of John Crowe Ransom, who grew up as the daughter of a neurosurgeon in Baton Rouge and lived through "the lovely solipsism of Southern girlhood" but could not maintain the image of the perky southern belle. "I don't believe that I have ever really felt that I was a native of any place. . . . I have made a small country of the society of my husband and my children, my mother and my sister, and my close friends. I rarely venture beyond its boundaries." The same might be said about Anne Tyler, although she does not classify herself as southern, was born elsewhere, and only raised "on the outskirts looking in."[27]

James Dickey offered some of the standard summations in the *Paris Review Interview*. "Due to their past, their history, and their rural background, southerners are lonely people. They very seldom have anyone to talk to. The result has been that when a southerner encounters another human being the southerner talks the stranger's head off. Add to this the very strong folklore and the legendary quality of local stories, anecdotes, and jokes, and you have the basis for southern poetry and also for southern fiction." But in the midst of so many quotations from southern women writers, Dickey's comments about them also bear repeating: "The women of the South have brought into American literature a unique mixture of domesticity and grotesquery. There have been two routes open to the southern woman writer. She could research a historic subject—such as Elizabeth Madox Roberts did in *The Great Meadow* which deals with the opening up of Kentucky—couple this with domestic images from her own life, and write her fiction out of these two considerations; or she could deal with eccentric village types such as Carson McCullers and Eudora Welty frequently do and Flannery O'Connor does to an extreme. The southern women writers of the two generations which produced our great ones were singularly immobile, but then so was Emily Brontë. They had little breadth of experience, but much penetration into a specific and still milieu. They are remarkable writers. But their scope is limited to the local and domestic with, in some cases, an admixture of the grotesque. I like it all."[28]

Margaret Walker likes living in Mississippi, but agrees with Dickey that there aren't many people to talk to, "nobody to raise an intellectual issue with you." Born the year Booker T. Washington died, she grew up in a home surrounded by books and music, went away to college and to work with the W.P.A. writers project in Chicago. She heard the story of her novel *Jubilee* from her grandmother.[29]

Andrew Lytle, who espoused the Agrarian view that southerners would become Americanized and lose their sense of general craftsmanship in favor of narrow specialties for material gains, told an interviewer for the *Chattahoochee Review* in the summer of 1988 that the national literature "has been dominated by southerners" for the last fifty years. Born in 1902, Lytle represents the same internalized South as Cleanth Brooks, born in 1906, whose typical southerner has "a belief in human imperfection and a genuine and never wavering disbelief in human perfection." But James Whitehead (born 1936), who has both Confederate and Union soldiers in his family background, also went to Vanderbilt, had Medgar Evers as one of his heroes, and calls his fictional football player Sonny Joiner "a secret Christian" who considers Billy Graham a gnostic. Whitehead has said Faulkner is like the humidity in Mississippi—"you don't avoid him, you grow up with him." He differentiates his perception of society from Walker Percy's, since Percy "writes about rich people," and notes that lively southern writing in the future may come from such areas as the Chicano part of Texas. Beth Henley, one of many Jackson, Mississippi, writers, says she writes about the South "because you can get away with making things more poetic. The style can just be stronger." But she doesn't want to come back and live down the road from Miss Welty, not just because Mississippi gives her hay fever but because "it would just be too quiet for me." Turner Cassity goes even further, calling present-day Jackson "an extension of Oklahoma City. Whatever the South was or was not, it was 80 years ago." He thinks the two great novels about the South are *War and Peace* and *Buddenbrooks!* Bobbie Ann Mason focuses on the superficial present-day South with its cancerous mobile homes, plastic restaurants, and Parthenon-like shopping malls, although she grew up on a dairy farm in Mayfield and says, "I still have my head in Kentucky." As a teenager in the 1950s, instead of listening to the war stories Confederate grandsons heard, she and her mother were active groupies, rushing around the country after such public figures as Smiley Burnett, Tony Martin, and the Hilltoppers, whose national fan club Mason headed. Ernest Gaines looked for black characters in southern writing and didn't find them the way he knew them, so he started reading not books by Faulkner, but by Russians and Europeans about peasant life in other places.[30]

Pat Conroy, who calls Thomas Wolfe his hero, remembers that his mother, Peg, tried to teach him that being southern "was a state of unearned grace and proof of a loving God." But Gail Godwin's Asheville was not Thomas Wolfe's, nor was his Pulpit Hill the same university for her as for Percy and Shelby Foote. She has used southern women as protagonists in her novels as well as analyzed the "southern belle" and "southern lady" for *Ms.* magazine, saying that in the South a growing girl can find "an image of womanhood already cut out for her, stitched securely by the practiced hands of tradition." In this she speaks for an ongoing regional sisterhood, echoing Ellen Glasgow's much earlier comment that her heroine's education was founded on the theory that "the less a girl knew about life the better prepared she would be to contend with it."[31]

Erskine Caldwell, who died in 1987 after publishing more than fifty books, admired regional writing since his life had been confined to the southern states and "that's what I've written about." He insisted that because of authentic southern experience he didn't need to invent scenes like two babies being suckled by a dog, or people beaten to death on the chain gang. Son of a Presbyterian minister but an agnostic himself, Caldwell said his famous character Ty Ty didn't really believe in God, either. "The only difficulty about regionalism now is the fact that it really doesn't exist anymore . . . we have all become slaves to this new universal Americanism."[32]

One could add to these a long list of southern exiles—who also have views about the South—from Walter Hines Page forward. Not many associate Max Bodenheim with his birthplace in Vicksburg. Alice Adams grew up surrounded by writers in Chapel Hill and attended a boarding school in Virginia, where polite conversation was "elevated to an almost religious principle," but Radcliffe attracted her away from the South. Lillian Hellman documented her southern roots in her two memoirs but lived mostly in New York. Al Young left Ocean Springs, Mississippi, when his family took the Chickenbone Special to Detroit; he has said that Kingfish Stevens and Rochester are one stereotype of blacks, "but the fist-waver is another." Willie Morris, who has made a profession of being from Yazoo City, Mississippi, edited in 1965 an issue of *Harper's*, "The South Today: 100 Years after Appomattox," but witnessed racial violence in the 1960s on his television screen in New York City. "I have mixed feelings about the New South," he said. "You can get off at the Atlanta airport, that whole modern cosmos, and you *still* know you're in the South. Yet I feel in my soul that Southern writing will endure."[33]

Elizabeth Hardwick says that being a southern writer is "a decision, not a fate," and although she grew up in Kentucky and had a fellowship to Louisiana State University at a time when it seemed magical to anyone interested in literature, she chose to leave the South for Columbia, and to leave the Calvinist view of man as well. Joan Williams has used in her novels the people she knew in Arkabutla, Tennessee, as well as her father's experiences on the Mississippi levees; and while she has called the South a limiting influence, her departure north also cut her off from her original material. When she visits nowadays, the contemporary South seems "much like anyplace else."[34] Yet Tarheel Washingtonians gather for an annual barbecue in the District of Columbia, and Mississippian New Yorkers have been holding a summer picnic in Central Park every summer since 1979, complete with watermelon-seed spitting contests and sculptures made of hominy grits.[35]

Representative testimony by southern writers could be quoted indefinitely, but surely the foregoing from many published interviews is sufficient to illustrate that there is no single monolithic South to be born into, grow up in, remember, or write about. Most interviewees find that answering questions about the South is like spitting into a whirlwind of presuppositions. There are many sub-souths being written about today, their subject matter modified by geography, age, gender, race, and economic class, and this diversity is apt to continue and spread.

The major geographic divisions with their effect on life and theme were documented by C. Hugh Holman in *The Roots of Southern Writing*.[36] Sea Island cotton and rice did not produce plantation culture near Asheville, and New Orleans always had more shipping than did Atlanta. Most southern stereotypes, in fact, refer to only one of many souths: the old, idealized plantation version—low country, cotton-growing, delta, or tidewater. Although there is a coastal south for Louisiana, geographically and culturally it is not identical with Kill Devil Hills in North Carolina. There is a mountainous, hardscrabble South that in recent years has seen different conflicts from those between Snopeses and Compsons as it turned into a tourist empire, with stylized Cherokee Indians and prefabricated chalets built along manmade ski slopes. (Once Lyndon B. Johnson visited Rocky Mount in eastern North Carolina and made loud speeches about T.V.A. and Appalachian poverty, not realizing that he was in flat tobacco country.) Downhill from this Appalachian South lies a piedmont, redclay, yeoman-farmer South that in the twentieth century has been steadily industrialized. In all of these Souths are small rural county seats which, despite chain grocers and pharmacies, still do not duplicate in spirit Atlanta or Nashville, and despite local history will never become as ornamental as Williamsburg. Natives of the rural upcountry South will walk as carefully as Yankees through cane-brake country, and when like tourists they bring home Spanish moss to hang in their crepe myrtle tree, it will not grow.

Nor do the clichéd assumptions about the southern past fit every sub-South equally. The stories some southerners tell their children (when they can be heard over television or jam boxes) may be about lost forefathers, brothers who wore either blue or gray uniforms and went to war against their own kin, freedmen in niggertown, millworkers on Lint Hill, grandmothers baking biscuits in detached kitchens or stirring laundry in a wash pot with an old broom handle after picking a hundred pounds of cotton per day, or unemployed weavers eating pintos and vinegar-onions at the diner while waiting for a job during the depression. The histories behind most southern families are not at all aristocratic.

Not only are there many geographic and historic Souths in reality, but all of them are held up to the mirror of the capital-S South as it has already been depicted by Faulkner, by W. J. Cash, in the photographs and text of James Agee and Walker Evans, by the Grand Old Opry, through country and jazz music, in Dogpatch and Tobacco Road and Tara and Flamingo Road and Yoknapatawpha, and so on.

"Southerners were invented as a coherent family of types in the early 19th century," said Jack Temple Kirby.[37] And they were not entirely invented by nonsoutherners. From Uncle Remus to Colonel Sanders, regional writers themselves have made it hard to tell the chicken from the egg because they have both collaborated with cliché and elaborated upon it. Specific predictions about the future of southern writing must be made within the assumption that writers will continue to reinvent the wheels-within-wheels of overlapping mythological and actual Souths because they—like Ezekiel—prefer to speak in visions and stories rather than make careful sociological studies or draw demographic charts. In fact, that may be the safest prediction about future southern writing— that even those writers who have secret ambitions to solve contemporary problems (blacks, feminists, closet Catholics, and Chicanos) will keep producing stories instead of submitting theses about social issues.

Writing in the New, Newer, Newest South

If there is no field guide to the various Souths or the southern types who live in them, John Reed analyzed many when he delivered Mercer's Lamar lecture in 1985. These, too, must be added to an invented population dwelling in an invented South which affects readers and writers alike.

For a writer, the presence of stereotypes presents certain advantages: fiction often has as one motive a desire to set the record straight, whether in Ernest Gaines's or Toni Morrison's creation of genuine black characters to correct Dilsey and Nigger Jim, or in the ways Larry McMurtry tore down and rebuilt the American cowboy in *Lonesome Dove.* Southern types may have been invented in the nineteenth century, but during the twentieth they have swarmed into Dixie's central casting office from life, literature, and popular culture—Uncle Tom, Sambo, Aunt Jemima, Amos and Andy, Richard Petty, Junior Johnson, Big Daddy, Amanda Wingfield, Blanche Du Bois, Minnie Pearl, Big Jim Folsom, Junior Samples, Mammy Yokum, Norma Rae, Rhett Butler, Moonbeam McSwine, Bubba, Merle Haggard, Gomer Pyle, Ernest T. Bass, Senator Phogbound, Loretta Lynn, Hank Williams, Lum and Abner, Step 'n Fetchit, Dolly Parton, and Butterfly McQueen, for example. Notice how few of these stereotypes represent the southern middle class, although half the southern labor force is now in white-collar jobs. Types give a writer something solid to push against, attack, overturn. Even those fictional characters who slide against the author's will into representative types or archetypes themselves would hardly be at home in one another's novels—picture Will Barrett buying Jeter Lester a drink, or Huck Finn escorting Frankie Addams to a junior high sockhop.

Almost as predictable as the New South's pop-culture caricatures are the recurring funeral elegies for the Old South itself, some of which have been alluded to in this chapter, since a dead South would kill off southern writing as a type of its own. The southern historian George Tindall has pointed out that the South has been scheduled to die over and over during American history. It was supposed to die because of the swift westward expansion and because of too much easy money produced in the Cotton Kingdom. Then it was supposed to be killed off by the railroads, then by secession, then by losing the Civil War. The end of slavery should have killed it and, if not, Reconstruction was certainly its deathbed. Populism rang a death knell; the South would never be the same after the arrival of the automobile and the national highway network. Mass communications were sure to put an end to distinctively southern speech and any spirit of regionalism. Surely the depression would prove fatal to the South. It died forever from the internationalizing results of World War II and, if not then, certainly it disappeared forever during the postwar boom. *Brown v. Topeka Board of Education* finally killed the South. No, the end of segregation did it. The arrival of suburbia destroyed the South as it had usually been defined. Politically the South died once it ceased to be solidly Democratic. Lately, like the murderers of Rasputin, the attacks of immigration, electronics, video, and federalism have been struggling to kill the South at long last.

Even this cursory glimpse of southern writers and their geographical sub-South worlds makes clear that change has only produced the destruction (or metamorphosis) of historical sub-Souths. We can excavate through the layers of change like Schliemann trying to dig down and unearth Homer's original Troy. Greensboro, North Carolina, is associated with O. Henry (1862–1910), but novelists Marianne Gingher and Candace Plynt in the 1980s seem to have no more in common with him than the Fayetteville/Fort Bragg Carson McCullers used in the 1940s resembles the setting of Tim McLaurin's novel of the 1980s, *The Acorn Plan*. Louis Rubin's boyhood memories of baseball in Charleston overlay the memories of DuBose Heyward's Catfish Row, and of the home ground of William Gilmore Simms, who liked to write about the Revolutionary War; and although Truman Capote and Harper Lee appear in each other's novels, they're not in the identical Monroeville, Alabama. The New Orleans of Harnett Kane, John Kennedy Toole, and George Washington Cable? How far down through Peter Taylor's stories of southern families in the 1930s would you have to dig before you uncovered the Memphis of Faulkner's grandfather?

Simply juxtaposing southern writers by locale makes clear that the new, or newer, Souths they write about have always differed because southern regions differ, and time has further changed each sub-South in more ways than parking lots and Big Mac hamburgers.

Which of those changes are showing up in southern literature? In every way, the region is now closer to national norms than it used to be. The satellite dish stands where the outhouse used to lean; after the tobacco curing barn gave way to the sharecropper's cabin, that was replaced by a rusting trailer, and now by an elaborate furnished mobile home that cost $35,000. In North or South, the following look much alike: airports, malls, hotel chains, fast food restaurants, television programs, most suburbs, highways, billboards, and city outskirts. The drive from New Jersey to Atlanta offers few surprises.

Despite televangelists like Jim and Tammy Bakker, Pat Robertson, Jerry Falwell, and Jimmy Swaggart, and even despite various scandals which should have reprinted old concepts of Original Sin in italics, the influence of religion on daily southern life continues to decline and thus becomes less vital to the themes of stories or poems. Visitors still remark that Sunday in the South is a day of subdued activity, that Sunday radio programs are dominated by local Jeremiahs whose cadence is sufficient to stop a pacemaker. But college-educated southerners no longer understand biblical allusions in literature because most of them grew up watching cartoons on Sunday mornings; few even use much secular literary allusion in their student stories and poems. Most sophomores find the themes of Flannery O'Connor bizarre.

Because of this decline, which only parallels the national decline of religion's vitality, Walter Sullivan has assigned to tomorrow's southern writer the same task facing other postmodern writers, to "compensate for the loss of belief that has taken place in society at large," by developing "in his own soul the values he once could draw from his culture." Prose technique, already skillfully functioning in the work of such writers as Bobbie Ann Mason and Cormac McCarthy, he says, will not in itself be enough.[38] Similar challenges, however, are being made daily to writers everywhere.

When television antennae began blooming on roofs in the French Quarter as well as down in Hoot Owl Holler, there were predictions that southern speech would be overrun by Walter Cronkite's accent, indeed, that the entire oral tradition was being supplanted in McLuhan's global village where any live picture might prove to be worth six or eight thousand words. Yet speech is still one distinctive southern quality, as even Daphne Athas concedes in her essay, "Why There Are No uthern Writers."[39] Accent, cadence, tone, colorful and anecdotal talk have passed into current literature as the southern version of "voice," especially in writers like Kaye Gibbons, Lee Smith, Jill McCorkle, and others. James Whitehead talks about writers taking the way people really speak and *using* it, not just duplicating. "It's a heightening . . . of the way people talk," he says, so there's a "mixture of levels of rhetoric" the way Anthony Burgess and Joyce Cary have mixed them in the British novel, and Mark Twain, Barry Hannah, and Harry Crews have continued to do in southern America.[40] Although southern natives fear they are undergoing a loss of distinctive dialect and accent, newcomers still rest their ears on softness after Brooklynese, still consider southerners great talkers and storytellers. Easy generalizations continue to be drawn about a sense of verbal rhythm exhibited by southerners of both races. Some critics also still detect in southern writing a distinctive usage of the concrete, a preference for the elemental, and an affection for the purely ornamental qualities of language. (On the contrary, as a teacher of southern college students, I observe every semester a decline in these virtues and a preference for the kind of prose conversation that non-southerners like George Orwell and E. B. White would also deplore.) But among published authors, southern voice and dialog continue to be a distinctive strength.

If in our archaeology of southern letters we were to dig down one layer of Memphis to Peter Taylor's upper-middle-class 1930s' families,

179

they would seem very old fashioned in their behavior, reticence, and mores. In our literary minimalist 1980s, too, Taylor's leisurely prose style would analyze more nuance than most of today's speed readers could absorb. Although southern writers are still exploring generations and families, and while in their fictional worlds family ties are sometimes stretched cobweb-thin across continents and after divorces, their narrators today are less often the heads of houses. The next voice you hear will be not only southern in tone and cadence but also cranky, female, adolescent, black, blue-collar, drunk, gay, and outlaw. Sometimes this voice twines around an authorial narrative that mixes rhetoric in White-head's manner, but frequently now a first-person storyteller does all the work: reporting events, giving overviews, making connections and analyses, and does all of these in the vernacular, like Huck Finn with punk hair. Novels and stories seem tape-recorded, often in present tense, so the oral tradition has metamorphosed into an oral voice that speaks the whole story directly behind the reader's ear, sometimes speaks it in street slang, while also providing solo musical accompaniment via descriptions that sound as if the narrator is only thinking aloud. Voice thus unifies and becomes a novel's prime structural device. The literal use of a series of tape-recorded transcriptions constituted Barry Hannah's second novel, *Nightwatch*. T. R. Pearson may be an exception, but the writing style of most southerners is becoming briefer and crisper, more like talk and less like the Psalms of David.

The writers themselves are no longer sons of the landed gentry educated in private schools, but have become what Daphne Athas called "defiantly plebeian" in their origins as well as their subject matter.[41] This shift again parallels national trends in a democracy where most "new" voices speak up in turn from population groups heretofore considered artistically mute. Louise Erdrich, for instance, certainly mixes rhetoric in her fiction while giving direct voice to contemporary Chippewa characters whose reservation life in North Dakota had not previously been rendered in American literature; nor had that on the Laguna Pueblo reservation until Leslie Silko came along. Again, plebeian fiction renders characters who themselves would be unlikely to read it. Tim McLaurin, a southern Nelson Algren, writes in his first novel of paratroopers, winos, and blue-collar workers who hang out on Hay Street in Fayetteville; Charlie Gaines's *Stay Hungry* brings into the novel form a cast of characters who lift weights in a Birmingham gym; Alice Walker's Celie wrote early letters to God that were nearly illiterate so her development as a character could be spiritual, sexual, *and* verbal, while Erskine Caldwell's characters changed very little. Harry Crews's

Marvin Molar has no speech, no hearing, and no legs. We need not expect to sit across library tables from these characters.

What new populations will be finding their niche in southern fiction in the next decade? Whitehead has already mentioned the Chicano culture on the Texas border. Besides the dammed-up literature that will continue to pour forth from southern blacks and women, there will probably be more stories and poems about Cubans and Haitians and illegal immigrants in general; the new Hispanic influx into bottom-rung southern jobs should eventually throw up writers, too, as these reproduce on their own the old clashes between cultures and histories. Although Klansmen and lynchings and Bull Connors will fade from plots, prejudice and discrimination will continue to create story conflict. The writers who explore themes such as isolation, loneliness, and alienation have two choices about emphasis; having stopped attributing these reactions to the history of this guilty region, they can either personify them in individuals or, like Walker Percy, cast them in a philosophical framework.

Like other Americans, southerners are moving to cities, so stock characters of farmers, sheriffs, local grocers, grandfathers who know about history as well as fishing holes, will also wane. Like Josephine Humphreys, many new southern writers have their own agendas of environmentalism, ecology, and city planning behind their writing— although almost nobody will say that directly, but will tell stories instead. Thus, since most of the new writers will not live in Andalusia, nor in Covington, Louisiana, or even in my small town of Pittsboro, North Carolina, their novels will use urban settings and characters, television, film, technology, perhaps will even explore the internationalism that has moved into the South along with world manufacturing for world markets. It is a safe prediction that there will be a broadening of scale. Daphne Athas, for instance, after publishing *Entering Ephesus* about growing up in Chapel Hill, then published *Cora*, which featured international intrigue and was mostly set in Greece. Mary Lee Settle has taken an area no larger than Yoknapatawpha, but extended it back before antebellum history, pioneer history, even before Indian history to primitive times; she has in other novels been exploring world mythologies and African-Mideastern religions in search of universal links. The themes of social novels like those of T. S. Stribling and Erskine Caldwell are being better handled now by television documentaries, so black writers who have a sense of mission are less likely to write essays like James Baldwin's, but to follow either the standard course (Wright's *Black Boy*, Gaines's *Jane Pittman*, Ellison's *Invisible Man*) of telling the community story through strong individuals—as the Jews did with Abra-

ham, Isaac, Moses, and David—or to bring into mainstream consciousness the whole subterranean river of African folklore in its American
derivations, as in 1980s novels by Alice Walker, Toni Morrison, Randall
Kenan.

For women writers, any battle over whether to go to the toilet in
Marilyn French's ladies' or women's room seemed trivial in a region so
recently recovered from white and colored water fountains. Southern
women have usually outwitted sexism by strategy, rather than confronting it head on. Thus the same prediction is often made today about the
battle between the southern sexes as was made in the 1950s about racial
conflict: that once legal and political battles had been fought, southern
blacks and whites were more likely than their northern counterparts to
achieve racial harmony because of their joint past and traditional cour-
tesy. I'm not so sure about southern sexism. There are so many thin,
almost translucent, masks of politeness still waiting to be peeled away
from the "Southern Belle's" face, and there is such a deep expression
of long-suffering patience to be wiped from the "Black Matriarch's"
countenance. Anger in national feminist fiction may peak and cool, even
while the temperature is still climbing slowly down in Dixie. After that
heatwave ends and the truce is made, I would like to live long enough
to read, then, the candid erotic poems southern black and white women
might write to southern men.

Because so many writers now teach their craft at colleges and universities, new southern writers emerge now from M.F.A. programs knowing more about writing technique than did Joseph Conrad when he
began. Walter Sullivan may thus be correct that since technique alone
is never enough, their emphasis and the reader's search will shift toward
discovering meaningful content. It may also shift from realistic writing
to more surreal or experimental uses of language.

It is not safe, though, to predict too much on the basis of reading
early manuscripts by southern college writers, who learn technique because it is the easiest thing to teach. Only wide reading and deep living
add the other dimensions, and so slowly! When Fred Chappell was interviewed in 1989 by the *Chattahoochee Review*, he was unwilling to locate
student fiction and prose in national literary patterns:

> I have read their teachers but they haven't . . . what they express is their
> individuality. Students by and large, and this is not a criticism, haven't
> read anything, so they have no tradition to put themselves into. They
> express themselves, but only in a limited way because pretty soon the
> obsessions that make one write run out; they dribble through your hands
> like sand, and you've got nothing left. . . . Students do not have the re-
> sources to fall back on. They are not a bit alike because what they express

is their own individualities which are very sharp and prickly . . . based on opinion rather than passion, so that they run out pretty shortly . . . .You are "feminist" or whatever. These are all political stances. Once you've expressed it, then you are liable to believe, "I have expressed myself." That is simply a skin rash that goes away or comes back or you die of it, but that is not important.[42]

Most of them want to be "different" from all the writers who came before, in every region, not knowing how typical is that desire.

In 1989, Knopf published *A Turn in the South* by V. S. Naipaul, the Indian novelist born in Trinidad, whose international characters and settings have so often been seen through eyes so chilly, ironic, and unremitting that readers wondered what he would make of the contemporary South. Certainly it was amazing that on his tour somebody mentioned General Sherman to him almost daily; I don't hear a mention of Sherman once a year, so assume Naipaul was occasionally the victim of Blount's Hushpuppy/Blackstrap Syndrome.

But in Naipaul's final pages, while poet James Applewhite acts as his host in eastern North Carolina, showing him fields of golden leaf in a decade when Tobacco Road is running all the way downhill to the Non-Smoking Area, Naipaul writes like a southerner—or else southerners share a lot with other cultures. When Applewhite, recalling his childhood, says that for art no landscape suffices like the first that one knew, Naipaul opines: "He couldn't have known how directly he was speaking to me (the scarcely bearable idea of the beginning of things now existing only in my heart, no longer existing physically in the ravaged, repopulated Trinidad of today)." After both men have criticized mechanization and ugly change, Naipaul says of Applewhite, "His past had been more or less abolished. But it was this past that gave him eyes for the landscape he now lived in," almost a paraphrase of Tate and others. After discussions with a fundamentalist preacher, Naipaul compares the reasons all religions revert to fundamentalism, whether Islam or Christianity—a need for security, "how to know the truth and hold on to one's soul at a time of great change."[43]

Some American writers born at my latitude who want to know the truth and how to hold onto their souls during times of great change may in the future revert to *literary* fundamentalism, may begin echoing, exaggerating, even inventing again what the South has been and is and how it has affected them. The temptation to go on quoting Allen Tate whether his words still apply or not is very great. Naipaul does some echoing of Tate himself: of the legacy of the southern land and last century's events, the heavy guilty history, the feeling southerners share of being deeply rooted and inextricably yoked, the "melancholy time

warp" that still encloses the region, and "the South's idea of itself."
These quotations appear on the jacket blurb, to make the book buyer
nod before buying.

Naipaul seems to have accepted the South's idea of itself and scrib-
bled it intact into his notebook after it dropped from the mouths of
southerners my age and older, most of them representative of particular
economic classes and particular sub-Souths. We native writers often
scribble down borrowed souths ourselves. I have never forgotten publishing my second novel, *The Scarlet Thread*, after a heady season during
which W. J. Cash spoke directly to me, and then reading William Peden's
review, which called it correctly "too much sieved through other books."
One disadvantage of living in this century and in this place—surrounded
by clichés and stereotypes, in the shadows of monumental giants of the
Southern Renascence, aided by faculties of southern scholars, is that
we may willingly press ourselves through their sieves. So did Naipaul;
while much of his southern tour is accurate and revealing, some of it
tastes of blackstrap and hushpuppies. He might have heard less of yesterday, more about tomorrow, had he heard from southern would-be
writers born, say, in the late 1960s, who don't know what a quonset
hut is, much less a mini ball, for whom the ambivalence of Appomattox
has been related to them in the Uncle Sam Revised Version by fathers
who served in Saigon. They seem to be coping with the same vague
dislocations and anxieties they will read about in junior or senior year
in John Fowles's British accent. Trends and fads, disco, reggae, heavy
metal, even literary deconstruction, reach the South more slowly; and
we slow-reacting writers may edge up to chaos and nihilism and technology and the global village and women's liberation and the third world
and materialism and abortion and the greenhouse effect more gradually
and obliquely than other American writers, wondering if we can still
tell stories rather than produce theses about social problems.

Like Jim Applewhite, we do use the past to give us eyes to see this
changing landscape we live in. But the young writers will soon use their
library cards to join us aging writers in reading not just our southern
compatriots, but Naipaul himself, and Márquez, Kundera, Rushdie,
Cortázar, Grass, Lessing, Hawkes, Nabokov, Barthelme, Pynchon, and
so on. Not only do we read national and international modern writers,
but we've read the one who lives and teaches in Maryland (a southerner?), John Barth. Barth hopes that today's ideal postmodernist "has
the first half of our century under his belt, but not on his back," which
certainly calls that old "burden" of southern history to mind. Now that
contemporary writers have either laid their burdens down, or swallowed
and digested them to nourish their own varied metabolic needs, perhaps

the regionalism of southern literature will become for readers what it has always aspired to be—a local means to universal ends, not a de facto minor league of letters recognizable by outdated obsessions.

Guy Owen once said that the whole story of the human heart could be told on one tobacco farm in eastern North Carolina. Certainly the future of southern literature lies in how well its writers can do the former, not in how accurately they reproduce the latter.

NOTES

1. Thomas W. Cutner, "Conference on Literature and Reading in the South and Reading in the South and Southwest, 1935," *Southern Review* 21 (Spring 1985): 299.

2. Eugene Ehrlich and Gorton Carruth, eds., *Oxford Literary Guide to the United States* (New York, 1982), p. 287. Wright fictionalized this memory in *Native Son*.

3. Quoted in John Shelton Reed, *Southern Folk: Native White Social Types, Plain and Fancy* (Athens, 1988), p. 65.

4. Michael O'Brien, *Rethinking the South* (Baltimore, 1988), p. 213.

5. Statistics cited in Southern Growth Policies Board, ed., *Halfway Home and a Long Way to Go* (Research Triangle Park, 1988), pp. 9–10.

6. Richard Kostelanetz, *Literary Politics in America* (Kansas City, Mo., 1981), pp. 17–34.

7. Walker Percy, "Questions They Never Asked Me," *Esquire* (December 1977): 170.

8. Lewis A. Lawson and Victor A. Kramer, eds., *Conversations with Walker Percy* (Jackson, 1985), p. 281.

9. Donald R. Noble, "The Future of Southern Writing" in *History of Southern Literature*, ed. Louis D. Rubin, Jr., et al. (Baton Rouge, 1985), pp. 578–88.

10. Allen Tate, ed., *Essays of Four Decades* (Chicago, 1968), p. 545; Walter Sullivan, *A Requiem for the Renascence* (Athens, 1976), p. 2; Twelve Southerners, *I'll Take My Stand: The South and the Agrarian Tradition* (New York, 1930), pp. i–xx.

11. Walter Sullivan, "The New Faustus" in *Southern Fiction Today: Renascence and Beyond*, ed. George Core (Athens, 1969), p. 11.

12. Roy Blount, Jr., "The Next President of the United States," in *The Prevailing South: Life and Politics in a Changing Culture*, ed. Dudley Clendinen (Atlanta, 1988), p. 234.

13. Quoted in George Tindall, "The Resurgence of Southern Identity," in *The American South*, ed. Louis D. Rubin, Jr. (Baton Rouge, 1980), p. 165.

14. Richard Gilman, "The Surface of the Earth: A Mastodon of a Novel" [book review], *New York Times Book Review*, June 29, 1975, p. 1.

15. Lawson and Kramer, eds., *Conversations with Percy*, p. 300.

16. Robert Bain, Joseph M. Flora, and Louis D. Rubin, eds., *Southern Writers: A Biographical Dictionary* (Baton Rouge, 1979); *A Directory of American Poets and Fiction Writers* (New York, 1989).

17. Quoted in Clendinen, ed., *The Prevailing South*, p. 222.

18. Rubin et al., eds., *History of Southern Literature*, p. 61.

19. Anne Tyler, "Still Just Writing," in *The Writer and Her Work*, ed. Janet Sternberg (New York, 1980), p. 11.

20. Percy, "Questions They Never Asked Me," p. 170.

21. Roy Blount, *What Men Don't Tell Women* (New York, 1984), p. 28.

22. Quoted in Margaret Bolsterli, "The Androgynous Bi-racial Vision of Berry Morgan," in *Women Writers of the Contemporary South*, ed. Peggy W. Prenshaw (Jackson, 1984); "Reynolds Price," in *Books, People*, ed. David McCullough (New York, 1981), p. 142; Alice Walker, "The Black Writer and the Southern Experience," in *In Search of Our Mothers' Gardens* (New York, 1983), p. 17.

23. Quoted in Clendinen, ed., *The Prevailing South*, p. 6; Philadelphia *Inquirer*, May 12, 1983, p. 12.

24. Josephine Humphreys, "A Disappearing Subject Called the South," in *The Prevailing South*, ed. Clendinen, p. 218.

25. Padgett Powell, "Hitting Back," in *A World Unsuspected: Portraits of Southern Childhood*, ed. Alex Harris (Chapel Hill, 1987), p. 12; "An Interview with Barry Hannah," in *Alive and Writing: Interviews with American Authors of the 1980s*, ed. Larry McCaffery and Sinda Gregory (Urbana, 1987), p. 112.

26. James Alan McPherson, "Going up to Atlanta," in *A World Unsuspected*, ed. Harris, p. 88.

27. Robb Forman Dew, "The Power and the Glory," ibid., p. 126; Tyler's quote in Laurie L. Brown, "Interviews with Seven Contemporary Writers," in *Women Writers*, ed. Penshaw, p. 3.

28. James Dickey interviewed by Franklin Ashley, *Paris Review Interview*, 5th series (New York, 1981), p. 281.

29. "Margaret Walker" in *Mississippi Writers Talking*, ed. John Griffin Jones (Jackson, 1982), vol. 2, p. 146.

30. Rubin et al., eds., *History of Southern Literature*, p. 263; "James Whitehead" in *Mississippi Writers*, ed. Jones, vol. 2, p. 194; "Beth Henley," ibid., vol. 1, p. 183; "Turner Cassity," ibid., vol. 1, pp. 190, 214; Bobbie Ann Mason, "Kentucky on Her Mind" in *The Writer as Celebrity: Intimate Interviews*, ed. Maralyn Lois Polak (New York, 1986), p. 17.

31. Pat Conroy, "Mama and Me: The Making of a Southern Son," in *The Prevailing South*, ed. Clendinen, p. 122; Gail Godwin, "The Southern Belle," *Ms.* (July 1975): 51; Ellen Glasgow, *The Woman Within* (New York, 1954).

32. "Erskine Caldwell," in *Listen to the Voices*, ed. Jo Braus (Dallas, 1988), p. 167.

33. Alice Adams, "Why I Write," in *First Person Singular*, ed. Joyce Carol Oates (Princeton, 1983), p. 274; "Al Young" in John O'Brien, *Interviews with Black Writers* (New York, 1973), p. 265; "Willie Morris" in *Mississippi Writers*, ed. Jones, vol. 2, p. 102.

34. Elizabeth Hardwick, *Writers at Work* in *Paris Review Interviews*, ed. George Plimpton (New York, 1986), vol. 7, p. 134; Joan Williams, "Interviews with Seven Contemporary Writers," in *Women Writers*, ed. Prenshaw, p. 280.

35. *New Yorker*, June 19, 1989, p. 8.

36. C. Hugh Holman, *The Roots of Southern Writing: Essays on the Literature of the American South* (Athens, 1972).

37. Jack Temple Kirby, *Media-Made Dixie: The South in the American Imagination* (Baton Rouge, 1978), p. 11.

38. Sullivan, *Requiem for the Renascence*, pp. 69–74.

39. Daphne Athas, "Why There Are No Southern Writers," pp. 295–306 in *Women Writers*, ed. Prenshaw.

40. "James Whitehead," in *Mississippi Writers*, ed. Jones, vol. 2, p. 164.

41. Athas, "Why There Are No Southern Writers," p. 305.

42. Tim Tarkington, "An Interview with Fred Chappell," *Chattahoochee Review* 10 (Winter 1989): 44–48.

43. V. S. Naipaul, *A Turn in the South* (New York, 1989), pp. 268, 276, 285.

7

Will Dixie Disappear?
Cultural Contours of a Region in Transition

HOWARD L. PRESTON

Ever since Waylon Jennings changed his duck-tail hair style to the blow-dry look of a Hollywood movie star, and the nation elected a president from the Deep South who referred to Italians as "Eye-talians," rumor has had it that the South is over.[1] Reports of the region's demise and alleged cultural extinction have, in fact, circulated for years. The most acclaimed came a little over a generation ago, when C. Vann Woodward of Yale University asked, "Is there nothing about the South that is immune from the disintegrating effect of nationalism and the pressure for conformity?" In his award-winning book, *The Burden of Southern History* (1960), Woodward recalled the righteous myths invented by southerners to fend off unwanted social change and surmised that because of stresses dictated by modernization and nationalism, younger southerners "may come to feel as uprooted as the immigrant." The only thing that the renowned southern historian could think of that offered any hope of avoiding total assimilation within the national culture was "the collective experience of Southern people," even if that experience was one of shared defeat, poverty, and ultimately guilt.[2]

In the decades since Woodward pondered this question, and especially since Vietnam and Watergate, much about the South has changed, and I wonder if Woodward's inquiry about the effects of modernization might be more appropriate now than when he voiced it. Today, the region can no longer be defined solely in terms of its social, political, and economic eccentricities. The late-twentieth-century South is as much a part of the American mainstream as any other section of the country. Writers who once focused primarily on the region's tumble-down housing and poorly educated school children as evidence of backwardness now direct attention to the gleam and glitter of new Sunbelt South cities where prospects for the future appear bright and optimistic.[3]

But does this mean that southernness is extinct, that the region has finally become a cultural colony of somewhere else, or that, as Hodding

Carter III has announced, "the South is purely and contemporaneously mainstream American"?[4] Has the South, well known for its racism, poverty, and penchant for religious fundamentalism and violence really disappeared and, like magic, in its place appeared the shiny, successful, surrealistic Sunbelt? To what extent have southerners weathered the storm of nationalism that Woodward saw eroding the region's provinciality? In the midst of the massive changes that the South has experienced, have southerners managed to retain their regional identity, or have they become the proverbial uprooted citizens that Woodward thought possible in 1960? And, in attempting to rid themselves of the worst aspects of their past, have southerners unwittingly embraced an entirely different set of myths, more national in scope, that have homogenized the South's culture and promise to remake the region into what Marshall Frady called "the inconclusive grumpiness of everywhere else?"[5]

The one provincialism invariably identified as the most characteristic of the South is race. In 1928 the historian Ulrich Bonnell Phillips, a native Georgian, raised the ire of many when he wrote in the *American Historical Review* that slavery was the central theme of southern history, and not surprisingly, that being a white southerner simply meant being a racist. In the 1930s, the North Carolina journalist Wilbur J. Cash came to a similar conclusion. In his famous study *The Mind of the South*, Cash observed that, among other things, race-baiting by political demagogues, which "whipped up the tastes and passions of [southern Democrats] with ever more personal and extravagant representations of the South in full gallop against . . . the Negro," could be singled out as the most firmly established aspect of the region's political history, all the way back to Andrew Jackson. This phenomenon of which both Phillips and Cash wrote can also be traced to as late as 1965, when North Carolina journalist Edwin M. Yoder wrote in *Harper's Magazine* that "even today, the enduring presence of Negroes in large numbers forbids . . . the practice of genuine interest politics. For whatever the South has chosen to accept in the way of racial practices," Yoder added, "it has not yet accepted in any state" the elevation of blacks to a high enough social status that they might be elected to political office in large numbers.[6]

Since the mid-1960s, however, this has proven to be hardly the case. Richard Arrington, a black man, is mayor of Birmingham, the very seedbed of white resistence in the former Confederate states during the early years of the civil rights movement. One hundred sixty-six other cities and towns spread out across the South, including Charlotte, New

Orleans, and Richmond, also elected black mayors. Blacks sit on county and city councils in both rural and urban areas of the South. They have been elected to school boards and to the judiciary, appointed to planning commissions, and entrusted with the responsibility of policing large cities and small towns as well as administering local governments.[7]

The issue of race in the South has also been muted by riots that took place during the late 1960s in American cities located far outside the South, by the racial unrest over school desegregation in the 1970s in South Boston, by the bigotry on display in Howard Beach that made headlines in newspapers across the country, and ultimately by the decision of many blacks, who lived elsewhere, to make the South their home. In 1975 only 43 percent of black Americans lived in the South, a decline since 1900 of 35 percent. By the mid-1970s, *Time* reported that this trend had been reversed and that countless well-educated, middle-class blacks were moving south in search of better educational opportunities for their children, a higher standard of living, and better jobs. By 1988, 55.9 percent of the nation's black population lived in the South, a 3.7 percent increase since 1980, and demographers believe that this emerging pattern of reverse migration will come into much sharper focus after the 1990 census. "I suspect," said Larry Long, chief analyst at the Census Bureau's Center for Demographic Studies, "that we will discover that the black middle class has such strong ties to Southern roots that they will retire to traditional areas of the rural South."[8]

Blacks and whites in the South are relating to one another today in the same way that Martin Luther King, Jr., did in the mid-1960s when he addressed Lyndon B. Johnson as "my fellow southerner." But while de jure segregation is a thing of the past, while a certain mutuality in recent years has grown between whites and blacks in the South, and while some blacks enjoy an unprecedented measure of economic prosperity, the region is by no means socially integrated. The highly visible success of some blacks who have done well in business or achieved recognition through election to public office has given rise to an indifference on the part of many whites to the continuing problems the vast majority of blacks in the South still face. Undeniably, much more progress toward racial harmony has been made since the 1960s than during the entire twentieth century. At the same time it is encouraging to see how far the region has come in this relatively short period; it is necessary, however, to understand that the civil rights movement is not over, and that in the far corners of the South, social change is resisted as strongly as ever.

Note the recent election of L. Douglas Wilder as governor of Virginia. In 1986, Wilder, the grandson of slaves, distinguished himself as the first black person to be elected since Reconstruction to a statewide political office—lieutenant governor of Virginia—in the South. Wilder ran a middle-of-the-road gubernatorial campaign, "re-thinking" his position on many sensitive issues like capital punishment along the way. Polls taken just prior to the 1989 fall election indicated that Wilder would win comfortably. But the election proved to be anything but comfortable, and Wilder's victory was not assured until the last precinct was counted. Apparently, as one observer put it, "some of Virginia's white voters are still racially prejudiced and, what's more, anxious to conceal it from pollsters."[9] Wilder's narrow victory may very well be the handwriting on the wall for other blacks in the South, like Andrew Young of Georgia, Harvey Gantt of North Carolina, and Mike Espy of Mississippi, who aspire to statewide political office.

Progress has been made. Wilder's election is proof of that, and the vast majority of white southerners have learned that the race relations of the future must be better than the past. But the issue of race itself, even to a soft-spoken, conciliatory man like Wilder who did everything he could in Virginia not to make *it* an issue, still remains prevalent and has not disappeared. Indicative of this is the political popularity of former Ku Klux Klan member David Duke in Louisiana.[10]

Nationally, the number of black elected officials increased by 5.8 percent in 1988, a change the Washington-based Joint Center for Political Studies attributed in part to an Alabama court decision that eliminated that state's at-large election system. Since the ruling, 252 blacks have been elected to seats in the 180 municipal and county jurisdictions mandated to abandon at-large elections. As of the fall of 1989, Alabama had the largest number, 694, of black-elected office-holders, followed closely by Mississippi with 646, Louisiana with 521, Georgia with 483, North Carolina with 449, Arkansas with 318, and Texas with 312. In South Carolina, 373 blacks were in publicly elected positions, an increase of 5.9 percent over 1988. Considering that the Palmetto State has the second largest black population in the nation, this modest improvement, however, is misleading. The ratio of blacks in public office to the total black population of the state is still exceptionally low, and observers attribute this situation to an unwillingness on the part of white voters to accept black candidates and to a failure by black office-seekers to broaden their political appeal to include whites.[11]

Another example of the stubbornness of racism in the South can be seen in rural Sumter County, Alabama, located in the western part of the state, adjacent to Mississippi. Sumter County school children were

191

as racially segregated in 1989 as they were the day the United States Supreme Court handed down its landmark *Brown v. Topeka Board of Education* decision. Black students in Sumter County attend a poorly funded public school system, and whites attend a network of private Christian academies. In the neighboring state of Mississippi the situation is not much better. Holmes County, dubiously recognized as the poorest county in the poorest state, had a public school system in 1986 of 4,300 students, only four of whom were white.[12] Like Sumter County, the overwhelming majority of Holmes County's white school-age children also are privately educated.

But even in some school districts in the Deep South where integrated classrooms have been the norm for almost twenty years, the vestiges of race consciousness are still apparent. At rural Pleasant Hill High School in Georgetown County, South Carolina, about thirty miles west of Myrtle Beach, for example, blacks and whites have been attending classes together harmoniously since 1970, the year the school integrated. In the spring of 1989, however, when the school hosted its annual "Magical Midnight Hour" prom, only blacks attended. The all-white Members Only club held its own private party in Myrtle Beach. "It's just life," said the father of one white Pleasant Hill High School student in a statement that sounded reminiscent of the 1950s. "I work with blacks every day. But if the good Lord had wanted us [blacks and whites] to be together, he would have made us one color."[13]

In recent years race has also figured into the decisions that major corporations, lured to the South by tax exemptions, cheap land, and cheap labor, have made in determining where in the region to build their branch plants and offices. Because of a belief that blacks pose a greater threat for unionization than whites, many of these industries have sought out "whiter" areas of the South in which to relocate. A 1983 Commission on Civil Rights report found that industry had rejected sixteen predominantly black counties in western Alabama as possible sites for factories.[14] That same year, the Southern Growth Policies Board documented that between 1977 and 1982 employment grew more than twice as fast in non-metropolitan counties in the South that were more than 75 percent white than in counties that were more than 50 percent black. Cases in point are the location of the Saturn automobile assembly plant in Maury County, Tennessee, and the decision by Toyota to build its facility in Scott County, Kentucky. The white populations of both of these counties are 93 percent and 83 percent respectively.[15] Futhermore, a poll taken in South Carolina for the *State* (Columbia) newspaper revealed that the majority of blacks and whites surveyed thought that racial discrimination and segregation still existed.[16] Most believed that more progress toward racial equality in housing, employment, and political representation was needed, and perhaps this same point of view applies to the entire South.

The vitriolic rhetoric of demagogues like James Vardaman and Theodore Bilbo of Mississippi, Lester Maddox and Eugene Talmadge of Georgia, and Cole Blease and Benjamin Tillman of South Carolina, which fanned the fires of racism and gained those who employed it untold political support, is politically extinct. Many whites who live in the South today are genuinely embarrassed by racial slurs against blacks and adamantly deplore the radical activities of racially motivated hate groups. As one writer put it, "the babykissing backwoodsman who drove his mules up to the court house square to quote the Bible, cuss the niggers, and claim the votes is an anachronism."[17] But race cannot be dismissed as no longer culturally distinctive of the South. Certainly it seems no longer important politically in Atlanta or Charlotte, but church attendance for the most part throughout the region remains strictly segregated, and so are funeral homes and cemeteries. Despite protests of black students attending the University of Mississippi, the Confederate Battle Flag and the song "Dixie," the very symbols of white supremacy, remain the official emblems of the university at sporting events. Gerrymandering and at-large elections to county and municipal public offices continue to keep many black southerners politically voiceless in certain areas.[18] Unarguably, the issue of race remains a persistent ingredient of southern culture and continues to play an important role in southern life and politics. The issue of race as a factor influencing day-to-day activities in much of the region is still, and will remain, very much alive. And in this respect at least, the South is not over, not by a long shot!

If race is one of the most distinguishable cultural characteristics of the South, two others are antebellum romanticism and southern cooking. In the nineteenth century, writers and artists cultivated a romantic image for the South as a place where the forces of industrialization had been kind, an image still very much a part of the region's identity. According to the myth, charm and social grace remain a functional part of everyday life below the Mason-Dixon line. Indicative of this century-old understanding of the South is the way in which the region continues to promote itself. For example, an advertisement by the Georgia Visitors' Bureau that appeared in a leading national magazine beckoned tourists with a scene of two wicker rocking chairs sitting empty on the veranda of a white-columned antebellum mansion. Carefully chosen words accompanied this romantic reminiscence: "A Look at the Side of Georgia That's Almost Gone With the Wind."[19]

To many Americans the South is not so much a place as it is a state of mind, and each year the seemingly insatiable appetite of those who want to relive the glories of the Lost Cause is fed a steady diet of third-rate novels and television serials. *Gone With the Wind* is the most popular movie ever shown on television, and a sequel to the 1936 novel by Margaret Mitchell is in the making and promises to earn both author, Alexandra Ripley, and a yet-to-be named publisher a fortune.[20] It is therefore apparent that, in the future, the image of the romantic Old South is not likely to lose its prominence atop the list of ways Americans want to remember and understand the region.

Also a part of the South's romantic image is its legendary hospitality, which many outsiders find most in evidence at dinnertime, when a feast of victuals is laid before them. Southern cooking is known worldwide and calls attention to a life-style of abundance that is unincumbered by want or modernization. Every serious cook, housewife and househusband alike, has at least one southern cookbook, and county fairs and church bake sales are famous for the fine food they display.

Joe Gray Taylor has written at length about the cultural idiosyncracies of southern cooking and has shown that as much as anything else, modernization has affected southerners' palates. According to Taylor, southerners' diet changed very little between the Civil War and the end of World War II, but since the war, greater mobility, in addition to radio and television, has introduced new products that have changed southern food preparation and eating habits. Ultimately, contemporary southerners' appetites for traditional southern dishes have been dulled, and their culinary standards lowered. But all is not lost. At the same time Taylor declares that southerners' tastebuds have been ravaged by an incessant diet of fast food, he finds that "the southern tradition in food has not disappeared. . . . The very fact that fried chicken is the most popular fast food," he allowed reassuringly, "is evidence of the survival of southern tastes. Standing along side the hamburger palaces, especially in the upper South, are little restaurants that still offer 'all the catfish you can eat' at a reasonable price. And that favorite of southerners, barbecue, is still to be had."[21]

Restaurants that offer diners mouth-watering barbecue entrées can be found throughout the South. Both pork and beef are used, but some southerners on occasion have been known to substitute possum and even armadillo. In South Carolina, pork barbecue is more pervasive than the palmetto tree, the state's symbol, which does not grow north of the fall line. South Carolina barbecue varies in different parts of the state, but because it is eaten in every county, two University of South Carolina geographers were enticed into dividing the state into four "barbecue regions," each with its own distinctive sauce.[22]

The curious practice of cooking meat outdoors over glowing coals in a pit is said to have started with Indians who inhabited the Southeast before European settlement. These Native Americans allegedly shared their gourmet secrets with early settlers, who during the antebellum period raised barbecuing to an art form. To many southern cooks steeped in the salivary subtleties that distinguish one sauce from another, barbecue is like fine wine. Recipes are closely guarded, and those who take their barbecue as seriously as their politics have been known to argue for hours, and with great emotion, over which sauce is best. From the standpoint of the kitchen, therefore, the South still exists as a distinctive part of the country. And despite efforts to capture a small measure of the region's culture in a bottle of barbecue sauce to market nationwide, southern cooking is not likely to disappear as a highly recognized and respected measure of life in the South.

Following race, romanticism, and cooking as persistent manifestations of cultural distinctiveness in the South is the widely held perception that the region remains by and large the most backward, isolated, and rural part of the country. No doubt there are places in the South that remain untouched by many aspects of modernization, but this widely held notion of backwardness has been given credence by the unsavory way that the South and southerners have been depicted in such popular films as *Deliverance* (1972) and *Mississippi Burning* (1988), and in such numerous long-running television programs as "The Real McCoys" (1958–62), "The Beverly Hillbillies" (1962–70), "Mayberry R.F.D." (1968–71), and "The Dukes of Hazzard" (1979–84). These and other programs, shown over and over again as reruns, portray southerners as intellectually backward and dim-witted, and their communities, if not politically corrupt, then lazy and devoid of progress.[23]

The two seemingly contradictory cultural characteristics that have long offered outsiders proof of the South's chronic backwardness are the bent southerners have for violent behavior and their long-standing zeal for fundamental religion. The notion that southerners are prone to become violent more often than residents of other parts of the country "is so pervasive," wrote the historian Sheldon Hackney, "that it compels the attention of anyone interested in understanding the South."[24] Scholars have found evidence of violent behavior on the part of southerners at every stage of the region's development. During the colonial period, eye-gouging was commonplace among backwoodsmen, and more "civilized" citizens settled differences by dueling.[25] In the antebellum South the violence carried out by masters and overseers attempting to keep slaves in line was an integral part of the master-slave relationship, and following the Civil War, the night-riding, hooded Ku Klux Klan, along with "Judge Lynch," appeared to keep "uppity," newly emancipated blacks "in their place."

To W. J. Cash, the South by the turn of the century had become so "solidly wedded to Negro-Lynching" that southerners observed the heinous practice ceremoniously as "an act of racial and patriotic expression, an act of chivalry, an act, indeed, having a definitely ritualistic value in respect to the entire southern sentiment."[26] By 1934, when Clemson Agricultural College sociologist H. C. Brearley tabulated the number of lynchings that had occurred in the United States between 1900 and 1930, this so-called "ritualism" had grown to monstrous proportions. Ninety percent of the 1,886 lynchings in the nation occurring during that thirty-year period were carried out in the eleven former Confederate states and Kentucky, and blacks were almost always the victims.

In explanation of southerners' violent tendencies, Brearley postulated that certain European feudal traditions were somehow more valued by southerners than by those who resided outside the region. He theorized that in the South this so-called "cavalier spirit" was manifest in southerners' loyalty to family, to class, and to community. In a society in which the preservation and perpetuation of these values was given highest priority, aggressive behavior was an attribute. One clear manifestation of this code of conduct is the violence leveled against blacks following the Civil War and during the early civil rights era of the 1950s and 1960s. During these times southerners felt that their "way of life" was clearly threatened, and as a means of denial, resorted to violence. "Directly and indirectly," Brearley wrote, "this feudal spirit increases the prevalence of homicide in the South. In an effort to secure or maintain status," he continued, "slayings occur every day among aristocrats, middle classes, 'poor whites,' and Negroes." Brearley believed that the feudal spirit helps explain the inordinately high rate of homicide in the South, as well as the fondness southerners have for firearms.[27]

During the depression, feuds over moonshining rights and other nefarious activities hatched by one backwoods, trigger-happy white family against another lent additional credence to Brearley's theory. Toward the middle of the twentieth century, as the South became more industrial, he saw little reason to believe that southerners would outgrow their violent predilections. "When industrial warfare occurs in a region where the participants are already predisposed to deeds of violence . . .

such conflicts may be expected to be especially destructive." As proof, he called attention to the bloodshed between textile workers and management in Marion and Gastonia, North Carolina, and in Harlan and Bell counties, Kentucky. But, in an attempt to offer hope for the future, Brearley optimistically allowed that "in a few more generations the evil effects of slavery and Reconstruction will have greatly abated. . . ."[28] Obviously, he had no way of foreseeing the ensuing civil rights struggle.

In the 1950s and 1960s, as wide-eyed Americans watched on television, the South proved itself conclusively to be the most violent section of the nation and its citizens to be the most unreasonable. School and church bombings in Birmingham, the riotous night of destruction at the University of Mississippi in Oxford over the enrollment of James Meredith that cost two journalists their lives, the brutal police attack against the civil rights marchers on the Edmund Pettus Bridge near Selma, the shooting of two students on the campus of South Carolina State College in Orangeburg, and ultimately the assassination of Martin Luther King, Jr., in Memphis galvanized public opinion against the region and confirmed what many Americans already suspected: southerners were undeniably the most violent of Americans.

The national attention that these and other events of the early civil rights movement received has had a mitigating effect on conspicuous displays of violence in the South. Overt violent behavior has become less tolerable, and although the rate of homicide and gun ownership in the region continues to be among the nation's highest, many residents rationally eschew private displays of violence as socially unacceptable. This does not necessarily mean that violence has vanished as a cultural characteristic of the South and that the region can no longer be identified as the most violent nationally. The sociologist John Shelton Reed found that in 1980 ten of the eighteen states with the highest rates of homicide were southern states, and that a better question than Is the South still the most violent part of the United States? might be, How much like the South has the rest of the country become?[29]

Although it is impossible to document scientifically the way sociologists calculate rates of homicides and per capita gun ownership, some observers have found the decline of criminal violence and the simultaneous upsurge of the popularity of football in the South to have an interesting correlation. "*Southern* football," commented writer Peter Schrag in 1972, "knows levels of meaning, intensity, and violence entirely foreign to other regions."[30] Reflecting on the many football games he had witnessed between the University of Texas Longhorns and the University of Oklahoma Sooners, Willie Morris compared the gridiron confrontation of these two institutions each autumn in Dallas's Cotton

197

Bowl to "the clashes of contemporary armies" and wrote that this particular rivalry has "the flow of history behind [it]."[31]

Since 1980, the universities comprising the Southeastern Conference have come closer to filling their football stadiums to capacity—98.5 percent in 1983—than any other major athletic federation in the country.[32] The intense loyalty shown by southerners to football, not only at the collegiate level but at the local high school level as well, goes far beyond mere game attendance and includes a year-round preoccupation with favorite team colors and logos displayed on everything from eyeglasses to automobile license tags. "Football is a passion around which we order our lives," allowed one University of Alabama fan. "Football holds us together—especially when we beat one of those big Northern schools."[33]

Every major southern university has its own "legends," and stories about football heroes abound and constitute a folklore of their own. Tuscaloosa, home of the University of Alabama's Crimson Tide, has perhaps the only museum in the country devoted to a football coach, Paul "Bear" Bryant. Furthermore, in 1970, with thirty years left in the century, southern sports writers voted University of Mississippi star Archie Manning "Quarterback of the Century," an honor not altogether foreign to a sports hero of Manning's stature. But after he had completed his senior season, his legendary status was raised to even greater heights. One evening while traveling through Canton, the Old Miss quarterback stopped in a restaurant to eat dinner. When he returned to the same restaurant three months later, the chair he sat in earlier was mounted on a tabletop and labeled "Archie Sat Here!"[34]

In their allegiance to football teams and their idolization of football heroes, southerners seem to be exhibiting the same sense of community and regional pride that social psychologists have identified as a part of the southern psyche. "Basketball players don't become folk heroes in the South, no matter how good they become," observed John F. Rooney, Jr., a geography professor at Oklahoma State University who has studied the phenomenon. "That's the difference. In emotional energy, the South is a one-sport region and football is the sport."[35] Perhaps one football coach put it best when he said, "Southern fans are more rabid [than other football fans]. They take football less as entertainment and more as a lifestyle."[36]

It is not clear to what extent southerners, in their passion for football, are acting out a need to express themselves in a violent manner. What is clear is that one of the most violent sports played in the United States enjoys its greatest success and has its greatest following in the one region that has historically embraced violence as an accepted means of self-expression. The South may well be, as University of Georgia sociologist Ira Robinson believes, "a phoenix dying to resurrect itself and football is for those who are dying."[37] But it remains a matter of speculation how closely related southerners' vicarious enjoyment of Saturday afternoon gridiron violence is to other historical forms of violence like lynching, which also had great spectator appeal in the South.

Southerners no longer carry an aura of violent backwardness, especially when the region is compared to the crime-infested cities of New York, Washington, Los Angeles, or Chicago. But for want of a better way to attract television sponsors and audiences to theaters across the country, every now and then Hollywood resurrects the image of the unwashed, uncivilized, uncouth, violence-prone, piney-woods redneck. *Easy Rider* (1969) and *Deliverance* (1972) provide ample evidence. In the first, southerners are characterized by a pickup-truck driving, bibjeaned Mississippi redneck who takes offense at the film's two heroes, both disciples of the counter-culture, and for no apparent reason save their long hair and beads kills them with a shotgun. The second movie goes even further by portraying rural southerners as degenerate, incestuous morons. Thus, violence as an acknowledged aspect of southern life and custom has become a part of late-twentieth-century American popular culture and promises to remain an acceptable and profitable way of personifying southernness in years to come.

While southerners have often in their history expressed violent tendencies, they have employed evangelical religion to temper their aggressiveness and quell their combative spirits. During the twentieth century this provincial theology has continually come under attack, and southerners have had to guard it defiantly against the erosive influences of the outside world. The struggle began as soon as improved roads reached into the isolated, back-wash communities where fundamentalism was practiced in earnest. The fear that contemporary thought is subversive and somehow leads to the destruction of evangelical Christendom is the cornerstone of this literal-minded faith. Central to its brand of theology, therefore, has been the firm belief that individual salvation is the highest religious priority and that a steadfast resistence is necessary against the encroachment of any kind of social gospel.

In the past, old-time southern religion was acted out with great zeal and intensity, and one need only read some of the stinging articles of H. L. Mencken in the 1920s to recall what it was like. In general, Mencken believed that organized religion stifled individual freedom and was a direct threat to those who sought new knowledge and enlightenment. The patent religious orthodoxy of the South, therefore, that denounced the reading of any book save the Holy Scriptures, that held gambling and dancing to result surely in damnation, that proclaimed any education beyond Bible study to be apostasy, and that even attacked Coca-Cola "as a levantine and Hell-sent narcotic" was fertile ground for Mencken's caustic pen. Speaking in tongues, holy dancing, emotional outbursts, highly charged sermons, and even snake handling—practices that Mencken labeled as tribal—continue to be a part of religious observances in the South, but they are not in the mainstream and are confined primarily to the Pentecostal church. Southerners subject to the cosmopolitan influences of urbanization, education, mass communication, and greater mobility have long since dispensed with them as unsophisticated and idolatrous. "It is all but impossible to conceive of [a] sweat-drenched child of God," wrote Thomas D. Clark in the early 1960s, "sitting in the sedate pews of a seminary-trained minister."[38] What has remained a consistent part of religious life in the South is that it continues to be overwhelmingly Protestant, philosophically fundamental, and profoundly evangelical. In 1976, *Time* estimated that of the thirty-two million Protestants in the South, twenty million considered themselves to be evangelicals. "Southerners are the most church-going people in the nation," the weekly news magazine allowed, "and from camp meeting through riverside baptisms to huge urban congregations, the tone and temper of Southern Protestantism is evangelical."[39]

Still a part of the religious landscape in the South are the philosophical distinctions southerners draw between the way they practice their faith and the way Protestants in other parts of the nation do. In 1983 the Presbyterian Church of the United States, organized in 1861 as the Presbyterian Church of the Confederacy, managed to reconcile its differences with its northern counterpart, the United Presbyterian Church of the United States of America. But unlike Presbyterians, the Baptist Church in America still has northern and southern wings whose members relate to different religious issues.

Southern Baptists, for example, believe strongly in abstinence from alcohol, and the pattern of counties which prohibit, and not just control or regulate, the sale and consumption of alcoholic beverages in the United States is reflective of this distinctive religious provincialism. In 1986, 243 counties located in fifteen states completely banned the use of alcohol, and more than half of the people living in these counties resided in the states of Kentucky, Tennessee, and Texas. None of South Carolina's forty-six counties totally ban the sale of liquor, but state law prohibits the public sale of intoxicating beverages on Sunday. Therefore, in 1989, when New Year's Eve fell on Sunday, South Carolinians who rang in 1990 at eating and drinking establishments that normally sold alcoholic beverages were forced to celebrate abstemiously.[40]

Many South Carolinians obviously still equate the consumption of "strong drink" with immorality. In February 1989, for example, a locally owned and operated Upstate grocery store chain applied to the South Carolina Alcoholic Beverage Control Commission for a license to sell beer and wine. This was the first time in the sixty-eight-year history of the business that the company had sought to sell alcoholic beverages. The decision was met with determined hostility from ministers like Pastor Allen Raines of the First Baptist Church of Union, South Carolina, who opposed granting the license because his church was located within a hundred feet of one of the stores and because he saw the sale of beer and wine to be a corrupting influence in his community.[41]

Where the evils of alcohol, tobacco, dancing, and gambling, however, were once the primary blasphemies of southerners' orthodoxy, new and more portentous secular demons have appeared more recently that threaten the faithful and occupy evangelicals' attention. Rock music and magazines, public school textbooks that teach evolution but fail to give equal attention to the biblical version of creation, prayer in public schools, and above all, abortion are the current issues of greatest importance. In the summer of 1986, Jimmy Swaggart, broadcasting from his Louisiana church studios, lashed out at Wal-Mart, K-Mart, and grocery stories for selling rock magazines that he claimed were demonic and could be purchased by children of any age. The widely known fundamentalist preacher opposes rock and roll of any kind—even the lyrics of the Christian vocalist Amy Grant—and is on record as saying, "You cannot claim the message of the annointed *with the music of the Devil!*" Shortly thereafter, Swaggart met with Wal-Mart executives and convinced them to remove all rock magazines from the shelves of the chain's more than nine hundred stores in twenty-two states.[42]

While fundamentalists have busied themselves fighting demonic rock and roll, three southern states have been embroiled in litigation over the issue of creationism versus evolutionism. In 1982 the Louisiana state legislature passed the Balanced Treatment for Creation-Science and Evolution-Science Act, which required the teaching of creationism whenever evolution was taught. The Louisiana statute defined the theory of "scientific creation" as "the belief that the origin of the elements, the galaxy, the solar system, of life, of all species of plants and animals, the origin of man, and the origin of all things and their processes and relationships were created *ex nihilo* and fixed by God."[43]

A United States district court did not even need a trial to declare this law contradictory to the Establishment Clause of the First Amendment, and after the Fifth Circuit Court of Appeals upheld the lower court's opinion, the United States Supreme Court, in a 7–2 decision, finalized the matter. Writing for the majority, Associate Justice William J. Brennan, Jr., stated that the law had a nonreligious purpose and was clearly an intent on the part of the Louisiana state legislature to advance a particular religious point of view.[44]

In Alabama and Tennessee the creationism controversy went farther. Christian fundamentalist parents claimed that every time their children were forced to read from certain textbooks they labeled as "godless," their right of religious freedom was violated. In August 1987, seven fundamentalist families in Hawkins County, Tennessee, won a suit against the local school board, and a United States district court judge required that any student who found certain textbooks published by Holt, Rinehart and Winston offensive to their faith could be excused from having to read them. The Alabama case involved forty-four textbooks in several different content areas and grade levels and was a continuation of litigation concerning school prayer and silent meditation. In this instance, fundamentalists sought to "purge from the classroom those things that serve to teach [that] salvation is through one's self rather than through a deity."[45] Education officials in both states immediately filed appeals and won.[46] The lower court victories, however, have given Christian fundamentalists cause to continue to press the position that secular humanism is, in fact, a religion and that creationism should be given equal treatment in public school classrooms. "The ruling in [the Tennessee case of] *Mozert v. Hawkins County Public Schools*," wrote a Massachusetts education official, "could be just the first trickle in a flood of litigation on the content of school curriculum."[47]

Christian fundamentalists have found support for their textbook cause outside the South, but the one issue that has galvanized strong support in their favor has been the position taken against abortion. In 1985, *U.S. News & World Report* found that the issue of abortion was "spurring a new fundamentalism," not only in the South but also across the nation, and Catholics and Protestants alike had united in vehement opposition to the Supreme Court's 1973 decision in *Roe v. Wade* legalizing abortion. Opposition to abortion, in fact, was found to be stronger in the Northeast, where one in three was against it, compared to one in five in the South. "Across the nation," reported the weekly news magazine, "abortion foes claim vocal allies in Southern-based TV preachers such as Jerry Falwell, Pat Robertson and Jimmy Swaggart."[48]

The electronic ministries of these and other fundamentalist preachers based in the South have breathed new life into Christian evangelism and have helped rally support against abortion and for other evangelical causes. This particular aspect of modernization, therefore, has helped to preserve rather than to erode Christian evangelism in the South. Televangelists' ability to reach directly into viewers' homes gives them enormous power, and their daily broadcasts, watched by millions, have helped blunt the forces of change and, to a certain extent, kept the old-time religion alive.[49] Whenever Jimmy Swaggart or Ernest Angley launches into an agitated, fretful sermon, one cannot help but be reminded of Mencken's description of the emotionally charged preacher he encountered at a camp-site service in the woods outside Dayton, Tennessee, in 1925.[50]

There are still reminders of this old-time religion and the importance southerners have given it. Christus Gardens, located near Gatlinburg, Tennessee, is the nation's most visited religious tourist attraction,[51] and occasionally messages to "Get Right with God" and "Jesus Saves" can be seen nailed to trees along rural roads and highways. Church affiliation in the South, for the most part, remains strictly segregated by race, and "the peripatetic revivalist," as Clark put it, is "as much a part of the southern scene as the motel and the barbecue stand."[52] John Shelton Reed documented the fact that, even today, southern Protestants are more than twice as likely as other American Protestants to believe in the Bible as the literal word of God and to watch religious television programs. In addition, Reed was able to show that, unlike most Americans, southerners still regard religion as a very important influence in their lives.[53] Indeed, the church has been and continues to be a major civil and social force among southerners, and as Atlanta-based pollster Claibourne Darden found, many of the old Bible Belt taboos against strong drink and gambling still endure in areas less affected by urbanization.[54]

In the last quarter century, rather than being weakened by modernization, Christian evangelism nationwide has experienced a resurgence that some foresee as eventually being as powerful as the great religious upheavals that rocked American society during the eighteenth and nineteenth centuries. Every five years since 1965, while more liberal Protestant denominations suffered a near 5 percent decline in membership, evangelical churches won converts at an average rate of 8 percent.[55] Millions of Americans, including former Surgeon General C. Everett Koop, former Secretary of the Interior Donald Hodel, and pollster George Gallop, Jr., consider themselves born-again Christians. In a society tortured by questions regarding sexuality, alcoholism, and drug abuse, the evangelical message that gives emphasis to the traditional values of family, home, temperance, and community indeed seems plausible to many less fundamental Christians. Consequently, like the old

203

days in the South when concerned evangelists flocked to their politicians to lobby for laws prohibiting the teaching of scientific evolution, the sale of liquor, or retail business on Sunday, we are still seeing, and are likely to see in the future, similar delegations of solicitous evangelists—and not just in southern states—approaching local lawmakers for protection against the corrupting magnetism of modernization.

Nowhere has modernization been more evident in the South than in the region's economy. The South remains the most rural part of the nation, but during the 1980s, this same traditionally agricultural region, where farmers within recent memory plowed their fields straight up and down hills instead of along landscape contours, grew into the most highly industrialized part of the country. This transformation came not so much with the growth of existing textile, tobacco, and paper-product industries, but in the diversification to new industries that produced petrochemicals, electronic parts, and aerospace equipment. More than 25 percent of the rural work force in the South held manufacturing jobs during the mid-1980s, compared to slightly more than 19 percent of labor nationally; and in 1987, 54 percent of the nation's counties that relied on manufacturing as their primary source of income were located in the rural South.[56]

The never-ending promotion of the South as a haven for industry has certainly paid dividends. But the prosperity long envisioned by Henry W. Grady and his flock of twentieth-century disciples has been an empty promise to most rural southerners, especially those in areas populated predominantly by blacks, and is fast becoming a broken promise to many others. In August of 1987, for example, South Carolina Governor Carroll Campbell gave his blessing to a group of South Korean investors headed by businessman H. S. Chung, who planned to renovate a rundown building in Jonesville, a small rural community of approximately two thousand people in the Upstate. After the Catawba Regional Planning Council helped the group secure a low-interest, start-up development loan from the government, Chung went public with plans to expand the small building in Jonesville to two hundred thousand square feet and begin operation of a textile facility that was to be called Jonesville Fancy Yarns. The factory was to employ two hundred, but within a year, Jonesville's ambitious hopes were dashed as Chung went back to South Korea without ever opening the plant or making the first payment on the $100,000 loan. "We had high expectations," lamented Jonesville mayor J. D. Addis, "but as it went along, we sort of had our doubts about the whole thing."[57]

When the South suddenly became the new American industrial frontier, many expected a marked improvement in the region's economy. But after almost two decades and countless experiences like that of Jonesville, southerners are anything but prosperous. North Carolinians, for example, may brag that their state has the nation's most industrialized labor force, but at the same time, they have to accept the dismal fact that Tarheel workers are the lowest paid of any industrial laborers in the country. More recently, rather than seeking new manufacturing firms, the rural South has found itself trying to hold onto the ones that it has attracted. As Jonesville sought to lure its first major manufacturer, many, many other communities in the piedmont were losing theirs. Between 1979 and 1985, the rural South found itself in bitter competition for industry with third-world developing nations. The irony here, as James C. Cobb has pointed out, is that cost-conscious corporate executives have discovered that, when compared to places like Thailand and Sri Lanka, the rural South, with all its incentives designed to attract industry, is not as attractive as it once seemed to be. What has emerged from the shift in economic fortunes from North to South, and now overseas, is what has been referred to as "a picture of progress and poverty existing side by side—with a widening gap between the winners and losers."[58]

In Florida between 1980 and 1985, manufacturing and related jobs increased by almost 850 percent. The same was true for Texas and eleven other large urban areas of the South. But for places like Jonesville that have been unsuccessful in attracting outside employers, and other small towns that have seen approximately three hundred thousand workers in textiles, apparel, primary metals, chemicals, coal mining, basic steel, and leather products lose their jobs, things are anything but bright. Many of these displaced workers have picked up and moved to larger towns and cities to find employment, leaving behind retirees and welfare recipients to inhabit the once-thriving communities. Thus, in the wake of industrialization, rural southerners, traditionally the poorest group in the country, have been able to raise their per capita income only to a mere 75 percent of the national average. The median annual wage for full-time workers in the South is $1,468 less for white males, $1,050 for white females, $6,678 for black males, and $2,263 for black females.[59]

Historically, this has meant poorly funded education programs and miserably inadequate public facilities. For example, in the small town of Blue Hill, a community of some forty tumble-down dwellings in the remote reaches of Jefferson County, Mississippi, it was not until 1989 that residents could enjoy the "luxury" of piped-in spigot water. And, according to Steven Beschloss, a writer for the Norfolk *Virginian-Pilot*, in 1987, some of the people in equally rural Tchula, Mississippi, "are wondering whether their homes will ever have running water and indoor toilets." No doubt, in this respect, the image of backwardness branded on the South cannot be disputed, for the region remains a colonial economy of the highest order. Between 1969 and 1976, 70 percent of the manufacturing companies that either relocated or built branch plants in the South were controlled from the North, and the newest carpetbaggers hail from overseas.[60]

The South in the 1980s has gained more jobs than it has lost, but this gain has not changed the financial situation for many southerners whose standard of living remains the lowest in the nation. Despite the South's new-found national dominance in manufacturing, the economic well-being that contemporary southern recruiters hoped would accompany industrialization, not unlike the experiences of their late-nineteenth- and early-twentieth-century predecessors, has been thus far only a pipe dream. Recent industrialization has not re-made the South into the vision of independence and progressiveness that prophets of the New South, past and present, said it would. If trends continue, this new industrial livelihood promises to make the region even more dependent, not only on the North for economic nourishment, but also on foreign countries. Perhaps too much has been given away in terms of low wages, guarantees against unionization, and tax exemptions to achieve for the rural South even a measure of the prosperity found elsewhere in the country. Even with industry instead of agriculture as the region's economic mainstay, rural southerners remain on the last rung of the economic ladder. In addition, with more and more industrial firms establishing overseas branches, the future does not seem to offer much hope. More than likely, struggling rural southerners will not be able to overcome the devastating poverty that has long plagued them, nor will the South be successful in ridding itself of the economic dependence that has been traditionally one of its prime cultural characteristics. In this sense, at least, the future seems more like the past.

Because it has been historically agricultural and slow to industrialize, the South has retained a certain small-town, rural identity long since swept away by modern forces of change in other parts of the country. Historiographically, the region has been portrayed predominantly from a rural perspective, and only recently have southern cities received the national acclaim, as well as the scholarly attention, that they deserve. Woodward's own observation in 1951 that "the sum total of urbanization in the South was comparatively unimportant" is indeed reflective of this long-established perception of the South as primarily agrarian and identifiably small-town.[61]

At the turn of the twentieth century, only one city in the South had grown to a population exceeding one hundred thousand. That was New Orleans, and although the last ninety years have brought sweeping changes to the urban South, citadels like Atlanta, Houston, and Dallas still do not epitomize the region as Boston does New England, Chicago the Midwest, or Los Angeles and San Francisco the West Coast. Twentieth-century metropolises with their gleaming skyscrapers and sprawling suburbs may very well characterize the ever-elusive Sunbelt South, but small towns with populations of 7,500 or fewer, whose pasts, in many cases, reach back into the eighteenth and early-nineteenth centuries, remain most culturally characteristic of the region. "The South is still an aggregate of small communities . . . that form the backbone of the region," claimed *Time* in 1976. "Both pilloried and praised by native writers, the small town remains the custodian of the Southern life-style."[62]

Characteristic of small towns in the South is a main street or courthouse square, encroached upon by chain stores and small industry more now than in the past. Also a part of the imagery is the existence of a few remaining antebellum mansions built and occupied by one family for several generations; a neighborhood containing large turn-of-the-century houses located close to a still-vibrant central business district that closes down on Wednesday afternoons; a collection of main street store fronts that over the years have housed a variety of businesses; a Confederate monument; an old railroad depot which once served as the gateway to the town; a cemetery in which the town's fathers are buried that is cared for by members of the DAR; and several large, columned, centrally located, well-attended Baptist and Methodist churches. In small towns, residents become familiar with these landmarks and commonly associate them with people. Death, therefore, in a small town like Yazoo City, Mississippi, where Willie Morris was raised, "is a different proposition from death in a large city. In a small town one associated death with landmarks, with places people had lived or places they spent most of their time. . . . Death in a small town deeply affected the whole community. For weeks or even years the physical presence of the dead person would be missed in specific places; his funeral itself would touch closely upon the life of the town."[63]

Community landmarks in towns across the South, therefore, evoke a vivid sense of place. They are the symbolic reminders of the past, providing small towns, in the South as well as in other parts of the country, with an unmistakable identity. For residents and visitors alike, their presence conveys the idea of a less transitory environment that begets stability and permanence. In a nation whose people thrive on mobility, move on average every five years, and consequently rarely put down roots or form lasting place-attachments, small towns where people live whose great grandfathers called the same place home are culturally distinctive.[64]

Small towns are commonly believed to have a certain innocence about them, reminiscent of Jeffersonian America that belies the city and all the problems that it represents. In small towns Americans have traditionally found enough virtue to justify a wholesale rejection of urban life and an uncritical acceptance of rural life. Neighborliness, garrulous behavior, shared values that center around families, an innate preoccupation with community-spirited "get-togethers," an openness toward strangers, and a leisurely attitude toward both work and play are the foundations of this life-style and part of the South's down-home image. To many observers, the presence of the past, indeed, can be felt in the small towns of the South, and southerners who reside in small communities learn their history as much by feeling it as by reading it. "The past [there]," as planner Kevin Lynch aptly put it, "is known, familiar, a possession in which [people] . . . feel secure."[65]

In the South small communities have helped residents form and preserve their identity; they have given definition to lives; and in a nation beset by rootlessness, they have helped them better cope with the uprooted feelings that Woodward foresaw. Small towns and rural homeplaces undoubtedly embody the strong and lasting attachments southerners have for place. Witness, for example, what one wayward southerner who rediscovered his roots in rural Virginia had to say about the compelling attachment of place that his relatives once called home. "One can see, as one drives through the South," wrote Don Anderson, who in 1981 was in charge of Norfolk's National Association for the Southern Poor, "the pale outline of its history. One strays from the modern interstate highways to old plantation houses or to households whose decor dates them back a century or so. There is a constant longing for former times, and the heart is stirred that here a village withstood a Federal advance, there a hero was born. The pendulum swings from the past to the present, and back into the past."[66]

The importance southerners assign place includes not only the built environment, but also the natural environment. Many writers have eloquently described Dixie's storybook landscape and referred to the reverence shown for the land. From William Faulkner and Eudora Welty to Reynolds Price and Olive Ann Burns, the land has played a prominent role in the region's literature. The characters of these and other southern writers caress the red, overworked soil with their hands and water it with the sweat of their brows. The land is something that has been fought over, died on, and relied upon for a living by generation after generation. The land, the soil, the out-of-doors, nature, or whatever southerners choose to call it, gives them a way to keep in touch with their past and even provides them with a means of geographically defining the contemporary South. By the very lay of the land, one contributor to the "Southern Journal" section of *Southern Living* magazine sublimely claimed that she could actually pinpoint where the North ended and the South began.[67]

This homage for the land has been attributed to the South's agrarian heritage, but it penetrates southern culture much deeper and with much broader definition. Southerners, both black and white, rich and poor, place enormous value on land ownership. Owning land deeded from one generation to members of the next has helped to reinforce all-important kinship loyalties and has provided a way for families to maintain a continuity with the past. Sydney Nathans has documented this phenomenon in his study of three generations of one black family that began in the 1840s, when 109 slaves were forced to leave their North Carolina home and migrate across South Carolina and Georgia to a newly opened cotton plantation in Alabama. After the Civil War, some of these 109 slaves eventually were granted title to a portion of the Alabama plantation and willed it to their children and grandchildren. After 150 years, according to Nathans, the community of blacks who own this land is still "marked by a notable continuity." From this home-place dozens of family members have begun their lives. The land, according to one community resident, has been like a "plant bed," and by holding on to it rather than succumbing to pressures to sell it, this particular black community has carried on a long and valuable family tradition.[68] A tendency, therefore, exists on the part of many southerners to view the land as something more than just real estate to be bought and sold.

In addition to the revelation of all sorts of ecological phenomena, from kudzu and fire ants to manatees, walking catfish, and fainting goats, the land is also known to have a certain spiritual and redemptive quality. After retiring to his native state of Arkansas, former New York *Times* correspondent Roy Reed wrote about an irresistible compulsion he felt to rejuvenate his life by taking up residence close to the land. Reed worked as a journalist in Atlanta, New Orleans, and London and discovered that what he called the "man-made reality" and "hedonistic caress" of urban life were creatively debilitating to his livelihood. He thus chose to retire on a rocky hill-side farm near the hamlet of Hogeye,

Arkansas. "For anyone brought up on duty, challenge, and self-provision," he determined, returning "to the reality of a smaller, more manageable" existence stirred the blood and renewed the instinct for hard work."[69]

Other observers, and even song writers, have alluded to southerners' love of the land by describing their obsession with hunting and fishing. One North Carolinian has written that, in the South, "a youngster of whatever education or social background expects to learn to hunt as a part of growing up. I suspect that what keeps calling the hunter to the field and the fisherman to the river may not be so much the meat as the chance of communion with the land."[70] In the hard-driving song "Dixie on My Mind," country musician Hank Williams, Jr., came to a similar conclusion. Complaining of being stranded in New York City, where life is "one big hassle," and anxious to return home to the South, he lamented:

> The thing, you know, that I miss most of all,
> Is the freedom of the rivers and the pine,
> They don't do much huntin' and fishin' up here, you know,
> But I have met a few squirrels and one porcupine.
> If this is the Promised Land,
> Then I've had all that I can stand,
> And I'm headed back below that Dixie line.[71]

Whether he appreciates country music or not, Jimmy Carter would probably agree. As a child growing up in the tiny southwest Georgia town of Plains, Carter developed an unrelenting fascination with the land as a place of recreation that has stayed with him throughout his life. In *An Outdoor Journal* Carter recalls some of the experiences he had as an outdoorsman. He writes of "a sense of order, truth, patience, beauty, and justice" that he gets from life on the land. "My father and all my ancestors did it [hunted and fished] before me," he confides. "It's been part of my life since childhood, and part of my identity, like being a southerner or a Baptist."[72]

This South is one of the heart, one that people long for, return to, and strive to preserve for future generations to enjoy and from which to glean their own identity. It seems reasonable to assume, therefore, that like the historic preservation movement that had its beginning in the South and is vital and growing, the importance southerners attach to place will last for many years to come and embrace future southerners just as it has those past and those present.

A large percentage of the residents of metropolitan areas like Atlanta and Houston are assimilated southerners. Residing in predominantly

Republican suburbs and commuting to jobs located in landscaped office parks, the acquisition of any identification with the traditional South has not come as easily as it has to those born and raised in the region, if indeed it has come at all. To this growing group of affluent people, southern culture is something that can be consumed. It comes in many forms: a one-hundred-dollar-a-head antebellum costume ball celebrating the fiftieth anniversary of the premier of *Gone With the Wind*; an antique rocking chair purchased in a small-town shop; a cassette tape in which Lewis Grizzard expounds on his boyhood in Moreland, Georgia; a Florence King paperback that provides comic relief from weeknight television; or a recipe plucked from the pages of *Southern Living*. Neither born nor raised in the region, the migration of these "outsiders" to the South has greatly watered-down regional distinctions and replaced them with a national cultural predictability and a mass-produced surrogate southernness. "The South is being etherized," wrote Marshall Frady in 1972, "subtly rendered pastless, memoryless, and vague of identity. What we are talking about is the passing of a sensibility—an event perhaps too wispy to define, but no less seismic . . . in its effect on the inner lives, the folk-geist, of a people. . . . Massively and uncomplainingly, the whole land is being trivialized. . . . The old pipe-organ range of prodigal possibilities for life there [in the South]—both gentle and barbarous, good and evil—has contracted to the comfortable monotone note of middle C."[73]

There can be no denying Frady's observation. But while southern identity may well be on the wane, it has not yet become, as John Shelton Reed found out, "useless and irrelevant" or even "doomed to an early extinction."[74] Some have claimed that what is happening in the South is not so much the result of a modern dominant culture aggressively imposing itself on a regional subculture as it is the widespread national acceptance of the regional subculture, that is, the "Southernization of America" instead of the "Americanization of the South."[75] To be sure, Charlie Daniels and his band play to sold-out audiences in New York as well as in Nashville, and Justin Wilson's public television program has been as enthusiastically received in Boston as in Baton Rouge.

In 1964 Howard Zinn wrote that the South was a regional embodiment of basic Americanism. The South's shortcomings, in other words, were really a microcosm of the nation's deficiencies, and the best description, according to Zinn, of the relationship between the South and the nation was that of "mirror-image" twins.[76] If he was right, and Americans have all along been "latent southerners," then it is not difficult to understand why southern culture has been so easily exported and is so resilient. Vietnam left many Americans with feelings of defeat, guilt, and repression. The South lived with this malaise long before the first American infantryman set foot in Southeast Asia, and this may also help to explain the adaptability of the region's culture. Still a place where people seem more in touch with their past, the region is commonly understood to be an anachronism where certain sensibilities associated with home, community, and family remain central to everyday life. In a seemingly rootless society caught up in drug addiction, fear of AIDS, public distrust of government, and rampant crime, many Americans have sought to reaffirm contact with traditional values and have looked to rural, small-town America to find some measure of reassurance. The song "Americana" by country musician Moe Bandy, about a forlorn trucker who forsakes the interstate highway for a less-traveled backroad and discovers the "real" America, perhaps best expresses these feelings. "Here's for courtin' at the Rexall soda fountain," he croons, "Like we did before they built the shopping mall. I saw so many reasons why I love this country, you know some things never really change at all."[77]

Inevitably, the future South will be less distinct than it is and will come to resemble more and more freeze-dried, fast-food, suburban America. Its unique regionalism, however, promises not to evaporate altogether and be replaced entirely by a national sameness, or even by an ersatz southernness. What seems more plausible is that like ethnic cultures elsewhere in the United States, attributes, customs, mannerisms, and even attitudes traditionally ascribed to the South will endure in the midst of a more dominant national or possibly even global culture. Thus the answer to Woodward's question seems to be "yes." There are things about the South that have withstood and will continue to withstand the tests of time and the pressures of conformity. Perhaps the most significant of these is the lasting recognition and steadfast conviction on the part of many that the South is indeed different. And this, more than anything else, may help the region to maintain a measure of its stubborn singularity.

NOTES

1. The quip about Waylon Jennings's hair came from James C. Cobb, "From Muskogee to Luckenbach: Country Music and the 'Southernization' of America," *Journal of Popular Culture* 16 (Winter 1982): 87. An Associated Press report in the Spartanburg, South Carolina, *Herald-Journal* offered additional documentation of the demise of a culturally distinct South: a Duke University botanist announced that as the global greenhouse effect causes temperatures worldwide to rise, kudzu, the vine that ate the South, would inevitably invade the North

(December 10, 1989, p. B12). See also, Joseph B. Cumming, Jr., "Been Down Home so Long It Looks Like up to Me," *Esquire* 76 (August 1971): 84.

2. C. Vann Woodward, *The Burden of Southern History* (Baton Rouge, 1960), pp. 25–31.

3. For one of the latest of these slick, self-serving articles about the South, see Doug Cumming, "Seven Wonders of the South," *Southpoint* 2 (February 1990): 30–45.

4. Hodding Carter III, "The End of the South," *Time*, August 6, 1990, p. 82.

5. Marshall Frady, "Gone with the Wind," *Newsweek*, July 28, 1975, p. 11.

6. Ulrich B. Phillips, "The Central Theme of Southern History," *American Historical Review* 34 (October 1928): 30–34; Wilbur J. Cash, *The Mind of the South* (New York, 1941), p. 252; Edwin M. Yoder, "W. J. Cash after a Quarter Century," *Harper's Magazine* 231 (September 1965): 16.

7. Cited in *Black Elected Officials: A National Roster*, 15th ed. (Washington, 1986), p. 21.

8. "Reverse Migration," *Time*, September 27, 1976, p. 50; "Black Migration in the South Rising," Spartanburg *Herald-Journal*, January 10, 1990, p. A3. The quote about future demographics for the South is found in Kenneth R. Weiss, "Many Northern Blacks Returning to New South," Spartanburg *Herald-Journal*, May 1, 1989, pp. A1, A7.

9. Frederick Allen, "The Color-Deaf Candidacy," *Southpoint* 2 (January 1990): 16.

10. Peter Applebome, "Klan's Ghost Haunts Louisiana Vote," New York *Times*, February 16, 1989, p. A22.

11. Statistics cited in "Ratio of Elected Blacks to Black Population Low," Spartanburg *Herald-Journal*, November 1, 1989, pp. B1, B2.

12. Steven Beschloss, "Prosperity's Broken Promise," *Southern Exposure* 15 (Fall 1987): 59.

13. Quoted in "Segregation Persists at High School Proms," Spartanburg *Herald-Journal*, March 25, 1989, p. B1.

14. James C. Cobb, "Y'all Come on Down: The Southern States' Pursuit of Industry," *Southern Exposure* 14 (n.d.): 22; Beschloss, "Prosperity's Broken Promise," p. 59.

15. Cited in Cobb, "Y'all Come on Down," p. 22.

16. Cited in Sally S. Huguley, "Study in Black and White," *Southern Exposure* 15 (Fall 1987): 66–67.

17. John Fischer, "Field Notes on a Changing South," *Harper's Magazine* 244 (April 1972): 18; Reg Murphy, "Not since Jefferson and Madison . . . ," *Saturday Review* 3 (September 1976): 3.

18. In 1989, Spartanburg County, South Carolina, for example, still elected its county commissioners at large, which, in effect, diluted the voting strength of blacks who live in the city of Spartanburg and in enclaves scattered throughout the county. In May 1991, after pressure from the NAACP and the U.S. Justice Department, commission members are to be elected from designated council districts.

19. *Saturday Evening Post* 261 (January-February 1989): 87.

20. Don O'Briant, "Frankly, My Dears, There's a Sequel," Atlanta *Constitution*, September 15, 1988, pp. 1A, 10A; Claudia Glenn Dowling, "The Further Adventures of Scarlet O'Hara," *Life* (May 1988): 26–32.

21. Joe Gray Taylor, *Eating, Drinking, and Visiting in the South* (Baton Rouge, 1982), p. 153.

22. Allie Patricia Wall and Ron L. Larne, *Hog Heaven: A Guide to South Carolina Barbecue* (Lexington, S.C., 1979), p. 13; Charles F. Kovacik and John Winberry, *South Carolina: A Geography* (Boulder, 1987), pp. 208–9.

23. Marsha G. McGee, "Prime-Time Dixie, Television's View of a 'Simple' South," *Journal of American Culture* 6 (Fall 1983): 100–109; Eric Peter Verschure, "Stumble, Bumble, Mumble: TV's Image of the South, " *Journal of Popular Culture* 16 (Winter 1982): 92–96.

24. Sheldon Hackney, "Southern Violence," *American Historical Review* 74 (February 1969): 906.

25. Elliot J. Gorn, "Gouge and Bite, Pull Hair and Scratch: The Social Significance of Fighting in the Southern Backcountry," *American Historical Review* 90 (February 1985): 18–43.

26. Cash, *Mind of the South*, p. 121.

27. H. C. Brearley, "The Pattern of Violence," in *Culture in the South*, ed. William T. Couch (Chapel Hill, 1934), pp. 679, 685–86. Two of the most recent attempts to explain the role violence has played in the history of the South are Herbert Shapiro, *White Violence and Black Response: From Reconstruction to Montgomery* (Amherst, 1988), and Ted Ownby, *Subduing Satan: Recreation, Religion, and Manhood in the Rural South, 1865–1920* (Chapel Hill, 1990).

28. Brearley, "Pattern of Violence," pp. 691-92.

29. John Shelton Reed, *The Enduring South: Subcultural Persistence in Mass Society* (Chapel Hill, 1986), p. 97.

30. Peter Schrag, "A Hesitant New South: Fragile Promise of the Last Frontier," *Saturday Review*, February 12, 1972, p. 55.

31. Willie Morris, "Texas-Oklahoma: Like the Clash of Armies," *Southern Living* 23 (September 1988): 14.

32. Cited in Gary Pomerantz, "Where Football Is King," Atlanta *Journal-Constitution*, November 25, 1988, p. 1C.

33. Quoted in "Eat 'Em Up, Get 'Em," *Time*, September 27, 1976, p. 81.

34. Pomerantz, "Where Football Is King," p. 1C.

35. Quoted in Kenneth R. Weiss, "For Whatever Reason, Football Rules the South," Spartanburg *Herald-Journal*, January 28, 1990, p. 1A.

36. Quoted in Pomerantz, "Where Football Is King," p. 8C.

37. Ibid.

38. Thomas D. Clark, *The Emerging South* (New York, 1961), p. 254.

39. "A Born-Again Faith," *Time*, September 28, 1976, p. 84.

40. Gerald L. Ingalls, "Remnants of Prohibition in the United States," *Southeastern Geographer* 27 (November 1987): 101–14; "Blue Laws Still Alive," Spartanburg *Herald-Journal*, December 31, 1989, p. A14.

41. "ABC Hearing Set for Grocery Store Application," Spartanburg *Herald-Journal*, March 10, 1989, pp. C1-C2.

42. Steven Wishnia, "Rockin' with the First Amendment," *The Nation* 244 (October 24, 1987): 6; Kathy Henderson, "Censorship of Sales Marketing?," *Seventeen* 46 (January 1987): 86.

43. Quoted in Thomas J. Flygare, "Supreme Court Strikes Down Louisiana Creationism Act," *Phi Delta Kappan* 69 (September 1987): 77.

44. *Aquillard v. Treen*, 634 F.S. 426 (E.D. Louisiana, 1985); 778 F.2d 2 (5th Circuit Court, 1985); *Edwards v. Aquillard*, 55 U.S.L.W. 4860.

45. Thomas J. Flygare, "Some Thoughts on the Tennessee Textbook Case," *Phi Delta Kappan* 67 (February 1986): 474–75; Perry A. Zirkel, "The Textbook Cases: Secularism on Appeal," *Phi Delta Kappan* 69 (December 1987): 309; *Jaffree v. Board of School Commissioners*, 554 F. Supplement, 1104, 1129, 41 (S.D. Alabama, 1983).

46. *Mozert v. Hawkins County Board of Education*, F.2d (6th Circuit, 1987); *Smith v. Board of School Commissioners*, F.2d (llth Circuit, 1987); see also "Fundamentalists Lose Two Textbook Cases in Federal Appeals Court," *Publishers Weekly*, September 11, 1987, p. 11.

47. Charles L. Glenn, "Textbook Controversies: A 'Disaster for the Public Schools?,' " *Phi Delta Kappan* 68 (February 1987): 451.

48. "New Strains on Dixie's Bible Belt," *U.S. News and World Report*, December 9, 1985, p. 59; see also "Change of Heart in Mississippi," *Christianity Today*, June 17, 1988, p. 63.

49. For an estimation of the number of Americans who regularly watch televised religious programs, see Stephen W. Tweedie, "Viewing the Bible Belt," *Journal of Culture* 11 (Spring 1978): 865–76.

50. Alistair Cooke, ed., *The Vintage Mencken* (New York, 1955), pp. 152–53.

51. Debra Lester, "New History Tells of Garden's Beginnings," Spartanburg *Herald-Journal*, November 11, 1989, p. C2.

52. Clark, *The Emerging South*, p. 254.

53. Reed, *The Enduring South*, p. 99.

54. Cited in "New Strains on Dixie's Bible Belt," p. 59.

55. "From Revival Tent to Mainstream," *U.S. News and World Report*, December 19, 1988, p. 54.

56. John Egerton, *The Americanization of Dixie: The Southernization of America* (New York, 1974), p. 105; Beschloss, "Prosperity's Broken Promise," pp. 57, 60.

57. "Was Promise of Jobs Just a Fancy Yarn?," Spartanburg *Herald-Journal*, December 2, 1988, pp. lA, 6A.

58. Beschloss, "Prosperity's Broken Promise," p. 5.

59. Cited in Stuart Rosenfeld, "A Divided South," *Southern Exposure* 14 (n.d.): 11.

60. Gregory Jaynes, "Taps for Blue Hill," *Life* (November 1989): 27; Beschloss, "Prosperity's Broken Promise," pp. 56–60; Cobb, "Y'all Come on Down," pp. 19–23.

61. C. Vann Woodward, *Origins of the New South, 1877–1913*, vol. 9: *A History of the South*, ed. Wendell Holmes Stephenson and E. Merton Coulter (Baton Rouge, 1951), p. 139.

62. "Small Town Soul," *Time*, September 27, 1976, p. 56. One recent article, " 'Southern Hospitality' Thrives in North Atlanta," Atlanta *Journal-Constitution*, July 29, 1990, p. 1, described the small communities north of Atlanta in Forsyth County as "points of reference" where "quality of life" and "southern hospitality" have their "truest meaning."

63. Willie Morris, *North Toward Home* (Boston, 1967), pp. 31–32.

64. Southern writers like Faulkner and Welty are famous for the sense of place their novels evoke, and many other writers have adopted this same idea. For example, see Warren Leamon, *Unheard Melodies* (Atlanta, 1990).

65. Kevin Lynch, *What Time Is This Place?* (Cambridge, 1972), p. 29.

66. Don Anderson, "At Daniel's Mountain," in *Why the South Will Survive: Fifteen Southerners Look at Their Region a Half Century after "I'll Take My Stand"* (Athens, 1981), p. 69.

67. Kathryn Ritter, "A Road into the South," *Southern Living* 23 (July 1988): 92.

68. Sydney Nathans, "Fortress without Walls: A Black Community after Slavery," in *Holding on to the Land and the Lord: Kinship, Ritual, Land Tenure, and Social Policy in the Rural South*, ed. Robert L. Hall and Carol B. Stack (Athens, 1982), pp. 55–65.

69. Roy Reed, *Looking for Hogeye* (Fayetteville, 1986), pp. 8–9.

70. Hamilton C. Horton, Jr., "The Enduring Soil," in *Why the South Will Survive*, pp. 58–59.

71. Hank Williams, Jr., "Dixie on My Mind," Electra/Asylum Records (1981).

72. Jimmy Carter, *An Outdoor Journal: Adventures and Reflections* (New York, 1988), pp. 5–7.

73. Frady, "Gone With the Wind" p. 57.

74. John Shelton Reed, *Southerners: The Social Psychology of Sectionalism* (Chapel Hill, 1983), pp. 108–9.

75. See Egerton, *The Americanization of Dixie*.

76. Howard Zinn, *The Southern Mystique* (New York, 1964), pp. 217–18.

77. Moe Bandy, "Americana," Curb Records (1988).

8

Tomorrow Seems Like Yesterday:
The South's Future in the Nation and the World

JAMES C. COBB

Yesterday, today, and tomorrow are "Is: Indivisible. . . . It's all now you see. Yesterday won't be over until tomorrow and tomorrow began ten thousand years ago."[1] What was true for young Chick Mallison in William Faulkner's *Intruder in the Dust* was truer still for a South that struggled for nearly a century to sort out the relationship between a distinctive past, a controversial present, and a glorious but elusive future. By the end of the 1960s, however, the region was caught up in a far-ranging process of regional, national, and global readjustment that lifted much of the weight of the past from the South's shoulders, only to replace it with a new burden—that of finding its way in a world where the embrace of American values no longer insured its success or even its survival.

"Tomorrow" may not have begun ten thousand years ago, but the future became an obsessive concern for the South's leaders long before the past did. The colonial South was portrayed time and again as an Edenic paradise with limitless potential. King Cotton was the mainstay of antebellum boosters, although there were those by the end of the period who could see an industrial future for the South.[2]

Picking up the post-Appomattox pieces of these dreams fell to Henry Grady, a Georgia editor and orator whose optimism and hyperbole became synonymous with the New South movement. Grady's ability to see the destruction of Atlanta as a fortuitous course correction that actually put the merrily rebuilding city on the right track set the tone for a succeeding generation of New South boosters who followed his lead by praising the region for its bounce-back from the war and the misfortunes of Reconstruction. Resurgent Klan activity, the lynching of Leo Frank (and hundreds of blacks who had even less of a chance), the Scopes trial, and even the foul slander of H. L. Mencken notwithstanding, "Looking Good and Getting Better" was the byword for Grady disciples like Edwin Mims. Mims surveyed a South on the brink of economic collapse in 1927 and promised that if the South followed the example of its more progressive leaders, "no one can have too high a hope of what can be achieved within the next quarter of a century. Freed from the limitations that have so long hampered it, and buoyant with the energy of a new life coursing through its veins, the South will press forward to a great destiny."[3]

Although boosters such as Mims were clearly in their ascendancy in the 1920s, there were those who begged to disagree. In 1929 the Nashville Agrarians produced *I'll Take My Stand*, a set of essays that offered a clear and comprehensive critique of industrialism and asked southerners if they truly wished to sacrifice their rural, agrarian life-style to the tyranny of industrialism. Despite its clarity and earnestness, *I'll Take My Stand* was a volume out of tune with its times. Boosterism was establishing an ever-broadening and tightening grip on the South by the end of the 1920s, and the economic disaster that began the next decade added even more desperation to the development push while focusing national attention on the apparent economic consequences of the South's long-standing adherence to agriculture.[4]

The depression years finally forced a nation that had been giving Dixie the benefit of considerable doubt to confront the distasteful realities of life below the Mason-Dixon line. The New South cry of opulence around the bend disappeared beneath a flood of exposés and reports, the most famous of which pronounced the region "The Nation's Number One Economic Problem." The New Deal marked the beginning of nearly a half century of bipartisan consensus that the federal government should subsidize, encourage, and facilitate in every way possible the South's entry into the American mainstream.[5]

The effort to assimilate the South, or render it assimilable, took on an even greater sense of urgency as the United States assumed the position of free-world leadership. With the nation apparently savoring the prospect of corrective intervention in the affairs of others, C. Vann Woodward suggested that southerners might draw on an experience with "failure, frustration, poverty, defeat and humiliation not shared by other Americans" and somehow resist the spell of the self-righteous invincibility that had seduced the rest of the nation. Woodward's hopes were dashed repeatedly over the next three decades as the South responded with "headlong precipitancy" to "the slogans of nationalism" and ultimately failed, as Woodward wrote, both its "fellow countrymen . . . and its own legitimate heritage."[6]

Woodward's disappointment was understandable, but even if southerners had raised a dissenting cry, the regional experience on which they drew would have undermined rather than bolstered their credibility as far as their target audience was concerned. Cold-war America, as

Woodward himself pointed out, "already lived in a post-industrial, post-modern, science fiction future unattainable by less fortunate folk." Its image bore but one significant blemish. A nation presenting itself "as a model for how democracy, power, opulence and virtue could be combined under one flag" could hardly tolerate within its own borders the poverty, repression, and general benightedness that had resulted from leaving the South's destiny in its own hands.[7]

To serve effectively as a global disciplinarian and leader-by-example, the nation had first to clean up around its own back door, or—specifically—its lower right-hand quadrant. Immanuel Wallerstein observed that once the United States became a "world hegemonic power," it was no longer acceptable to "the dominant political forces of the U.S. federal state to have a 'backward' geographical zone, just as it was no longer in its interest to have the denial of political rights to minorities such as the blacks. The homogenization of America was an urgent political (and diplomatic) need of the U.S. federal state."[8] Most southern leaders showed no inclination to resist the national myths of innocence and omnipotence, but few appeared to realize that their region would be on both the giving and receiving end of the national commitment to an Americanized world.

With economic, political, legal, and social trends pointing toward the need to accelerate the South's convergence with the remainder of American society, a revisionist impulse began to manifest itself on the scholarly horizon. Whereas previous generations who studied the South had largely contented themselves, as Vann Woodward saw it, with "vindicating, justifying, rationalizing and often celebrating the present order," a new group of scholars led by Woodward and political scientist V. O. Key turned the study of the South on its head by blaming the misdeeds of the past for the region's obvious failure to fulfill the long-standing prophecy of good and plenty. In the process they identified the specific areas where the undoing of these misdeeds might contribute to a more acceptable, Americanized version of the New South.[9]

Presented in synthesis, Woodward and Key's analyses might be summarized as "how self-serving late nineteenth-century white elites managed to keep the South out of the American mainstream." Woodward and Key depicted a South that limped into the twentieth century hamstrung by disfranchisement and segregation; a near-barbaric, one-party political system; and an inefficient, labor-intensive agriculture featuring an exploitive and outdated system of credit and tenancy. The two scholars saw the prevailing social philosophy as what Woodward termed "juleps for the few and pellagra for the crew." Concerns that Henry Grady and other advocates of industrial development might somehow dilute this splendid mixture of inequality, poverty, and depravity evaporated as the New South strategists built on what Numan Bartley described as a "shortsighted . . . alliance with northeastern capitalism" established by the post-Reconstruction Redeemer governments. According to prevailing wisdom, this active effort to promote the colonization of the South by both northern and foreign capital shackled the region with a low-wage, resource-exploitive, socially indifferent industrial sector that was at times barely distinguishable from the dominant agricultural component.[10]

The belief that the Woodward-Key synthesis identified the essential causes of the South's failure to embrace its rightful future was seldom challenged, although economist William H. Nicholls recast the synthesis in essentially cultural terms before focusing on its role in retarding the South's economic progress. Others contended that instead of the ascendant bourgeois elite described by Woodward, it was a tenacious planter oligarchy that had actually erected the matrix of institutional and cultural barriers standing between the South and its tomorrow. Jonathan Wiener and Dwight Billings argued for planter persistence in the South comparable to that of the Junkers in Prussia and blamed planters for the South's failure to modernize along the classical lines followed by England and the northern United States. In so doing, however, these scholars simply shifted the blame for the South's woes from one set of villains to another. The essential conditions that held the South back remained constant, regardless of whether they appeared to serve the interests of a business or an agricultural elite.[11]

There was a disagreement over who constructed the obstacles that blocked the South's advance, but the consensus strategy for clearing the path to the future focused first on the modernization of the South's economy. It was widely held among liberal journalists and social scientists that the coming of cities and factories to Dixie would quickly eradicate a host of regional ills ranging from pellagra to political irresponsibility. Indeed, a close reading of this literature suggests that the forthcoming encounter between an advancing wave of smokestacks and skyscrapers on the one hand and the entrenched forces of ignorance and degradation on the other would make *Godzilla v. The Thing* seem like a schoolyard scuffle. At any rate, urban-industrial development would mean curtains for Jim Crow; the end of disfranchisement and a racially preoccupied one-party politics; and, finally, institutional advancement on a broad front ranging from public education to health care and all the necessary infrastructural services.[12]

These changes came much more slowly than had been anticipated. Urbanization and industrialization had been grossly overrated as agents of social change, and, of course, ignorance and degradation gave their usual good account of themselves. Finally, however, thanks in part to federal intervention that coincided with the South's economic transformation, by the middle of the 1970s it appeared that the critically debilitating conditions outlined in the Woodward-Key synthesis had been either neutralized, minimized, or eradicated. The South's economy was a mainstay of the supposedly booming Sunbelt. Blacks were enfranchised; schools and lunch counters were integrated; Republicans no longer needed the protection of the game warden, but actually sought office and won on many occasions.

As seemed typical of the region's historical fortunes, however, just as many southerners were tuning up for a few verses of "Shall We Gather at the Mainstream," the achievement of parity with the North was both overshadowed and tainted by the reality of northern decline. Deindustrialization, racial tension, environment pollution, and outmigration took their toll against a national backdrop of defeat and disillusionment fostered by the back-to-back debacles of Vietnam and Watergate. So significant and shocking was this national fall from grace that, instead of praising the South for its achievements, critical observers like John Egerton worried that Dixie and the nation were not "exchanging strengths as much as they are exchanging sins."[13]

The traumatic confrontation with defeat, economic stagnation, and moral imperfection led to what Woodward described as a withering of "self-righteousness along the Maine-Michigan axis." Hence, it was not so surprising that the 1970s emerged as a decade characterized by widespread empathy, tolerance, and, briefly, even a fascination for people and things southern. As Texan Larry L. King summed it up, "We Ain't Trash No More!"[14]

Not only did the nation elect a southern president (albeit by the skin of his prodigious choppers) but Americans also generally seemed to embrace the region's culture and mores during the decade. Country music achieved the long-sought crossover into the pop market so often that, for awhile at least, Luckenbach, Texas, seemed almost as fascinating as New York, New York. And, for an equally brief moment, Jimmy Carter appeared to represent a grown-up John-Boy Walton, whose television family seemed to affirm all that was good about southern life. "The Waltons" offered alienated, second-generation rat-racers outside the South a vision of personal connectedness—in Jack Kirby's words, "a small tractable world where place, people, and extended family ties are real." The appeal of "The Waltons" did not come without costs, however, as Kirby noted: "In reversing the po-white, Tobacco Road stereotype the show's success also "created a national reference

221

whose very southerness began to evaporate." At the same time, while it was gratifying to hear John Denver thank God he was a country boy, it was a bit unsettling to see the title "Country Entertainer of the Year" go to Olivia Newton-John, whose "country" was actually Australia.[15]

The nation's embrace of the South also robbed it of its uncalculating, almost countercultural, innocence that seemed to coexist remarkably well with its once-unfailing instincts for depravity. On the screen, Robert Altman used the country music industry and its Nashville mecca to show that Watergate-era America was as rotten at the bottom—among the plain folk—as it was up top where the politicians hung out. Likewise, on television's "Dallas," J. R. Ewing and his fellow Texas good ol' boys robbed, swindled, and seduced at a pace that would have put any of the old (or new) northern robber barons to shame.[16]

Basking in the first glow of southern ascendancy and savoring the North's misfortune in none-too-well concealed fashion, some southerners had called on the South to give guidance to a stricken nation. Those who suggested that the South had the credentials for such leadership, however, seldom went beyond vague references to basic everyday American staples such as manners, localism, personalism, or love of family.

For example, in the conclusion to his history of the South, I. A. Newby warned that if the South were to be totally immersed in the mainstream, "the nation would lose an important element of pluralism and particularism and southerners a way of life whose best qualities had much to offer in an age of standardization and alienation." Like so many statements of this sort, Newby's argument was long on the subjunctive and short on the substantive, a fact that became more obvious as he continued: "The southerner's traditional attachment to locality and family and his sense of history *might have* helped him and other Americans mitigate the rootlessness and anxieties of mass urban society, just as his conservatism *might have* braked the headlong rush toward undirected 'progress'. . . . His respect for tradition and institutions and constitutionalism *might have* helped limit the growth of government power or at least reduced the likelihood of its abuse. His sense of the tragic *might have* blunted the excessive optimism of liberals and their exaggerated faith in social reform and the periodic disillusionments this produced." Even when Newby's statements appeared more confident in tone, the reader was left to search for specifics: "As it was, his personalism and mannerliness did help the South ease aspects of the racial problem that baffled more liberal northern communities."[17]

Georgia-born Joseph B. Cumming responded to such celebrations of southern values by pointing out that "these values can be used to thwart the better impulses of the human spirit. I have seen honor stiff-arm honesty, hospitality suffocate friendliness, graciousness out-gesture generosity and natural sympathy." As for a South ready to lead the rest of the nation, Cumming sadly observed: "I would like to believe this version of the vision, but I cannot. The South I know just isn't equipped for existential voyages. It lacks the Pilgrim soul."[18]

Cumming's judgment may have been a bit harsh, but after attempting to feed on the South for a while, a still-hungry nation seemed to discover that, in terms of its staying power, the great southern love feast was the emotional and psychological equivalent of a stereotypical Chinese meal. Jimmy Carter's ostentatious humility soon grew boring, while his low-key, but definitely Southern Baptist, sermonizing about the need for patience, restraint, and lowered expectations breached the fine line between preaching and meddling to a generation hooked on instant gratification and general self-indulgence. Hence, Americans turned to a new leader, a prophet not just of plenty, but of more than enough. By 1980, Carter's regional identity was of less importance to the great majority of voters than his uninspiring leadership. Meanwhile, Woodward's hopes to the contrary notwithstanding, white southerners were no more tolerant than their counterparts elsewhere of the Georgian's inability to neutralize forces and events beyond his control. It was worth noting that Carter's southernness was something of an issue in 1976, but it came up infrequently if at all in 1980. Only the more paranoid professional southerners believed it did him any harm, and with returns from the South suggesting that even Miss Lillian may have opted for someone closer to her own age, there was certainly no reason to suspect that it did him any good.[19]

In the final analysis, America'a willingness to embrace the South in the 1970s and 1980s was the product of both changes in the region itself and in the nation and world at large. The South had faced its greatest pressures for reform during the Kennedy-Johnson years when the nation was playing its self-assigned role as world policeman and all-around moral arbiter. The ensuing decade of disillusionment, defeat, economic decline, and retreat from leadership shook the nation's self-confidence and suggested a new world environment in which America's claims to moral supremacy and military might were suspect.

As the nation passed into what Wallerstein called its "post-hegemonic" phase, the matter of Americanizing the South seemed much less urgent.[20] To Reagan-era strategists, military prowess was no problem so long as money was no object. Moral superiority was easier to assert than to establish, however, and they opted for the former. This strategy entailed a moratorium on nitpicking about civil rights, poverty, and other issues of sensitivity to both recently Republicanized southern whites and a large number of their northern counterparts as well. In fact, racial woes were too common throughout the nation to allow for much finger-pointing by even the most uncompromising northern liberal. Hence, the Reagan administration's attitude toward the status quo in Dixie was *Bonzo* in triplicate, hearing, seeing, and, especially, speaking no evil.

Had Bonzo been willing to risk it, even he could have pointed out that the South of the 1980s was still some distance from the South it was supposed to become. In fact, in terms of what it should have been, the South of the 1980s hardly made any sense at all. It was the most industrialized region in the country, but it remained the poorest. Most of its population lived in metropolitan areas, but most of its industry was in the country. Manufacturers rated it the best place in the nation in which to operate a business, while labor spokespersons condemned it as the worst place to work. Dixie finally had two-party politics, but in presidential elections, at least, almost all blacks were in one party and the majority of whites were in the other.[21]

In short, despite the changes it had undergone, the contemporary South seemed hardly less contradictory and paradoxical than the one W. J. Cash confronted when he wrote that only a madman would venture prophecies about the region's future "in the face of forces sweeping over the world in the fateful year of 1940." Cash would soon be gone, but, nearly fifty years later, his warning that global forces will play a major role in shaping the South's future rings truer than ever.[22]

For example, the Reagan administration might have moved to reclaim world military and moral dominance through expensive weaponry and cheap talk, but regaining economic preeminence was not so simple. As its massive trade deficit grew, the United States became Japan's favorite colony and the South its favorite regional investment center. Southern leaders who thought they had bought industries found, alas, that they had only rented them, as footloose firms nurtured by subsidies, tax breaks, and other past favors showed their gratitude by disdaining national loyalties and scouring the globe for the easiest pickings available. When the growth of manufacturing employment slowed significantly, the shift to jobs in services held the line against high unemployment but masked the slippage of thousands of workers into lower-income and poverty categories.[23]

As this phenomenon affected more and more southerners, progress wrought by integration and equal opportunity measures would be tested by increased competition for jobs concentrated in metropolitan areas where the poor and unskilled of both races seemed destined to congregate. Similarly, the racial divisions that continued to mark the region even in an era of two-party politics were unlikely to narrow in the face of increased economic competition. (For a great many whites, the answer to What does Jesse want? was Everything you've got!) Hence, for the Democrats, the task of recapturing the votes of lower-income whites without alienating the party's long-suffering black loyalists loomed ever larger and more intimidating. Meanwhile, for the Republicans, the persistent racial conservatism of lower-class whites and the growth of the South's white middle class pointed to a promising future indeed.[24]

The emergence of a middle class was a much-anticipated development that seemed to promise rational, responsive government at the state and local level. In reality, however, the South's failure to develop a viable, color-blind coalition of have-nots such as the one Key anticipated left the region's ascendant bourgeoisie free to fashion policies attuned to its particular preferences about services, amenities, and facilities without undue concern for programs designed to respond to the needs of low-income, working-class southerners of either race. Urbanization and immigration by Republicans from other regions helped to moderate the flat-earthism of the rank-and-file, home-grown GOP, but as radical a development as it might have seemed to those who remembered the years when white Republicans were hardly known south of Appalachia, there was actually little evidence at the end of the 1980s to dispute the observations of Numan Bartley and Hugh Graham in 1975 that the Republican conquest of Dixie might amount to little more than a "quite traditional southern triumph under a new partisan label, of the South's more dominant social conservatism over her game but historically outweighed populism."[25]

The self-interested bourgeois conservatism of the new generation of southern leaders was reinforced by the commitment of business and professional leaders at the city and county level to the gospel of economic growth which had emerged in the post-World War II years as an all-consuming regional passion. The growth ethos dictated a rigid fiscal frugality forsaken only when industries needed subsidies or when expenditures for services or infrastructure seemed to promise a guaranteed return in growth. This same commitment demanded wholehearted opposition to expensive benefit or compensation plans for workers and, of course, rock-ribbed opposition to organized labor. Stunned political pundits who had visions of frost forming around the edges of Hell the first time they saw Strom Thurmond shaking hands with blacks will know it is truly time to start outfitting departed sinners with ice skates when he embraces his first union official.[26]

225

Convinced that the South would follow the same development path as the North, many Sunbelt-era observers hoped their region would avoid the "mistakes" that left the North vulnerable to urban decay, environmental despoilation, labor unrest, and a host of other problems. In essence, this view restated the earlier sentiments of Louis Rubin and others that the South would find "a way to control industrialism, to admit it only on the South's terms and then only such industrialism as it will need." A similar notion was expressed in non-Western societies that somehow the developing nation can accept only those aspects of industrial and commercial development that it wants and needs, reject the rest, and thereby produce a society that will "surpass the best that the West has ever achieved." The development-mad South showed no such inclination to selectivity whatsoever, of course. For example, Alabama Governor Guy Hunt has found it appropriate to cite the opening of a new factory employing eight people as a tribute to the fundamental wisdom of the United States Constitution.[27]

Such affection for industrial employers was common across a South that, despite its progress, was still home to areas that had little else to offer. More than a century ago, Henry Grady sought to dramatize the economic dependence of the South with the story of a funeral in Pickens County, Georgia, where everything from the clothes worn by the deceased to the shovel that dug the grave was imported from the North. Except for the corpse, Grady pointed out, the only thing the South provided for the entire affair was a hole in the ground.[28]

In 1987, Alabama and Mississippi officials joined forces in the tumultuous courtship of the ultra-space-age, $4.4 billion, superconducting supercollider, hoping to lure the project—later awarded to Texas—to the prairie region of north central Mississippi near the Alabama line. The spirit of cooperation across state lines was admirable and sensible. Moreover, if the powers that be had favored this unlikely location with the magnificent facility, officials of both states promised huge outlays—$2.1 billion for Mississippi, which spent $2.5 million alone on its effort to promote the Mississippi site—for improvements in roads, public facilities, and secondary and higher education. The real hopes of the promoters lay, however, not so much in their Wimpy-like "pay-you-Tuesday-for-a-hamburger-today" assurances, but in "Selma Chalk," a subsoil material that was soft and easily removed (the project requires a gigantic fifty-three-mile circular tunnel) but extremely stable—hence, the tunnel would not collapse. For all their after-the-fact promises, a century after Henry Grady breathed his last, all Alabama and Mississippi could offer as a front-end enticement to this high-tech facility was still the hole in the ground. Elsewhere, the glittering high-tech firms that once spurned the South entirely had a highly localized impact on the Raleigh-Durham-Chapel Hill "Research Triangle" area. Most of the new manufacturing jobs created in Dixie by these firms, however, were low-wage, low-skill positions, many of them filled by union-shy former employees of garment or food-processing plants.[29]

With so many areas struggling for survival while others appeared to be courting disaster through overdevelopment, it was not surprising that economic concerns would predominate as the South faced the future. The region had never suffered, after all, for lack of comment on its economic condition. What was striking, however, was the appearance on the endangered-species list of that once-familiar creature, the regional soul-searcher. In 1940 an ambivalent, emotionally exhausted Cash fretted that the South's "capacity for adjustment" would soon be tested, and expressed the fervent hope that its "virtues will tower over and conquer its faults."[30] In the late 1980s, however, outside of a few committed symposia-goers, virtually no one sat up late worrying about the South or tried to nag it into being something other that what it was.

It seemed at one point to Faulkner's Chick Mallison that the North consisted of "massed uncountable faces looking down at him and his in fading amazement and outrage and frustration and most curious of all, gullibility, a volitionless, almost helpless capacity and eagerness to believe anything about the South not even provided it be derogatory but merely bizarre enough and strange enough." If the 1980s to date are any indication, however, southern problems, southern characteristics, perhaps the whole notion of southernness itself, may have become too irrelevant to capture the attention of those outside the South. Should this condition prove permanent, there is reason to question whether southernness has much of a future even inside the South. After he had used his revolver to dispatch a somewhat daffy old southern matron, Flannery O'Connor's character "the Misfit" observed that "she would of been a good woman . . . if it had been somebody there to shoot her every minute of her life." As the 1980s drew to a close, it remained to be seen whether a region which was no longer "under the gun" of national scrutiny and assessment would continue to behave in any way that rendered it identifiable as the South.[31]

Believing that southernness would disappear as soon as southerners knew better and could do better, social scientists had once predicted that economic and educational progress would eventually cleanse Dixie-ites of their distinctive regional traits. John Shelton Reed has presented convincing evidence and arguments that this has not occurred. Reed found that those southerners with income and educational levels nearest

227

the national norm are the ones who guard their regional identities most jealously. Upwardly mobile southerners whose parents once fought over the *Sears and Roebuck Catalog* now contest their spouses for the first glance at *Southern Living*. In this regard, they are comparable to other ethnic groups who have struggled for cultural absorption only to spurn it at the very moment it becomes achievable. This rejection of such a long-sought goal results from the realization that assimilation may bring cultural anonymity and the loss of any significant group identification.[32]

Reed's ethnicity theory provided some hope that cultural southern-ness might feed for a time on the sheer determination of southerners to keep it alive, but the larger question remained as to whether any such subgroup identity could survive through simple self-assertion so long as the larger society neither challenged it nor recognized it as especially significant. If this indifference persists, it may not be long before southerners will be unable, as Roy Blount put it, to "get a charge out of being typical."[33]

In this regard, there is particular cause for concern in the once-rich area of southern literature, where in recent decades we have witnessed a decided waning of what Fred Hobson called the southern "rage to explain." As the twentieth century unfolded, the accelerating effort to industrialize and the growing likelihood of sweeping racial changes left southern writers in a position analogous to that of their counterparts in developing regions around the world. In these societies, the threat of economic and cultural Westernization induced in sensitive observers a genuine sense of ambivalence about changes that threatened to destroy what was good as well as what was bad about the old ways. (In Russia, for example, these tensions led to a schism between the Westernizers and the Slavophiles, who in some ways approximated Chapel Hill's regionalists on the one hand and Nashville's Agrarians on the other.) Both William Faulkner and Flannery O'Connor showed great concern about the cultural upheaval that might accompany the Americanization of Dixie. O'Connor worried, for example, "that everyday we are getting more and more like the rest of the country, that we are being forced out, not only of our many sins but our few virtues." Once the pressures for change were gone, however, there was no longer any particularly urgent reason for southern intellectuals to contemplate the question of which aspects of the South's culture should be demolished and which should be preserved.[34]

The literary South did indeed, as Walker Percy suggested, resemble a man who had finally recovered from a lifelong toothache only to find that without this all-consuming pain, he had nothing to occupy his energies and concentration. The need to explain the South and its failure to embrace its Americanized destiny had been the throbbing obsession that drove southern writers to their best work, but in the contemporary setting, Percy wrote, "the peculiar isolation and disabilities under which the South labored so long and which served some southern writers so well . . . are now things of the past."[35]

Apparently forgetting the ancient maxim that one good barbecue joint counts for more than a dozen skyscrapers, a number of observers saw an entire South symbolized by an Atlanta lost—ironically, through triumph rather than defeat—to the Yankees for a second and final time. Pining for the old demagogues and degenerates he used to flay so mercilessly, Marshall Frady worried that the South had undergone a "cultural lobotomy." This was certainly not the case with the country singer who asserted, "I'd rather have a bottle in front of me than a frontal lobotomy," but on the other hand, Sonny and Bob, the Osborne Brothers, who sang that "Georgia mules and country boys are fading fast away," were but two members of the "Disappearing Dixie" school that flourished in the post–World War II years. George Tindall argued, however, that it was not the South that had vanished but the ever-beckoning American mainstream. It is tempting to accept this explanation if only because one can imagine Hank Williams, Jr., singing "When I finally got to the mainstream, the doggone thing was dry." Still, a more accurate description might be that the mainstream, which had always seemed to be receding, began to shift rapidly southward in the late 1960s and continued to do so until the perennially unworthy candidate for salvation suddenly found itself not so much baptized as swamped. As David Donald saw it, instead of the South finally rejoining the rest of the nation, "the United States has finally decided to rejoin the South."[36]

Acceptance of this interpretation does not mean that the long-standing debate over distinctiveness that has sustained the careers of several southernologists is settled, but it does mean that it is probably over. Like a tree crashing to earth in the midst of a deserted forest, statistical or analytical evidence about homicides, illiteracy, or even the availability of grits no longer leaves any audible impression on the great mass of Americans who apparently could care less whether the South has retained its uniqueness. By October 1990, *The Encyclopedia of Southern Culture* had sold nearly forty-five thousand copies, but despite the national and international publicity it received, the majority of its sales were below the Mason-Dixon line. Southerners may continue to dote on their own distinctiveness yet awhile, but scholars and writers who pursue this market are not likely to find preaching only to the converted nearly so lucrative as have certain television evangelists within their region.

The question of whether a rapidly changing global and national economic and ideological context has produced an Americanized South or a Southernized America is less important than the fact that the mainstreaming of Dixie swept away one of its great regional burdens—not the irrelevant, aristocratic past that never was or the poverty and brutality that should not have been, but the dominant and intimidating future that absolutely had to be—and left the South without a destiny to anticipate or dread.

The result of these changes, of the untimely demise of the South's alternately alluring and intimidating future, is that many southerners now seem to share Edwin M. Yoder's sense of "burden and exertion" in trying to keep the South alive. "How long," Yoder asked (to no apparent response), "has it been since we heard something genuinely novel said about the South or the southern experience?" Certainly, much of what passed for "southern" literature in the 1980s was actually little more than syrupy doses of days gone by. The success enjoyed by such writers as Ferrol Sams and Olive Ann Burns indicated that there was indeed a market for such work, but critics could only hope that the market would soon reach saturation.[37]

This is not to say that the South did not continue to turn out more than its share of talented writers in the 1970s and 1980s, but many of the best of them showed no particular interest in establishing a regional identification for themselves or their work. When Mississippian Richard Ford returned to his home state, he found that he could "live here and treat the South as if it were any place else in the United States" while resisting the spell of "southernness with a capital 'S' and all of the baggage that goes with it." While living in the Magnolia State, Ford proved his point by writing a widely acclaimed novel about a New Jersey sportswriter as well as a book of short stories set in Montana. Ellen Douglas, another Mississippi writer, demonstrated in *Can't Quit You Baby* that she could tell the tale of the relationship between two southern women, one black, one white, and make the story simply one of two humans sharing their grief and struggle and drawing courage from each other.[38]

On the one hand, it was troubling to think that a morally and economically rehabilitated South might no longer produce a distinctive regional literature. On the other, however, southern writers were now better positioned to follow the lead of William Faulkner and more recently, Walker Percy, who repeatedly demonstrated that modern life subjects not just southerners or Americans but all of humanity to what

230

he calls "deep dislocation in their lives that has nothing to do with poverty, ignorance and discrimination." Indeed, Percy explained that "what increasingly engages the southern novelist as much as his Connecticut counterpart are no longer Faulkner's Snopeses or O'Connor's crackers or Wright's black underclass but their successful grandchildren who are going nuts in Atlanta condominiums."[39]

In the interest of accuracy, these grandchildren are more likely going nuts in Atlanta traffic trying to get to their condominiums, but Percy's point is, of course, valid. Whether the new breed of writers who happen to be southern will succeed in making much sense out of modern life is anybody's guess, but they have at least as good a perspective on it as anyone else now that, as Percy put it, "the virtues and faults of the South are the virtues and faults of the nation, no more and no less."[40]

There is also cause for optimism concerning the study of southern history. For approximately half a century, historians have devoted much energy to using the past to explain the differences between the South that is and the South that should be. That eminent and ever-insightful humanist Lewis Grizzard once referred to an entire subgroup of southerners as "the kind of folks who think the moonshot's fake and wrestling's real." Similarly, studying Dixie through lenses bearing the decidedly rosy tint of the larger national success story, many southern historians have sought to explain how a region with such a logical, well-defined, Americanized future could be bogged down in such an irrational, untenable, and un-American present. In the process, they have often advanced regional explanations for globally induced historical influences and ascribed to various regional interest groups and governing classes power to do evil far beyond their capacity, if not their intent.[41]

Writing in 1952, C. Vann Woodward indicated that, for most Americans outside the South, "history" was "something unpleasant that happens to other people." At the time Woodward wrote, "the collective will" of the United States had never been "confronted by complete frustration. Whether by luck, by abundant resources, by ingenuity, by technology, by organizing cleverness or by sheer force of arms," Woodward observed, "America has been able to overcome every major historic crises—economic, political, or foreign—with which it has had to cope." Seen in this light, Woodward pointed out, it was not the South, but the remainder of the nation whose experiences stood apart from the rest of the world.[42]

Despite what Wallerstein described as Ronald Reagan's "Canute-like efforts to order the ocean to recede," by the end of the 1980s the United States confronted a demanding adjustment to its "slow economic and hence geopolitical decline in the world system."[43] Deny it as many Americans might, the nation had actually begun in the late 1960s to lose its Teflon coating and to share with the rest of the world, including the South, the sobering experience of having history "happen" to it. Daunting as this prospect might be to American society at large, it was good news at least for those who struggled to make a living by poring over a southern past that should now become much more usable to those who try to anticipate not only the South's destiny, but that of the entire nation as well.

It was more than a little ironic that after decades of having the glorious national past serve as the model for its future, the South's somewhat less inspiring history should suddenly offer a wealth of insights into the contemporary and future experiences of the nation at large. For example, the antebellum South had been home to a class of exploitive capitalists whose resources and assets were so mobile that they seldom took an interest in developing the economies of whatever localities they happened to occupy at the time. As Gavin Wright has pointed out, the behavior of these antebellum slaveholders, "labor-lords" as Wright called them, strongly parallels that of many modern corporate and industrial executives whose firms are not so much multinational as post-national in that, because of their technologically enhanced mobility, borders and national allegiances mean less to them than the opportunity to minimize their costs and maximize their profits.[44]

Whereas the South had once banked too heavily on its ability to dominate the world market for cotton, so at the height of its economic achievement did the United States seem to assume that it had established a permanent claim on the most lucrative sectors of the global manufacturing economy. In the case of both the South and the nation, a tumble from their lofty perches forced their leaders to court external investment as a means of reviving their economies. These policies ultimately left these leaders and those who sought to advise or criticize them pondering the question of how to restore economic independence in the long run while contriving to promote economic colonization in the meantime. Likewise, an American society that mocked in hindsight the shortsightedness of southern leaders in banking so heavily on a volatile world cotton market made little headway in freeing itself from the influences of a fluctuating world market for oil.

Those concerned with the relative economic slippage of the United States in recent decades might well profit from a reconsideration of the importance of technology, resources, demographics, and—most importantly, timing—to any nation's economic and geopolitical stature. These factors served the rest of the nation well in the late nineteenth and early twentieth centuries, but they figured less positively in the South's efforts to pull itself into the economic and social mainstream of American society. These efforts put the South in competition with, first, a comparatively advantaged North and then, finally, an emerging third world teeming with cheaper labor and driven by even more desperate poverty to welcome any and all employers and investors with open arms.[45]

Unfortunately, the third-world instability that troubled American foreign policy experts so deeply in the 1980s was linked directly to the ability of these nations to compete with the United States for their share of new industrial jobs. A number of insights into the difficulties of underdeveloped regions and the frustrated efforts of American leaders to aid them and encourage reform of their economic and social and political systems are available in an analysis of the impact of federal policy on the South. For nearly a century after the abortive Reconstruction experiment, federal assistance and relief programs often functioned not so much to eliminate the inequities in southern society as to confirm them.[46]

In the Mississippi Delta, for example, federal assistance funded levee construction that increased the productivity and value of planters' landholdings. Emergency relief assistance from Washington sustained black refugees from the disastrous 1927 flood while they were held in concentration camps by local planters. During the New Deal, relief programs and Agricultural Adjustment Administration (AAA) crop-reduction efforts remained under local white control. The relief programs provided support for farm labor during non-peak periods, only to be shut off completely when planters needed their choppers and pickers again. AAA and subsequent acreage-reduction subsidies soon helped to push the income of larger planters well into six figures. Beginning with AAA, the government's acreage-reduction programs stimulated the mechanization and consolidation of agriculture, in the process setting off a massive displacement of peasant laborers comparable to the enclosure movement that swept across industrializing England.[47]

In the 1960s federal policies operated at cross purposes on a number of fronts. A $1 per hour minimum-wage law encouraged further mechanization, as did continuing subsidy programs. The result was further labor displacement at a time when blacks were attempting to claim the social and political equality guaranteed by Washington. All the while, welfare programs remained in the grip of local whites who used their control of these agencies to coerce further outmigration or submission to local white authority. By the 1980s, many of those blacks who had not found a place on the welfare rolls in a northern ghetto led a strikingly similar existence on the margin in a Delta where government transfer payments were the major source of income. More than a century after the first Reconstruction and two decades after the second one, the legacy of federal policies in the Delta was that of continuing economic disparity and a crippling dependence on a federal government that now filled the provider's role once played by the planter.[48]

Some of the foregoing comparisons may seem a bit strained, but the overarching similarity between the South's past and the nation's contemporary and likely future experience is an undeniable sense of powerlessness, a feeling that one's destiny is being shaped by impersonal and inexorable influences totally beyond one's control. For all of the progress the South has made in recent decades, the experience of confronting the similarities between the South's past and the nation's future is nonetheless a humbling one for a society that for so long viewed the South as an embarrassingly backward region that hung like a millstone around the neck of a progressive colossus. The real purpose of a cold comparative analysis, however, is not to take the remainder of the nation down a peg or two so much as it is to demonstrate the importance of the broader economic and geopolitical context in shaping the nature and direction of any society.

Immanuel Wallerstein has argued that the key to understanding southern culture was the realization that instead of a simple mass of taboos, rituals, and peculiarities passing intact and unchallenged from one generation to the next, "southern culture" was subject to the changing inputs generated by the larger national society and the even larger global context—the "world system" as Wallerstein called it. The same was true, of course, of the national culture against which the South had been so long assessed and, until recently, found wanting. The extent to which the South and the nation had always shared a culture and a past was subject to debate, but, for better or worse, the two were certain to share the future.[49]

Chick Mallison realized that "tomorrow night is nothing but one long sleepless wrestle with yesterday's omissions and regrets."[50] Likewise, the recent history of the American South demonstrates nothing so much as the fact that while the errors of the past can be corrected, the rapid flow of national and international events cannot be switched to pause while the legacy of these mistakes is erased. A broadened perspective on the past promises not so much to lighten the burden of southern history as to redistribute its weight, so that efforts to anticipate the region's future will consider that future less a challenge to the South's ability to measure up to national fantasies than in a test of capacity of the entire nation to cope with global realities.

NOTES

1. William Faulkner, *Intruder in the Dust* (New York, 1948), p. 194.

2. Charles P. Roland, "The South, America's Will-o-the-Wisp Eden," *Louisiana History* 11 (1970): 101–19.

3. Edwin Mims, *The Advancing South* (New York, 1927), p. 315.

4. Twelve Southerners, *I'll Take My Stand: The South and the Agrarian Tradition* (New York, 1930). See also William C. Harvard and Walter Sullivan, eds., *A Band of Prophets: The Vanderbilt Agrarians after Fifty Years* (Baton Rouge, 1982).

5. See the National Emergency Council, *Report on Economic Conditions of the South* (Washington, 1938); and James C. Cobb and Michael J. Namorato, eds, *The New Deal and the South* (Jackson, 1984), p. 14.

6. C. Vann Woodward, "The Irony of Southern History," in *The Burden of Southern History* (Baton Rouge, 1960), pp. 167–92 and *Thinking Back: The Perils of Writing History* (Baton Rouge, 1986), pp. 114–17; Tennant S. McWilliams, *The New South Faces the World: Foreign Affairs and the Southern Sense of Self* (Baton Rouge, 1988), pp. 4–5.

7. Woodward, *Thinking Back*, p. 102.

8. Immanuel Wallerstein, "What Can One Mean by Southern Culture?" in *The Evolution of Southern Culture*, ed. Numan V. Bartley (Athens, 1988), pp. 11–12.

9. Woodward, *Thinking Back*, p. 23; V. O. Key, Jr., *Southern Politics in State and Nation* (New York, 1949).

10. C. Vann Woodward "New South Fraud Is Papered by Old South-Myth," Washington *Post*, July 9, 1961. Hugh Davis Graham, "Southern Politics since World War II," in *Interpreting Southern History: Historiograpical Essays in Honor of Sanford W. Higginbotham*, ed. John B. Boles and Evelyn Thomas Nolen (Baton Rouge, 1987), pp. 390–91.

11. William H. Nicholls, *Southern Tradition and Regional Progress* (Chapel Hill, 1960); Jonathon M. Weiner, *Social Origins of the New South: Alabama, 1860–1885* (Baton Rouge, 1978); Dwight B. Billings, Jr., *Planters and the Making of a New South: Class, Politics, and Development in North Carolina* (Chapel Hill, 1979).

12. For example, see J. Milton Yinger and George E. Simpson, "Can Segregation Survive in an Industrial Society?," *Antioch Review* 28 (March 1958): 15–24. See also James C. Cobb, "Urbanization and the Changing South: A Review of Literature," *South Atlantic Urban Studies* 1 (1977): 253–66.

13. John Egerton, *The Americanization of Dixie: The Southernization of America* (New York, 1974), p. xx.

14. C. Vann Woodward, "The South Tomorrow," *Time*, September 27, 1976, p. 98; Larry L. King, "We Ain't Trash No More!," *Esquire* 126 (November 1976): 88–90, 152–56.

15. Jack Temple Kirby, *Media Made Dixie: The South in the American Imagination* (Athens, 1986), pp. 146, 171; James C. Cobb, "From Muskogee to Luckenbach: Country Music and the 'Southernization' of America," *Journal of Popular Culture* 16 (Winter, 1982): 87.

16. Cobb, "From Muskogee to Luckenbach," p. 90.

17. For the suggestion that the South could play a leadership role, see Samuel S. Hill et al., *Religion and the Solid South* (Nashville, 1972), p. 208; Indus A. Newby, *The South: A History* (New York, 1978), p. 505, emphasis added.

18. Joseph B. Cumming, "Been Down Home So Long It Looks Like Up to Me," *Esquire* 76 (August 1976): 111.

19. Kirby, *Media-Made Dixie*, pp. 172–73.

20. Wallerstein, "What Can One Mean," p. 12.

21. For a effort to explain these contradictions, see James C. Cobb, *Industrialization and Southern Society, 1877–1984* (Lexington, Ky., 1984), pp. 136–64.

22. Wilbur J. Cash, *The Mind of the South* (New York, 1941), p. 440.

23. On job loss and the shift to services in Alabama, see Birmingham *Post-Herald*, September 22, 1987. See also, James C. Cobb, "Y'all Come on Down: The Southern States' Pursuit of Industry," *Southern Exposure* 14 (n.d.): 22.

24. Birmingham *Post-Herald*, January 13, 1989.

25. Numan V. Bartley and Hugh D. Graham, *Southern Politics and the Second Reconstruction* (Baltimore, 1975), p. 200.

26. On Strom Thurmond's attitude toward unions, see Washington *Post*, April 30, 1978.

27. Louis D. Rubin, Jr., "An Image of the South" in *The New South Creed: A Study In Southern Mythmaking*, ed. Louis D. Rubin and Paul M. Gaston (Baton Rouge, 1983), pp. 70–71; Louis D. Rubin, Jr. and James Jackson Kilpatrick, eds., *The Lasting South: Fourteen Southerners Look at Their Home* (Chicago, 1957), p. 15; Mary Matossian, "Ideologies of Delayed Industrialization" in *Political Development and Social Change*, ed. Jason L. Finkle and Richard W. Gable (New York, 1966), p. 175; Tuscaloosa *News*, June 8, 1988.

28. Paul M. Gaston, *The New South Creed: A Study in Southern Mythmaking* (New York, 1970), pp. 70–71.

29. Jackson *Clarion-Ledger*, December 30, 1987. On low-wage jobs in high-tech industries, see Marc Miller, "The Low Down on High Tech," *Southern Exposure* 14 (n.d.): 35–39.

30. Cash, *Mind of the South*, p. 440.

31. Flannery O'Connor, "A Good Man Is Hard to Find" in Flannery O'Connor, *The Complete Stories* (New York, 1978), p. 133; Faulkner, *Intruder in the Dust*, p. 153.

32. See John Shelton Reed, *Southerners: The Social Psychology of Sectionalism* (Chapel Hill, 1983).

33. Roy Blount, Jr., *What Men Don't Tell Women* (New York, 1984), pp. 28–29.

34. Fred Hobson, *Tell about the South: The Southern Rage to Explain* (Baton Rouge, 1983); Nicholas V. Riasanovsky, *Russia and the West in the Teaching of*

the Slavophiles: A Study of Romantic Ideology (Cambridge, 1952); Flannery O'Connor, "The Fiction Writer and His Country," in *The Living Novel: A Symposium,* ed. Granville Hicks (New York, 1957), p. 159.

35. Walker Percy, "Southern Comfort," *Harper's* 258 (January 1979): 80.

36. James C. Cobb, "Cracklins and Caviar: The Enigma of Sunbelt Georgia," *Georgia Historical Quarterly* 68 (Spring 1984): 19–39; Marshall Frady, "Gone With the Wind," *Newsweek,* July 28, 1975, p. 11; George B. Tindall, "Beyond the Mainstream," in *The Ethnic Southerners* (Baton Rouge, 1974). Donald is quoted in New York *Times* (August 30, 1976). See also Charles P. Roland, "The Ever-Vanishing South," *Journal of Southern History* 48 (February 1982): 3–20.

37. Edwin M. Yoder, Jr., "The Dixification of Dixie," in *Dixie Dateline: A Journalistic Portrait of the Contemporary South,* ed. John B. Boles (Houston, 1983), p. 160; Ferrol Sams, *Run with the Horseman* (Atlanta, 1982); Olive Ann Burns, *Cold Sassy Tree* (New York, 1984).

38. W. Hampton Sides, "Interview, Richard Ford: Debunking the Mystique of the Southern Writer," *Memphis* 10 (February 1986): 42, 49; Richard Ford, *The Sportswriter* (New York, 1986); Ellen Douglas, *Can't Quit You Baby* (New York, 1988).

39. Percy, "Southern Comfort," p. 83.

40. Ibid., p. 83.

41. For an argument in favor of a more "globalized" approach to the study of southern history, see James C. Cobb, "Beyond Planters and Industrialists: A New Perspective on the New South," *Journal of Southern History* 54 (February 1988): 45-68.

42. Woodward, "The Irony of Southern History," pp. 167–70.

43. Wallerstein, "What Can One Mean," p. 12.

44. Gavin Wright, *Old South, New South: Revolutions in the Southern Economy since the Civil War* (New York, 1986), p. 273.

45. For a suggestive examination of third-world development strategies, see James A. Caporaso, "The State's Role in Third World Economic Growth," *Annals of the American Academy of Political Science* 449 (January 1982): 103–11.

46. For critical treatments of the impact of federal agricultural policy in the South, see Pete Daniel, *Breaking the Land: The Transformation of Cotton, Tobacco, and Rice Cultures since 1880* (Urbana, 1985) and Jack Temple Kirby, *Rural Worlds Lost: The American South, 1920–1960* (Baton Rouge, 1987).

47. On the use of federal flood relief to maintain labor control, see Pete Daniel, *Deep'n as It Come: The 1927 Mississippi River Flood* (New York, 1977), pp. 105–9. On planter control of the AAA and the resultant labor displacement, see Daniel, "The Transformation of the Rural South, 1930 to the Present," *Agriculture History* 55 (July 1981): 231–48.

48. For a summary assessment of the impact on the minimum-wage law on the Mississippi Delta, see Jackson *Clarion-Ledger,* December 17, 1980. See also, Memphis *Commercial Appeal,* May 4, 7, and 8, 1986.

49. Wallerstein, "What Can One Mean," p. 12.

50. Faulkner, *Intruder in the Dust,* p. 195.

Contributors

DORIS BETTS, Alumni Distinguished Professor of English at the University of North Carolina-Chapel Hill, is both an award-winning writer and an authority on southern literature. She has written four novels, three collections of short stories, and scores of short stories, poetry, articles, and essays. Her work appears in dozens of journals and anthologies. Her awards include a Guggenheim Fellowship in Creative Writing, the Medal of Merit in the Short Story by the American Academy of Arts and Letters, and she is a three-time recipient of the Sir Walter Raleigh Award in Fiction.

JAMES C. COBB, Bernadotte Schmitt Professor of History at the University of Tennessee, has written widely on the impact of economic development upon southern society. His books include *The Selling of the South: The Southern Crusade for Industrial Development, 1930–1980, Industrialization and Southern Society, 1877–1984, The New Deal and the South,* and volumes 3 and 4 of *Perspectives on the American South.* Two other books, *The Great Copper Basin: An Economic and Environmental History* and *The Last South: Society, Politics, and Culture in the Mississippi Delta from the Antebellum Era to the Present,* are forthcoming.

JOE P. DUNN, professor of history and politics at Converse College, is a Vietnam War specialist and has written on a wide range of other subjects. In addition to *Teaching the Vietnam War: Resources and Assessments,* he has extensive anthology and journal publications on Vietnam, recent U.S. political history, national security, and various world affairs topics.

DAVID R. GOLDFIELD, Robert Lee Bailey Professor of History at the University of North Carolina at Charlotte, is a specialist on urban history and the American South. His book *Cotton Fields and Skyscrapers: Southern City and Region, 1607–1980* won the 1983 Mayflower Cup Award. He has published a number of article and anthology contributions, and among his other books are *Urban Growth in the Age of Sectionalism: Virginia, 1847–1861* and *Promised Land: The South Since 1945.*

ALEXANDER P. LAMIS, associate professor of political science at Case Western Reserve University, is an authority on southern politics. His *The Two-Party South* won the 1985 V. O. Key Book Award; he also has contributed several articles and chapters in anthologies. Before entering academia, Lamis, who also has a law degree, was a newspaper and television journalist.

ROBERT C. McMATH, JR., professor of history and associate dean of the Ivan Allen College of Management, Policy, and International Affairs at the Georgia

Institute of Technology, has focused on Populism, rural America, and the economic, industrial, and technological development of the South. Among his many books are *Populist Vanguard: A History of the Southern Farmers' Alliance, Toward a New South?: Studies in Post-Civil War Southern Communities,* and *Engineering the New South: Georgia Tech, 1885–1985.* He is editor of *Proletarian Aristocrat: The Autobiography of William Greene Raoul.*

HOWARD L. PRESTON, a member of the adjunct faculty at Converse College, has written several articles on the South for journals and anthologies and two books: *Automobile Age Atlanta: The Making of a Southern Metropolis, 1900–1935* and *Dirt Roads to Dixie: Accessibility and Modernization in the South, 1895–1935.*

HOWARD N. RABINOWITZ, professor of history at the University of New Mexico, has published extensively on black history and southern race relations. His *Race Relations in the Urban South, 1865–1890* was nominated for the Pulitzer Prize. He edited *Southern Black Leaders of the Reconstruction Era,* has many articles and anthology contributions, and his *The First New South, 1877–1920* is forthcoming.

MARGARET RIPLEY WOLFE, professor of history at East Tennessee State University, specializes in American social themes, urban history, and the history of southern women. The former president of the Southern Association for Women Historians (1984), she is the author of *Lucius Polk Brown and Progressive Food and Drug Control: Tennessee and New York City, 1908–1920* and *Kingsport, Tennessee: A Planned American City* as well as numerous articles in professional journals and anthologies. She is presently writing an interpretive history of southern women for the *New Perspectives on the South* series.

Index

Abbot, Willis John, on Charleston, South
  Carolina, 23
Abortion, 202
Abramowitz, Alan I., 65
Acquired Immune Deficiency Syndrome
  (AIDS), statistics on, 148
Adams, Alice, 174
Affirmative Action, 110, 142
Agee, James, 176
Agribusiness, 89
Agricultural Adjustment Act, 25
Agricultural Adjustment Administration
  (AAA), 233
Agriculture, southern revolutions of, 88;
  subsidies of, 89
Aiken, Conrad, 171
Ailes, Roger, 61
Air conditioning, 36
Alcoholic beverages, prohibition of,
  200–201
All the King's Men, 165
Allen, Walter, on economic status of
  blacks, 115
Altman, Robert, 222
American Association of University
  Women (AAUW), 125
American Colonization Society, 104
Ames, Jessie Daniel, 133
Anderson, Don, on importance of place
  in South, 208
"Andyomics," 34
Angley, Ernest, 203
Applewhite, James, 183, 184
Arnow, Harriet, 171
Arrington, Richard, 40, 189
Ashmore, Harry, 2; on race relations in
  South, 114
Askew, Reuben, 55
Astor, Irene, 129
Astor, Nancy Langhorne, 129
Athas, Daphne, 179, 180, 181

Atlanta, 16–17, 21, 24, 25, 31, 32, 40,
  41, 82, 123; and Scarlett O'Hara, 42;
  annexations, 21; Cumberland-Galleria
  complex, 37; demographic changes in,
  31; public school desegregation in,
  29; suburbs of, 33; wages in during
  1930s, 25; twentieth-century
  advancements of, 21
Atlanta *Constitution,* 82
Atlanta Woman's Club, 19
A Turn in the South, 183–84
Atwater, Lee, and Willie Horton issue, 61
Atwood, Margaret, 149
Automobility, and end of South, 177;
  in rural South, 18
Ayers, H. Brant, 3

Backwardness of South, imagery of in
  films and television programs, 195;
  in education, 159; in intellectual
  pursuits, 159. *See also,* Violence
Baker, Paula, on women and domestic
  politics, 135
Baker, Tod A., 3
Bakker, Jim and Tammy, 178
Baliles, Gerald L., 139
Bandy, Moe, 212
Barbecue, 195; in South Carolina,
  194–95
Barth, John, 184
Bartley, Numan, 3, 225; on New South
  strategies, 220
Bentsen, Lloyd, 58; on being a "Southern
  Democrat," 78n.20; on Willie Horton
  issue, 79n.25
Berlin, Ira, 101
Beschloss, Steven, on impoverished
  South, 206
"Beverly Hillbillies," 195
Bilbo, Theodore, 107, 193
Billings, Dwight, on planter economy,
  220

Birmingham, Alabama, 21, 33, 41; River
Chase development, 37; Tutweiler
Hotel, 33
Black, Earl and Merle, 2
Blackmun, Harry, on *Roe v. Wade*
decision, 140
Blacks, achievements of, 27–29; and
Hispanics, 114; as artists and writers,
169; attracted to South, 113, 114;
church life of, 27–28; communities of,
28; demographics of, 107, 110, 114;
disfranchisement of, 106, 107; during
Reconstruction, 105; economic
prospects of, 112; education of,
191–92; enfranchisement of, 103;
free, 103; future economic status of,
115; future political power of, 114,
115; future problems of, 116–17; in
public office, 111, 189–91; in urban
areas, 45n.43, 108; migrations of, 29,
108–9, 111, 113, 190; protests of, 28;
residential segregation of, 112,
115–16; reverse migration of, 30,
190; rights of in Northern colonies,
101, 102. *See also* Segregation
Blackwelder, Julia Kirk, 133
Blount, Roy, Jr., 166, 170, 228
Bombeck, Erma, 127, 128
Brodsky, David, 3
Brooks, Cleanth, 173. *See also* Nashville
Agrarians
Bodenheim, Max, 174
Boosterism, 218
Bork, Robert, 69, 143, 148, 157n.118
Bowen, David R., on black-white coalition
politics in South, 56–57
Bowen, Margaret, 129
Brown v. Board of Education (1954), 109,
166, 192
Brown, Rita Mae, 171
Bryant, Paul "Bear," 198
Brearley, H. C., on violence, 196–97
Burns, Olive Ann, 208, 230
Busbee, George, 55; on high-tech
employment in South, 91
Bush, George Herbert Walker, 57, 58,
62, 139, 155n.85
Byrd, William, 158

Cable, George Washington, 164, 178

Calhoun, Richard J., 3
Caldwell, Erskine, 174, 180, 181
Campbell, Carroll, 204
Capote, Truman, 165, 178
Carmichael, Stokely, on women's role in
civil rights protests, 142
Carter, Hodding III, on disappearing
South, 189
Carter, Jimmy, 47, 64, 66; as John-Boy
Walton, 221; fall from national grace,
223; on importance of the land, 210;
toasts Deng Xiaoping, 83
Carter, Judy, 127
Carter, Rosalynn, 123
Cash, Wilbur J., 2, 176, 184, 224, 227;
on Greensboro and Charlotte, North
Carolina, 21; on race, 189; on
violence, 196
Cason, Sandra, 141
Cassity, Turner, 173
Catawba Regional Planning Commission,
204
Cauley, T. J., 83
"Cavalier Spirit," in southern society,
197
Center for Demographic Studies, on
reverse migration of blacks to South,
190
Center for the Study of Southern Culture
(University of Mississippi), 161
Chafe, William H., on American
feminism, 141
Chappell, Fred, 182
Charleston, South Carolina, 23–24, 42;
historic consciousness in, 24
Charlotte, North Carolina, 18, 21, 111;
Dilworth (suburb), 24
Charlton, David L., 82
Cheatam, Annie, 125
Cheek, Joel O., 21
Cherokee County, Georgia,
changes in, 35–36
Child care, statistics on, 146
Chiles, Lawton, 63
City planning, 20
Cities, revitalization of, 32–33
Civil Rights Act of 1875, 106; of 1964,
142
Civil Rights Movement, historic sites of,
33; primary goal of, 117; in urban
South, 28

Civil Rights Restoration Act of 1988, 143
Clark, Robert, 111
Clark, Septima Poinsette, 129
Clark, Thomas D., 2; on religion in
  South, 200, 203
Clay, Henry, 104
Clemson College, opens textile school, 87
Clendinen, Dudley, 3
Clinton, Catherine, 134
Coca-Cola, Inc., 34
Collins, Martha Layne, 129
Commerce, Georgia, 20
Congressional Quarterly Weekly Report, 62
Congressional Reconstruction, 105
Conrad, Joseph, 182
Conroy, Pat, 174
Converse College, 134
Converse, Dexter Edgar, 84
Cooking, southern, 194–95
Chopin, Kate, 164
Cott, Nancy F., on definition of
  feminism, 151
Cotton gin, 81, 97n.32
Country music, 221
Cramer, Stuart, 86
Creationism, in Alabama, 202; in
  Louisiana, 201–2; in Tennessee, 202.
  See also Evangelism; Fundamentalism;
  Religion
Crews, Harry, 179, 180
Cumming, Joseph B., 222
Cushman, Pauline, 129

"Dallas," 222
Dallas, Texas, 40, 41; Las Colinas
  development, 37
Daniels, Charlie, 211
Darden, Claibourne, 203
Davidson, Donald, on Southern Literary
  Renascence, 164
Davidson, Nicholas, 128, 145
Davis, Edith Luckett, 125
Degler, Carl, 2, 128; on American
  history, 130
Deliverance, 195
Democratic party, and blacks, 109; and
  liberalism, 65; and segregation,
  53–54; and "southern moderates,"
  55; black-white coalition politics of,
  55, 63, 67, 68; demise of, 63, 67; in

future, 63–64, 68–70; index of
  strength, 64; restructuring of, 55–56;
  resurgence of, 63; strength from
  1932–86, 53
Demography in South, changing, 30, 35,
  190, 210; in Florida, 51; in Virginia
  suburbs of Washington, D.C., 51
Demos, John, on women's history, 133
Denton, Nancy A., on residential
  segregation, 112
Denver, John, 222
Desegregation, of public schools, 116;
  of cities, 116–17
Dew, Robb Forman, 172
Dickey, James, 166, 172
Dinkins, David, 112
*Directory of American Poets and Fiction
  Writers,* 168
Dixon, Thomas, 164
Doe v. Bolton (1973), 140
Doherty, J. C., 41
Dole, Elizabeth, 139
Donald, David, 229
Douglas, Ellen, 230
Douglass, Frederick, on racial
  segregation, 103
Dowdy, Wayne, 55, 63
Dukakis, Michael, 57, 58, 66; seen as
  liberal, 58–61
Duke, David, 191
"Dukes of Hazzard," 166, 195

Easy Rider, 199
Economic development in South, federal
  involvement in, 25–26; since World
  War II, 46n.47
Economic Policy Council, on priorities
  for working mothers, 145
Education, reforms in urban South, 20
Edmonds, Richard H., 107; on attracting
  manufacturing to South, 88
Egerton, John, 2, 67, 221
Eisler, Riane, 134
Ellis, Mary Carolyn, 136, 137
Encyclopedia of Southern Culture, 229
Equal Credit Opportunity Act, 143
Equal Employment Opportunity
  Commission (EEOC), 142
Equal Pay Act of 1963, 142

Equal Rights Amendment, 143, 148; southern states and ratification of, 135
Erdrich, Louise, 180
Espy, Mike, 111, 191
Evangelism, *see* Creationism; Fundamentalism; Religion
Evans, Walker, 176

Falwell, Jerry, 178, 202
Farley, Reynolds, on economic status of blacks, 115
Faulkner, William, 164–65, 176, 178, 208, 217, 227, 228, 230; on southern economy, 90
Federal Emergency Relief Administration, 25
Federal Equitable Pay Practices Act, 143
Feminism, definition of, 151n.26
Fite, Gilbert, 89
Florida, 1988 elections in, 63. *See also* Demography
Folson, Jim, Jr., on Michael Dukakis, 58
Foner, Eric, on Reconstruction, 106
Food, *see* Cooking
Football, as manifestation of violent behavior, 197–99; Southeastern Conference attendance statistics, 198
Ford, Richard, 230
Fox-Genovese, Elizabeth, 134
Foxfire, 160
Frady, Marshall, on disappearing South, 189, 211, 229
Frank, Leo, 217
Frederick, Carolyn, 137
Fuller, Paul E., 133
Fundamentalism, religious, 166. *See also* Creationism; Evangelism; Religion

Gaines, Charlie, 180
Gaines, Ernest, 167, 173
Gallop, George, Jr., 203
Galveston, Texas, commission form of government inaugurated in, 19
Gantt, Harvey, 191
Gardner, Ava, 129
Geil, Janet Zollinger, on women and the future, 126
George Draper Company, and Northrop automatic loom, 86

Georgia Visitors' Bureau, 193
Gibbons, Kaye, 179
Gilman, Richard, on *The Surface of the Earth,* 166–67
Gingher, Marianne, 178
Giovanni, Nikki, 124
Glasgow, Ellen, 174
Global economy, 34
Godwin, Gail, 174
Goldwater, Barry, and 1964 presidential election, 55
Grady, Henry W., 4, 88, 91, 94, 107, 217, 219, 226; on southern urbanization, 16; vision of, 82–83
Graham, Bob, 55
Graham, Hugh, on Republican party in South, 225
Grant, Amy, 201
Grantham, Dewey W., 2; on southern women, 139
Grau, Shirley Ann, 160, 167
Gregg, William, 84
Great Migration, 107
Greensboro, North Carolina, 18, 21, 33
Greenville, South Carolina, 17, 18
Greenwood, Mississippi, 33
Griffiths, Martha W., 126, 142
Grizzard, Lewis, 211, 231
Guterbock, Thomas M., 137
Gwinnett County, Georgia, growth of, 35

Hackney, Sheldon, on violence, 195
Hall, Eula, 129
Hall, Jacquelyn Dowd, 133, 134
Hall, Lyman, 87
Hamer, Fannie Lou, 129
Hannah, Barry, 171, 179, 180
Hardwick, Elizabeth, on being a southern writer, 175
Harman, Willis W., 124, 144–45
Harris, Joe Frank, 55
Harris, Joel Chandler, 164, 169
Hart, Gary, 129
Harvard, William C., 3
Hawks, Joanne V., 136, 137
Hellbroner, Robert L., on history and the future, 125
Helms, Jesse, 92
Henley, Beth, 173
Hewlett, Sylvia Ann, 145

Heyward, DuBose, 24, 178
High-tech industry, 39, 90, 91;
employment of southerners in,
99n.51; exportation to South, 92–93;
in Florida and North Carolina, 40,
205
Hightower, Jim, on attracting new
industry to South, 94
Historic Preservation, 32, 33; beginnings
of, 23
Hite, Shere, 148
Hobson, Fred, 2, 228
Hodel, Donald, 203
Hodges, Luther, 91
Hollings, Ernest F., 57–58, 69
Holman, C. Hugh, 175
Holmes County, Mississippi, 191
Hood, Mary, on Cherokee County,
Georgia, 35–36
Houston, Texas, 25, 40
Human Papilloma Virus (HIV), 148
Humphreys, Josephine, 171, 181
Hunt, Guy, 226
Hunt, James B., 55, 91
Hutner, Frances C., on equal pay for
women, 146
"Hypersegregation," 112. *See also*
Segregation; Race

I-85, 37
Ickes, Harold, 109
I'll Take My Stand, 164, 218
In the Heat of the Night, 158
Industrial workers in South, wages of,
205. *See also* High-tech industry
Industrialization, as cure for South's ills,
220; in rural South, 204–6
Institute of Southern Studies (University
of South Carolina), 161

Jackson, Jesse, 57–58; on economic
agenda for Democratic party, 78n.12
Jackson, Maynard, 32, 34
Jackson, Mississippi, 33
Jefferson County, Mississippi, 205
Jefferson, Thomas, and slave trade, 102
Jennings, Waylon, 144, 188
Jim Crow laws, 220
Johnson, Lady Bird, 123, 127

Johnson, Lyndon, 110, 190; and
Executive Order 11246, 142
Joint Center for Political Studies, on
black elected officials in South, 191
Jones, Jacqueline, 133
Jonesville, South Carolina, 204
Jordan, Barbara, 148
Jordan, Winthrop, 101
J. P. Stevens, Inc., 39

Kane, Harnett, 178
Kennedy, Anthony, 140
Kenner, Hugh, 161
Kerber, Linda K., on women, 130
Key, V. O., Jr., 2, 217, 219; on
dissolution of one-party South, 70; on
public opinion, 77; on southern
politics, 49–51; on voter rationality,
71, 80n.40
King, Coretta Scott, 127
King Cotton, 217
King, Larry L., 221
King, Martin Luther, Jr., 149, 165, 190
King, Mary, 141, 144
Kirby, Jack Temple, 176, 221
K-Mart, 201
Koop, C. Everett, 203
Kostelanetz, Richard, 160–61
Kudzu, 212n.1

Land, importance southerners assign to,
208–10
Lander, Ernest M., 3
Lea, James F., 3
Lebsock, Suzanne, 133
Lee, Harper, 178
Leinberger, Christopher, on "out-town"
developments, 37
Leiserson, Avery, 3
Lerner, Gerda, 133; on historiography,
134
Library of Southern Literature, 159
Lincoln, Abraham, on slavery, 104
Little Rock, Arkansas, 40, 42
Lott, Trent, 63
Louisiana Writers' Guild, 160
Louisville, Kentucky, racial segregation
in, 116–17
Lowell Shops, 85
Luckenbach, Texas, 221

Lynch, Kevin, 208
Lynchings, statistics on, 196
Lytle, Andrew Nelson, 173. *See also*
    Nashville Agrarians

Mack, Connie, 63
Mackay, Alexander on Richmond, 14
MacKay, Buddy, 63
Madison County, Alabama, self-
    promotion of, 42
Madison, James, 104
Makepeace, George, 84
Manning, Archie, 198
Mason, Bobbie Ann, 158, 173, 179
Massey, Douglas A., on residential
    segregation, 112
Maury County, Tennessee, Saturn
    assembly plant, 192
May, Henry F., 126
"Mayberry RFD," 195
McCarthy, Cormac, 179
McCorkie, Jill, 179
McCullers, Carson, 165, 172
McFee, Michael, 161
McKern, Sharon, on women in history,
    133
McKinney, John C., 3
McLaurin, Tim, 178, 180
McMurtry, Larry, 177
McNeely, Dave, on Ann Richards, 138
McPherson, James Alan, 167, 171
McWhiney, Grady, 128
Mechanization, of farming in South,
    88–89, 90
Memphis, Tennessee, 25; description of,
    32; Peabody Hotel, 33
Mencken, H. L., 158, 217; on religion,
    199–200, 203
Meredith, James, 165
Merrill, Henry, 84; manufacturing
    operations of, 85
Metropolitan Atlanta Council for
    Economic Development
    (MACFED), 38
Meyer, Agnes, on urban South, 26
Miami, Florida, Edward De Bartolo
    development, 37
Mill villages, and southern workers, 87;
    boom of, 85–86; in Piedmont, 17–18,
    84; social aspects of, 18

Mims, Edwin, 217–18
The Mind of the South, see Cash, Wilbur J.
Mississippi Burning, 195
Mississippi, Delta, 233; 1988 elections in,
    63; University of, 193
Mitchell, Broadus, 96n.16
Mitchell, Margaret, 194
Mobile, Alabama, descriptions of, 15, 24;
    population of, 26
Mohl, Raymond A., 3
Mondale, Walter, 57, 76
Monroe, James, reinterment of in
    Richmond, 12
Moreland, Laurence W., 3
Morgan, Berry, 170
Morgan, Edmund, on racism, 102
Morris, Willie, on death in small towns,
    206; on life in the New South, 174;
    on football in South, 197
Moyers, Bill, on Ronald Reagan and race
    issue in South, 79n.24
Mozert v. Hawkins County Public Schools,
    202
Myers, Gustavus, 14–15

Naipaul, V. S., 183–84
Nashville Agrarians, 83, 169, 218
Nashville, Tennessee, 24, 41; Maxwell
    House Hotel, 21
Nathans, Sydney, on importance of land
    ownership in South, 209
National Association for the
    Advancement of Colored People
    (NAACP), 109
National Association for the Southern
    Poor, 208
National Opinion Research Center, on
    women in politics, 137
National Organization for Women
    (NOW), 143, 148; on child care, 146
Naylor, Thomas N., 3
Nelson, Willie, 144
Newby, I. A., on southerners' sense of
    history, 222
New Orleans, Louisiana, 33
"New Reconstruction," 110
New South, 23, 42, 217; Americanized
    version of, 219; failure of, 24;
    strategies, 220
Newton-John, Olivia, 222

Nicholls, William H., 220
Nixon, Richard M., and Executive Order 11478, 142; and 1972 reelection, 55
Noble, Donald R., on the future of southern writing, 163
Norfolk, Virginia, 33, 40; population of, 26

O'Brien, Michael, 2, 159
O'Connor, Flannery, 159, 168, 169, 172, 179, 227, 228
O'Connor, Sandra Day, 140
Olmsted, Frederick Law, Jr., 24
Olmsted, Frederick Law, Sr., on Richmond, Virginia, 11

Page, Arthur W., on Piedmont mill villages, 18
Page, Nelson, 164
Parks, Rosa Louise, 129
Pascagoula, Mississippi, population of, 26
Percy, Walker, 161, 162–63, 181, 228–29, 230–31; on South, 169
Pettigrew, Thomas, 110
Place, importance of in South, 207–10
Plynt, Candace, 178
Poe, Edgar Allen, 164, 169
Politics, southern, in future, 68–70; nationalization of, 67–68; one-party system, 50. *See also* Democratic party; Republican party
Porter, Katherine Anne, 165
Portman, John, 32
Powell, Mary Clare, 125
Powell, Padgett, 171
Prayer, in public schools, 77
Presidential Reconstruction, 105
Price, Reynolds, 166, 170, 171, 208. *See also The Surface of the Earth*
Progressivism, in South, 43n.22
Public works, in southern cities, 20
Public Works Administration, 25

Race, as factor in 1988 elections, 62; as factor in 1989 Virginia gubernatorial election, 112, 190–91; as part of southern culture, 189–93; issue of, 70; at the University of Mississippi, 193. *See also* Maury County,

Tennessee; Segregation; Scott County, Kentucky; Virginia; Watson, Tom
Race relations in South, accommodations toward blacks 29; during World War I, 107–8; from 1865–1900, 104–7; from 1900–1954, 109; from 1954 to present, 109–11
Race riots, in northern cities, 104, 108, 109; in southern cities, 108
Raleigh, North Carolina, War Memorial Auditorium, 109
Ransom, John Crowe, 162, 172
Raoul, William Green, 86–87
Reagan, Nancy Davis, 125
Reagan, Ronald, 57; and "New Southern Strategy," 61–62
"Real McCoys," 195
Reed, John Shelton, 2, 8, 42, 161, 176; on homicide rates in southern states, 197; on religion in South, 203; on retention of southern imagery, 227–28; on southern culture, 42
Reed, Roy, on importance of the land, 209–10
Regan, Donald T., on Nancy Reagan, 125
Rehnquist, William, 140
Religion, Baptist, 200, evangelical, 199, 202–4; "Old-Time," 199–200, 203; Presbyterian, 200
Republican party, 4; and black-white coalition politics in South, 57; and middle-class white southerners, 225; and 1988 elections in South, 62; and Reconstruction, 105; compared to North, 65–66; conservatism of, 225; "down-ticket" elections in South, 65, 66–67; uneven growth in South, 55
Research Triangle Park, North Carolina, 30, 91, 92, 227
Richards, Ann, 138
Richmond, Virginia, 11–12, 14, 23, 27, 33; Hollywood Cemetery, 12; Monument Avenue, 11; Mosque Theatre, 109; 1860 black population of, 27
Ripley, Alexandra, 194
Roanoke, Virginia, 20
Robb, Charles, 55
Roberts, Elizabeth Madox, 172
Robertson, Pat, 178, 202

Robinson, Ira, on football, 198–99
Rock Hill, South Carolina, early
  description of, 22
Roe v. Wade (1973), 140, 202. *See also*
  Abortion
Romanticism, antebellum, in advertising,
  193.
Rooney, John F., on football, 198
Roosevelt, Eleanor, 109
Roswell Manufacturing Company, 84
Rubin, Louis, 160, 168, 178; on
  Southern Literary Renascence, 165
Rustin, Bayard, 109

Sabato, Larry (political scientist), on 1989
  Virginia gubernatorial campaign,
  111–12
Sams, Ferrol, 230
Sanford, Terry, 55
Savannah, Georgia, 33; in 1879, 24
Scalia, Antonin, 140
Schrag, Peter, on football, 197
Scott, Anne Firor, 133; on southern
  women, 130
Scott, County, Kentucky, Toyota assembly
  plant, 192
Scott, Joan W., 131–32
Second Reconstruction, 51
Seddon, Rhea, 124
Segregation, racial, by federal
  government, 109; de factor, 108, 110;
  de jure, 105, 107, 108;
  demonstrations against, 109; during
  Reconstruction, 105; early forms of,
  103; in Georgetown County, South
  Carolina, 192; in residential settings
  in South, 112, 115–16; in rural school
  districts in South, 191–92; in urban
  South, 20, 24, 27, 108
Seneca Falls Convention, goals of, 141
Seward, William, 104
Sharecropping, 107
Simms, William Gilmore, 158, 164, 178
Simpson, Lewis, on Southern Literary
  Renascence, 165
"Sit-down strikes," in Alexandria,
  Virginia, 109
Skuube, Michael, 168
Slater, Samuel, manufacturing system of,
  84

Slave trade, 102
Slavery, abolition of, 103; as
  Constitutional Convention issue, 102;
  during American revolution, 102;
  expansion of, 102; in Chesapeake
  region, 101; in North, 104; in
  northern colonies, 101, 102; in South,
  101–3
Small towns, imagery of, 25, 207–8
Smith, Howard W., 142
Smith, Lee, 171, 179
Smith, Stephen A., 2
Sommers, Tish, 126
Soul on Ice, 165
Souter, David, 155n.85
South, announced deaths of, 177–78;
  and Reagan administration policies,
  224; and the arts, 161–62; and third
  world, 205, 233; Americanization of,
  217–19; colonization of 220; cultural
  barriers of, 220; current economic
  concerns of, 227; economic
  modernization of, 220; endless literary
  variety of, 175; federal assistance to,
  233–34; high-tech industrialization in,
  226–27; influence of religion in, 178,
  199–200; national embrace of,
  221–22; of 1980s, 224; Republican
  party in, 225; sterotypical, 175, 177;
  support of intellectuals, 158
South Carolina Alcoholic Beverage
  Control Commission, 201
South Carolina, future of, 1; future
  politics in, 68; cotton cultivation
  in, 26
Southern Association for Women
  Historians, 134
Southern Growth Policies Board, 90;
  1980 report of, 43
Southern Historical Association, 130
Southern history, and race relations, 100;
  as positive force, 41; sexual
  polarization of, 148. *See also*
  Woodward, C. Vann
Southern hospitality, 194, 216n.62
Southern Literary Journal, 161
Southern Literary Renascence, 169
Southern literature, and blacks, 181; and
  geographic sub-Souths, 175; and
  locale, 178; and women writers, 182;

distinctiveness of, 164; future of, 176, 181
Southern Living, 12, 209, 211, 228
Southern Quarterly, 161
Southern Review, 161
Southern stereotypes, examples of, 177
Southern Studies, 161
Southern Writers: A Biographical Dictionary, 168
Southern writers, critics of, 169; list of during nineteenth century, 164; list of during 1970s, 167; list of during 1980s, 167–68; styles of, 180
Southernness, disappearance of, 227; irrelevancy of, 227
Southernologists, 229, 232
Spartanburg, South Carolina, 84, 134
Spartanburg County, South Carolina, at large elections in, 214n.18; international investment in, 37
Spelman College, 123
Spivey, Ted, 159
Spruill, Julia Cherry, 133
Staunton, Virginia, city manager system inaugurated in, 19–20
Steed, Robert P., 3
Steele, Mary Lee, 167, 181
Strategies to Elevate People (STEP), 41
Stribling, T. S., 181
Stuart, J. E. B., 23
Student Nonviolent Coordinating Committee (SNCC), 141–42
Sturrock, David, 66; on future "down-ticket" elections, 67–68
Styron, William, 161
Sullivan, Walter, 3, 179, 182; on southern literature, 164, 165
Sumter County, Alabama, 191–92
Sunbelt, 221; problems in, 1, 31–32; pursuit of culture in, 160; term coined, 29
Super Tuesday, 58, 78n.13
Supply Side Economics, 90
The Surface of the Earth, 166–67
Swaggart, Jimmy, 129, 178, 202, 203; on rock and roll, 201
Swansbrough, Robert H., 3
Swift, Graham, 124

Tate, Allen, 158, 159, 160, 162, 163, 164, 165, 169, 171, 183

Taylor, Joe Gray, 194
Taylor, Peter, 178, 179–80
Tchula, Mississippi, 205–6
Televangalism, 202–3. *See also* Creationism; Evangelism; Fundamentalism; Religion
Terman, Frederick, 91, 99n.48
Terry, Mary Sue, 139
Textile industry, boom of in Piedmont, 85–86; during 1920s, 18; educational programs for, 87; technology of, 86. *See also* Ware Shoals, South Carolina; Whitmire, South Carolina
Thalhimer, William, 15
Thornburgh v. American College of Obstetricians and Gynecologists (1986),140
Thurmond, Strom, 225–26
Timrod, Henry, 158
Tindall, George, 2, 4, 5, 94; on disappearance of South, 229; on future South, 42
Toner, Robin, on Michael Dukakis, 58
Toole, John Kennedy, 178
Toyota automobile assembly plant, Scott County, Kentucky, 192
Trowbridge, John T., on Charleston, South Carolina, 23
Tubman, Harriet, 129
Turner, Nat, 103
Twain, Mark, 9, 164, 179
Tyler, Anne, 167, 169

Unemployment, in rural South, 38
Union, South Carolina, First Baptist Church of, 201
Urban middle class, in South, emergence of, 18–19
Urban sprawl, 38
Urbanization, and European immigrants in South, 14–15; and late-nineteenth-century suburbanization, 45n.33; and "out-towns," 37; and reform, 19–20; and slavery, 12; as cure for South's economic ills, 220; as influence on southern writers, 159; compared to other parts of U.S., 40–41; during antebellum period, 12–16; during early twentieth century, 21–22; during Great Depression and World War II,

25–28; during post-Civil War, 16–18; in Piedmont, 44n.15; in South from 1880 to 1910, 19; in South since 1950, 29–31

Vardaman, James K., 107, 193
Vesey, Denmark, 103
Violence, as a part of southern culture, 195–99; domestic, 146; during colonial period, 295; during antebellum period, 196; during early twentieth century, 196; during 1950s and 1960s; in Alabama, 197; in Bell and Harlan counties, Kentucky, 197; in films, 199; in Gastonia and Marion, North Carolina, 197; in Mississippi, 197; in 1989 Virginia gubernatorial election, 190–91
Volunteerism, in urban South, 41
Voting Rights Act of 1965, 32, 110, 111

Walker, Alice, 167, 170, 180, 182
Walker, Margaret, 173
Wallace, George, 58, 165
Wallerstein, Immanuel, 219, 223, 231; on southern culture, 234
Wal-Mart, 36, 201
Ware Shoals, South Carolina, decline of, 38–39
Warren, Robert Penn, 165
Watson, Tom, 107; on attempts to attract northern capital to South, 83; on race, 70
Watters, Pat, 2
Webster, Daniel, 104
Webster v. Reproductive Health Services (1989), 140
Welty, Eudora, 160, 162, 165, 167, 172, 208
What Men Don't Tell Women, 170
White supremacy, in present-day South, 113–14
White, Vanna, 129
Whitehead, James, 179, 180, 181; on future of southern literature, 173
Whites, southern, politics of, 76
Whitmire, South Carolina, economic problems of, 39
Whitin Machine Works, 85; and Stuart W. Cramer, 86

Wiener, Jonathan, on planter economy, 220
Wilder, L. Douglas, 111–12, 114, 115, 139, 191
Williams, Hank, Jr., 210, 229
Wilmington, North Carolina, in 1879, 24
Wilson, Justin, 211
Winston-Salem, North Carolina, 37
Winter, William, 55
Wolfe, Thomas, 165, 174; on Asheville, North Carolina, 22; on life in the South, 25
Women, and abortion, 139–40; and academics, 135; and AIDS, 148; and child care, 146; and demands on time, 137–38; and domestic politics, 135; and equal pay, 146; and equal rights, 135, 148; and feminist label, 128; and future, 134–35; and hysterectomies, 156n.111; and image of southern lady, 128; and issue of equality, 76, 127; and legal rights, 136; and poverty, 146; and race relations, 143; and Reagan Revolution, 140; and reproductive freedom, 139, 140; and suffrage, 132, 141; and southern literature, 182; and southern men, 144; and veneral disease, 148; as reformers, 132; common thread among, 130; during Progressive Era, 141; in Carolina backcountry, 129; in politics, 137; in positions of authority, 138; in southern history, 143; in southern state legislatures, 136–37; in southern states, 147; life expectancy of, 147, 151n.29; sexual harassment of, 147
Women's Educational Equity Act of 1974 (WEEA), 143
Women's movement, 141
Women's studies, 128
Woodville, Mississippi, 39
Woodward, C. Vann, 94, 110, 218–19, 221; on antisouthernism, 159; on disappearing South, 188; on early twentieth-century South, 219; on rural identity of South, 206; on southern history, 231
Works Progress Administration, 25
Wright, Richard, 158